Exploring Neurodiversity Through Virtual Reality

Sarune Savickaite

Exploring Neurodiversity Through Virtual Reality

Breaking Power Imbalances in Experimental Research

palgrave
macmillan

Sarune Savickaite
Department of Psychology
University of Exeter
Exeter, UK

ISBN 978-3-032-19635-4 ISBN 978-3-032-19636-1 (eBook)
https://doi.org/10.1007/978-3-032-19636-1

This Palgrave Macmillan imprint is published by the registered company Springer Nature Switzerland AG.
The registered company address is: Gewerbestrasse 11, 6330 Cham, Switzerland

What kept me hammering away… nothing is more important than being able to express myself.
— Naoki Higashida, *The Reason I Jump*.

To my family—
and to my grandfather, Juozas, whom I never met but who remains a compass for learning no matter the challenges;
to my parents, whose unconditional support has steadied every path I have taken—
this book is for you.

Preface

This book is the result of years of work, starting with my master's and doctoral studies and continuing to grow as one of the main initiatives of my academic career. I hope it will likewise keep evolving and changing, much like my research has and my interest in perception, technology, and neurodiversity has.

The beginning of this research can be traced back to when I was a postgraduate student at the University of Glasgow. It was there that I first met my PhD supervisor, Dr. David Simmons. Having studied psychophysics, stereovision, and cognition as an undergraduate, I initially anticipated investigating visual perception and perceptual disparities within a traditional experimental context. But at the time, David was doing research on autism, and through our early conversations—especially those that connected my background as an artist with my interest in autistic savant artists like Stephen Wiltshire—we found a common interest that became the basis for this project.

Later, Professor Neil McDonnell, my secondary supervisor, joined the team. He brought his knowledge of virtual reality with him. I have always been interested in technology and the potential of three-dimensional digital worlds. This junction of art, cognition, and technology provided me with a distinctive opportunity to integrate several aspects of my experience and enthusiasm into a cohesive study program. This area of work—using virtual reality to learn about neurodiversity—was very new at the time, but it has now evolved into a highly rewarding and exciting job. Thus, I have found my place in an interdisciplinary field by using new technologies to look at how autistic individuals and other neurodivergent groups see the world differently and how these qualities are spread throughout the population. I hope that you may feel my passion in the following pages.

The title of this book is meant to be broad, covering things like neurodiversity, virtual reality, and variances in perception. These ideas are connected and can be used to look at how people think and perceive things differently. The book's goal is to give readers an idea of the bigger research world I work in and to show them how much can be learned in this niche—how rich and varied the data can be, and how it can help people of all diagnostic labels and differences express themselves through art, symbols, and visual communication.

I present virtual reality (VR) as a distinctive research instrument for examining perceptual and cognitive disparities. Although few studies have employed open-ended, creative, or arts-based methodologies to explore the human condition using VR, my research posits that VR provides a unique amalgamation of control and immersion, facilitating profound insights into lived experiences. The research in this book is founded on a person-centered, arts-based, and participatory paradigm that puts neurodivergent people and their points of view at the center.

In this book, I showcase the viewpoints of participants and the artworks they produced during our investigations, emphasizing the significance of non-verbal and experiential modes of expression. One of the main goals is to fix the power imbalances in traditional research, where standardized methodologies generally favor verbal communication and regular assessment systems. Immersive technologies and arts-based methodologies, on the other hand, can challenge existing hierarchies and create spaces that are more open and welcoming to everyone. These methods not only include participants in a more significant way, but they also reveal perceptual and cognitive distinctions that may have been missed before, especially among those who do not primarily communicate through language.

In this approach, the book helps us comprehend neurodiverse experiences in a more nuanced way and shows us how to do research that includes everyone. What sets this work apart is that it uses arts-based research approaches, such as VR sketching exercises, and it focuses on helping neurodivergent people communicate and be creative. It fills a vacuum in existing VR and neurodiversity research, which typically ignores perceptual and cognitive aspects. It shows how VR may be used as a research tool and a possible therapy tool, both of which help people learn in new and easy-to-understand ways.

In the first chapter, neurodiversity and neurodivergence are discussed. It is explained how these terms will be utilized throughout the remainder of the book, as well as how they are connected to conditions such as autism, attention-deficit/hyperactivity disorder (ADHD), synesthesia, and aphantasia.

Within the framework of the neurodiversity paradigm, Chap. 2 focuses on perceptual differences, with a particular emphasis on autism. However, it also discusses other conditions that are related to autism that fall under the neural diversity spectrum.

Chapter 3 explores the application of virtual reality as a research instrument, emphasizing its utilization in neurodivergent studies and elucidating the advantages of the arts-based techniques I advocate. This chapter discusses the research framework and experimental methods I established during my studies. These are designed to be relevant for the benefit of other researchers as well.

In Chap. 4, we take a look at drawing, first as a general practice and then as an activity that is carried out in virtual reality. Presented here is one of the first few initial studies that I conducted as part of my research, which investigated the experiences of persons who are artistically minded and who use virtual reality drawing tools.

Virtual reality (VR) is examined in Chap. 5 as a means of communication and creation. Studies that included autistic individuals and those with attention-deficit/hyperactivity disorder (ADHD), synesthesia, and aphantasia are explored in more detail. In this chapter, I also discuss the ways in which these experimental protocols can assist us in gaining a deeper understanding of communication and creativity in the context of neurodiversity.

In Chap. 6, I examine the merits and drawbacks of virtual reality (VR), addressing concerns related to accessibility and representation, alongside emerging methodologies that are currently under development.

It is discussed in the final chapter that drawing is a global practice that may transcend borders of language and culture, regardless of whether or not it is done with the assistance of technology. The chapter concludes by discussing the significance of intersectionality and the decolonization of neurodivergence, and it makes a plea for a vision of neurodiversity/neurodivergence beyond the limited two-dimensional spectrum and that encompasses a larger range of experiences instead.

Positionality

I am neurodivergent. As a woman of Eastern European origin (Lithuanian/Baltic) who has spent the most of her life in the United Kingdom and is nearing 40, I possess a distinct viewpoint about the concept of neurodivergence and my position within it. I was diagnosed with anxiety and depression when I was a teenager, and I have experienced various therapeutic approaches and taken medicine on and off since then. My diagnosis has changed since to Generalized Anxiety Disorder (GAD), and I can see a lot of obsessive-compulsive (OCD) behaviors that go along with it. In this way, I may be on the edges of the "neurodivergent spectrum," which I shall discuss further in the first chapter. There is a significant likelihood that I, like numerous other women, have been misdiagnosed, given that neurodivergence and anxiety frequently present differently in women and are generally under-recognized.

For now, I feel comfortable identifying as neurodivergent in a general rather than in a specific diagnostic group. As I will contend subsequently, it might be challenging—and possibly unwarranted—to restrict one's identity to a singular title. I possess hyperphantasia, indicating that I frequently visualize concepts as imagery. This tendency has influenced both my research and the manner in which I convey my ideas, frequently utilizing diagrams and other visual aids. I will discuss the nuanced world of aphantasic and hyperphantasic experiences later in the book.

It has not been long since I started talking about my personal neurodivergence and journey that got me here. In my culture, people did not talk about mental health very much, and I owe a lot to my parents for being there for me when things were tough. My journey of self-understanding is still ongoing, but I believe that it is important to recognize the researcher's positionality in qualitative research on neurodivergence. My lived experience will always affect how I interpret things, but I have stayed true to the scientific method and objectivity in all of the empirical work I present in this book as much as possible.

Anyone who is interested in neurodivergent perception, virtual reality, or creative or arts-based ways of expressing themselves should read this book. It is also for people who want to connect their inner worlds in ways more than just words, including through technology, visual communication, or shared human experience. I hope that the work presented here not only helps people understand neurodiversity better, but also encourages more creative, kind, and open-minded ways of doing research, teaching, and communicating with each other.

Exeter, UK Sarune Savickaite

Acknowledgments

I am deeply grateful to the University of Glasgow for providing me with a stimulating academic environment and exceptional resources to pursue my PhD research. And now, University of Exeter, where I have recently joined as associate lecturer and continue to explore neurodivergent perceptual differences, cognition and immersive technologies.

I would like to extend my sincere gratitude to the Economic and Social Research Council (ESRC) for providing funding for my doctoral research. The financial support received from ESRC has been instrumental in enabling me to conduct rigorous research that has the potential to make a positive impact on society. A lot of the research I discuss in this book came from this doctoral research project.

I would like to express my gratitude to my PhD supervisors—Dr David Simmons and Dr Neil McDonnell—for their guidance, support, and encouragement throughout my doctoral research. Their expertise and insights have been instrumental in shaping my research direction and in helping me achieve my academic goals. I would also like to thank my mentors—Prof Catherine Lido, Dr Ioanna Kapantai and Prof Hazel Mycroft, for guiding me through some difficult times, particularly during my ECR journey overall.

I am also grateful to my collaborators for their contributions to my research and beyond. Their expertise and willingness to share their knowledge have greatly enriched my research and helped me develop a deeper understanding of my research topic. To fellow PhD students, Elliot Millington and Tammy-Ann Husselman, and undergraduate and postgraduate students: Kimberley McNaughton, Elisa Gaillard, Jo Amaya,

Rebecca Airlie, Claire Morrison, Rebecca Taylor, Emma Hayashibara, Alicia Quick, Emily Smith, Hanan Khalif, Laurel Hilliker, Han Li. I have learned from you as much as you from me.

Finally, I would like to acknowledge my family and friends for their love, support, and encouragement throughout my academic journey. Their unwavering support and belief in me have been a constant source of motivation and inspiration.

I also want to extend my thanks to all of our participants who have taken time to take part in the studies we ran and share their diagnostic journeys, perceptual experiences, and lived experiences. Because of these interactions, often through drawings and conversations, I have learned to accept my own neurodivergence and discuss my lived experiences more openly as well.

And finally, I must thank my constant companion, my cat—Mimi. She was with me every step of this challenging journey and consoled me at times I did not even know I needed consolation. She is certainly the most caring pet and deserves her own picture in my book.

Competing Interests The author has no competing interests to declare that are relevant to the content of this manuscript.

Contents

List of Figures

CHAPTER 1

Mapping Inner Worlds: Understanding Neurodiversity Through Perception

In this first chapter, I will set the scene for neurodiversity. This is an ongoing topic about the broader spectrum of cognitive and perceptual differences among individuals. "Neurodivergence" has also arisen as a more inclusive and specific term, frequently referring to conditions such as autism, ADHD, dyslexia, dyspraxia, or OCD, as well as some mental health issues. The discussion of neurodiversity, neurodivergence, and numerous neurotypes is vast. It also extends into disability theory, philosophical disputes, and nomenclature, which are considerably beyond the scope of this work. I will briefly present the important components that I believe are relevant to the context of this work, and throughout the book, I will mention some of the key sources where readers can research more. However, there is insufficient scope in this opening chapter, or even in this book, to address all potential possibilities of this discourse.

One key message I hope to emphasize is that, while the majority of existing research has focused on specific neurodivergent conditions, most commonly autism and ADHD, this is simply because these conditions receive the most research attention, particularly in the sensory aspects that I am most interested in. They also represent communities that are most open to discussing their circumstances and lived experiences. However, as someone who considers myself to be on the neurodivergent spectrum, albeit more gently, as someone diagnosed with generalized anxiety disorder and OCD, I believe that, based on my personal experience, many

S. Savickaite, *Exploring Neurodiversity Through Virtual Reality*,
https://doi.org/10.1007/978-3-032-19636-1_1

sensory sensitivities, perceptual aspects, and cognitive differences and similarities cross multiple diagnostic labels. This also encompasses the conditions I will explore alongside autism and ADHD, such as synesthesia and aphantasia, as well as individual characteristics like a propensity for visual thinking.

I strongly believe, and encourage readers to consider, that the neurotype, or how an individual identifies (diagnosed or not), will include a spectrum of variants that can encompass numerous conditions, whether these are related solely to specific traits or a formal diagnosis. This is not to belittle the diagnostic procedure; there are times when it is necessary and critical. However, this book highlights the value of lived experience and the ability to articulate ideas that are frequently difficult to express. These questions frequently go beyond the greater discussion about what constitutes "impairment" or which diagnostic criteria we accept. I intend to portray this as a fundamentally human yearning for connection—to find methods to express ourselves, particularly when neurodivergent sensory sensitivities or perceptual and cognitive difficulties often make spoken communication challenging.

Although this book is part of a much larger conversation about neurodiversity and neurodivergence, it will discuss several significant theories and theoretical aspects to provide context. The objective, however, is not to focus on support needs or the argument over verbal vs non-verbal expression within neurodivergent groups—though these conversations, which are frequently centered on autistic experiences, are still important to the paradigm proposed here. It is critical to recognize communication as something that can be expressed in methods other than words. Human experiences, perceptual distinctions, inner sensations, and inner worlds may be unavailable to others, but we nevertheless want to relate to others and explain them. I hope that this becomes the book's ultimate goal: to investigate how we might connect with individuals who communicate effectively across several mediums, as well as those who struggle to articulate their experiences vocally and may require alternate means.

Although this may appear ambitious, it is intended as a beginning step toward explaining how the methods used in the studies I present, as well as related work, provide early tools for developing more cohesive and holistic approaches to communication. These include think-aloud methods, art-based expression, novel technologies, and other innovative ways that have the potential to change how we think about research and interaction with our participants. In many circumstances, participants should be viewed as co-creators rather than passive recipients of information. This power imbalance will be addressed throughout the book, particularly in discussions of how emerging technologies and methodologies might assist closing the gap between researcher and participant and improve communication.

Neurodiversity, Neurodivergence, and Neurotypes

Neurodiversity denotes the neurological or neurocognitive diversity inherently present among the human population. Judy Singer first used the term in a book published in 1993 called "Neurodiversity." It refers to a growing socio-political movement that supports the recognition and inclusion of natural neurocognitive diversity in society. It is important to acknowledge that this movement has not been, and continues to be, impervious to specific exclusionary forces. The movement started with autistic people who could talk, but even though it has grown to encompass many other conditions, autistic people (and more lately, those with ADHD) still seem to be the most visible part of it.

For the objectives of this book, I will employ the subsequent definitions. I acknowledge that there are widespread disagreement and ongoing discourse regarding the precise definitions of these terms, but such disputes go beyond the purview of this book.

Neurodiversity denotes the inherent diversity in human brains and minds, including a broad spectrum of cognitive styles, sensory perceptions, and information processing methods. It emphasizes that neurological variations constitute a standard aspect of human variability rather than deficiencies or illnesses.

Neurodivergent refers to persons whose cognitive processes deviate from the "norm," termed "neurotypical." This includes individuals who are autistic, have ADHD, dyslexia, dyspraxia, or possess other neurological variations.

Neurotype denotes an individual's distinct cognitive profile or method of perceiving the environment, encompassing both neurotypical and neurodivergent classifications. It delineates the overarching pattern of an individual's cognitive processes and perceptions of the environment.

Neurodiversity is a term that developed within the autism community to articulate the concept that variations in neurological functioning are both normal and significant. The concept is founded on the fact that people think in various ways. But it has also been used to advocate a wider idea: a set of concepts that will help a social movement battle against unfair policies and attitudes (May, 2025).

A significant aspect of neurodiversity theory is its normative assertion: neurodiversities ought to be regarded as differences rather than impairments, necessitating societal accommodation rather than treatment. A more nuanced perspective that considers "cognitive continuity" between neurotypical and atypical experiences should provide philosophy with a more robust foundation. This moves the attention away from comparisons about minorities or biodiversity and toward differences in personality qualities. This encourages a more flexible and inclusive approach that emphasizes shared humanity and encourages compassion, respect, and support (May, 2025).

This perspective serves as an enhancement to the neurodiversity model rather than a repudiation of it. Chapman (2020) argues, "neurodiversity means a lot of different things to different people."

People sometimes use the words "neurodiversity" and "neurodivergence" to mean the same thing. To clarify the semantic distinction, it is accurate to assert that all individuals are neurodiverse, although it is not feasible for all to be neurodivergent. For anything or someone to be divergent, there must be something or someone else that is not divergent (Legault et al., 2021). Individuals are quantitatively classified as neurodivergent when their neurological or neurocognitive profile resides at the periphery of that profile's statistical distribution (in this context, the criterion is a specific point or threshold on the distribution); they are qualitatively deemed neurodivergent when qualitative criteria (e.g., a set of necessary and sufficient conditions, including those outlined in the DSM-5—see Fig. 1.1 for some conditions commonly classed as neurodivergent) delineate what constitutes a normal neurocognitive profile. In other words, when such criteria establish the definition of "normalcy." These criteria, whether quantitative or qualitative, are typically selected for medical, practical, economic, or moral reasons, based on the belief that one type is "more functional," "more evolutionarily adapted," "easier to interact with," "less resource demanding," or "more characteristic of a life worth living," among other factors.

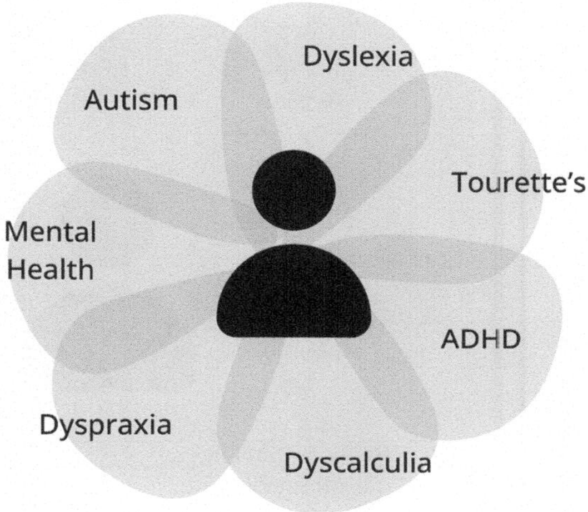

Fig. 1.1 A visual illustration of the diversity of neurodivergent profiles. The diagram emphasizes that neurodiversity is multifaceted and individual

Even though neurodivergent people may have limitations or "problems", it is not necessary to pathologize their differences. According to the social model of disability, many difficulties stem from societal inadequacies in accommodation rather than from the individual. Den Houting (2019) observes that, even for those with significant support requirements, disability can frequently be mitigated or circumvented through environmental modifications and the availability of suitable equipment. This stance supports the notion that neurodivergent individuals necessitate accommodation rather than intervention (May, 2025). Figure 1.2 illustrates some of the characteristics that can be perceived as disadvantages as well as advantages for many neurodivergent individuals, and this varies greatly across conditions and populations.

Dahlstrom (2023) emphasizes that neurodiversity is frequently a misconstrued and obscured aspect of diversity. Being neurodivergent does not mean you are less than others; it just means you work differently than most people. Because neurodivergence is often not evident, many people hide their condition because they are afraid of being evaluated in social or professional situations. This hiding (or masking) can make it harder to get the accommodations you need and put more stress on your mind. Executive dysfunction and sensory processing variations are examined as essential characteristics influencing lived experiences. For example, sensory hypersensitivity affects most autistic adults and can make many places

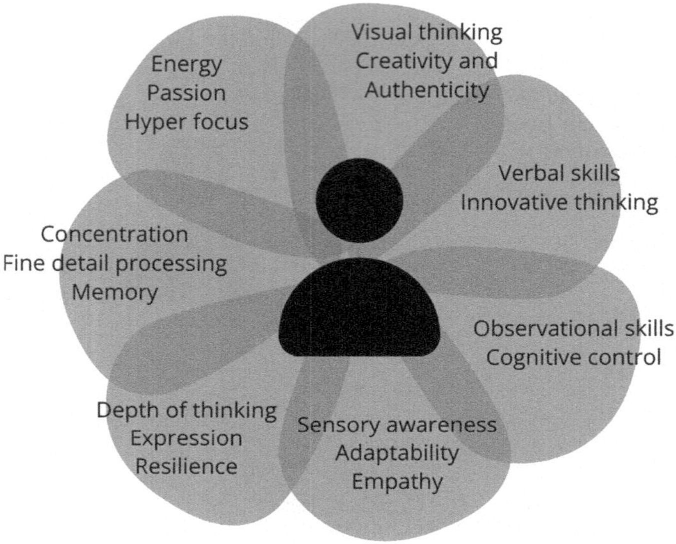

Fig. 1.2 This figure illustrates some strengths and positive characteristics often associated with neurodivergent individuals

overwhelming. Manning and Scerif (2023) assert that comprehending perceptual variability necessitates an examination of the interactions among various influences, from sensory encoding to decision execution, throughout development. The authors advocate for a more dynamic model of perceptual decision-making that acknowledges developmental timing and neurodiversity as essential elements, emphasizing both convergence and divergence between conditions such as autism and dyslexia.

Historically prevalent narratives—mind-blindness, inflexible Theory of Mind frameworks, and functionality classifications like "high/low functioning"—are criticized as inadequate and frequently empirically unreliable. Furthermore, Milton et al. (2023) posit the "double empathy problem" as a fundamental corrective, asserting that communication failures are relational and bi-directional, rather than indicative of a unilateral autistic "weakness". This perspective posits that autism is more accurately characterized as a distinct difference, frequently sensory in nature, that influences social interactions, rather than as a mostly social condition with secondary sensory characteristics.

Robinson (2017) promotes individual perspectives and autoethnographic methodologies. Since all research is imbued with values, elucidating positionality is epistemically advantageous: first-person narratives reveal deficiencies in third-person accounts and aid in combating hermeneutical injustice, which refers to the systemic exclusion of groups from the interpretation of their own experiences. This book warns against making diagnostic categories too distinct and points out that comorbidity (such ADHD, OCD, epilepsy, or intellectual disability) makes it harder to say that autism is a "disability" on its own. The primary normative inquiry is: what is the precise object of concern—autism per se, comorbid illnesses, or societal structures that facilitate these differences?

Perception and Development

Perception is a vital element of human development, arising from the interplay of biological maturation, experiential learning, and social context. It allows individuals to perceive, analyze, and respond to sensory stimuli in manners that shape their learning, relationships, and identity over the course of their lives (Johnson & Hannon, 2015). People often think of perception as just seeing and hearing, but it is actually a dynamic process that changes over time.

Perceptual abilities develop prenatally and expand significantly during infancy. Newborns are sensitive to patterns with a lot of contrast, and they are drawn to faces very early on, which is important for their social and emotional development later (Johnson & Hannon, 2015). At birth, babies' hearing is also very advanced. They can tell the difference between small changes in speech sounds and respond to the rhythm and tone of language, which sets the stage for later language learning (Werker & Tees, 1984). The tactile and proprioceptive systems help newborns learn about their bodies and the world around them. Touch teaches kids about the properties of things and helps them become more aware of space. These early experiences are very important for developing motor skills, building relationships, and growing intellectually.

As children grow up, their ability to combine information from different senses (multisensory integration) gets better. This lets them do more complex tasks like reading, picking up on social cues, coordinating movement, and finding their way around (Bremner et al., 2012). Perceptual acuity and sensory-motor coordination frequently reach their peak during adolescence. Young individuals exhibit enhanced speed and accuracy in their responses to stimuli. Hormonal and cognitive changes make teens more likely to be affected by environments that are too much for them to handle, especially those that are emotionally or socially demanding (Steinberg, 2005).

Adulthood is frequently marked by perceptual stability, although a gradual decline in sensory function commences. Presbyopia, the inability to focus on nearby objects, and high-frequency hearing loss are two prevalent age-related alterations. Adults often utilize experience-based reasoning, contextual information, and behavioral techniques to compensate, indicating that perception is flexible and susceptible to change (Salthouse, 2010). In later life, declines become more evident: cataracts, glaucoma, and presbycusis can hinder vision and hearing, while diminished cognitive processing may affect reaction time and recognition accuracy (Lindenberger & Baltes, 1994). Nonetheless, perceptual plasticity endures. Older people can stay independent and have a good quality of life with the help of cognitive training, assistive technology, and changes to their environment.

Recognizing perceptual development throughout the lifespan highlights the importance of age-appropriate support. Early interventions, including sensory integration techniques and enriched environments, can enhance early development, while adaptations in later life foster autonomy and emotional well-being (Johnson & Hannon, 2015). Perception is a fundamental aspect of human development, arising from the interaction of biological maturation, experiential accumulation, and sociocultural context. It enables individuals to perceive, interpret, and react to sensory stimuli in manners that influence learning, interpersonal relationships, and identity across the lifespan (Johnson & Hannon, 2015). People often talk about perception in terms of seeing and hearing, but it is better to think of it as a dynamic process that changes over time and involves many senses.

While many people follow a broadly similar developmental trajectory, neurodivergent people, both those with recognized conditions and those without formal diagnoses, may perceive the sensory world in qualitatively different ways. These disparities are more than just challenges; they reflect diverse perceptual styles that might present both obstacles and opportunities. Some people have increased sensitivity (hypersensitivity) to sensory input such as loud noises, bright lights, or strong odors, which can cause discomfort, avoidance behaviors, or problems in busy surroundings. Others may be hyposensitive, meaning they respond less to sensory information and prefer powerful stimulation like deep pressure, spinning, or high-intensity movement. In rare circumstances, sensory channels become actively entwined: for example, people with synesthesia may consistently perceive colors when listening to music or reading text, indicating stable cross-modal associations (Cytowic, 2002). These variances can influence learning, preferences emotional control, and social involvement.

On a larger scale, creating sensory-inclusive spaces encourages involvement and well-being. Designing flexible rules, quiet zones, and changeable lighting not only benefits persons with sensory problems, but also enhances overall comfort. Finally, empathy, education, and inclusive design create communities in which various perceptual experiences are recognized, supported, and cherished.

Chapter Conclusion

This chapter has set the conceptual foundations for understanding neurodiversity through perception, framing it both as a descriptive account of human cognitive and sensory variation and as a normative paradigm that challenges deficit-based models and rigid notions of "normalcy." By drawing together philosophy, disability studies, developmental psychology, and first-person perspectives, it has argued that perceptual differences are dynamic, multisensory, and shaped across the lifespan by biological maturation, experience, and sociocultural context—often cutting across diagnostic categories such as autism, ADHD, OCD, synesthesia, and aphantasia in ways that complicate classification and simplistic explanations. Emphasizing communication as more than speech, the chapter positioned lived experience, positionality, and the relational nature of misunderstanding (including the double empathy problem) as central to both ethical research and inclusive practice.

References

Bremner, A. J., et al. (2012). Multisensory development. In *Oxford handbook of developmental psychology*. https://doi.org/10.1093/oxfordhb/9780199958450.013.020

Chapman, R. (2020). The reality of autism: On the metaphysics of disorder and diversity. *Philosophical Psychology, 33*(6), 799–819. https://doi.org/10.1080/09515089.2020.1748610

Cytowic, R. (2002). *Synesthesia: A union of the senses*. MIT Press.

Dahlstrom, A. (2023). Neurodiversity in the workplace: Understanding invisible disabilities. *Harvard Business Review*.

Den Houting, J. (2019). Neurodiversity: An insider's perspective. *Autism, 23*(2), 271–273. https://doi.org/10.1177/1362361318820762

Johnson, S. P., & Hannon, E. E. (2015). Developmental changes in perception and cognition. In *The Oxford handbook of cognitive psychology*. https://doi.org/10.1093/oxfordhb/9780199958450.013.022

Legault, M., Bourdon, J. N., & Poirier, P. (2021). From neurodiversity to neurodivergence: The role of epistemic and cognitive marginalization. *Synthese, 199*(5), 12843–12868.

Lindenberger, U., & Baltes, P. (1994). Sensory functioning and intelligence in old age. *Psychology and Aging, 9*(3), 339–355. https://doi.org/10.1037/0882-7974.9.3.339

Manning, C., & Scerif, G. (2023). Understanding perceptual decisions by studying development and neurodiversity. *Current Directions in Psychological Science, 32*(4), 300–306. https://doi.org/10.1177/09637214231162369

May, J. (2025). Neurodiversity with nuance. *Neuroethics, 18*(2), 30.

Milton, D. E. M., Waldock, K. E., & Keates, N. (2023). Autism and the 'double empathy problem'. In *Conversations on empathy: Interdisciplinary perspectives on empathy, imagination and othering* (pp. 78–97). Routledge.

Robinson, S. A. (2017). Express yourself: An auto-ethnographic poetic account. *International Journal for Talent Development and Creativity., 5*, 149–154.

Salthouse, T. (2010). *Major issues in cognitive aging*. Oxford University Press.

Steinberg, L. (2005). Cognitive and affective development in adolescence. *Trends in Cognitive Sciences, 9*(2), 69–74. https://doi.org/10.1016/j.tics.2004.12.005

Werker, J. F., & Tees, R. C. (1984). Cross-language speech perception. *Infant Behavior and Development, 7*, 49–63. https://doi.org/10.1016/S0163-6383(84)80022-3

CHAPTER 2

The Architecture of Difference: Theoretical Perspectives on Neurodivergent Cognition

Our visual system combines numerous pieces of information to generate a meaningful perception of the world (Goldstein & Brockmole, 2016). The ability to notice and analyze such emergent visual patterns is commonly referred to as "perceptual organisation" (Wagemans et al., 2012). Individual experiences are private and inaccessible to experimenters; yet, diverse processing styles can be studied. For example, global processing involves extracting the "gist" of a visual image, whereas local processing concentrates on the specific information (Simmons & Todorova, 2018). We all blend local pieces of perception to obtain general meaning, but how we use this information to understand our surroundings varies.

Individual differences in local and global processing have been found since infancy (Freeseman et al., 1993). Gender (Sadler-Smith, 2011), race (McKone et al., 2010), and mood have all been shown to influence our preferred processing mode. These differences also apply to neurodivergent populations, with distinct preferences reported in Obsessive-Compulsive Disorder (Yovel et al., 2005), schizophrenia (Johnson et al., 2005), eating disorders (Li et al., 2015; Lopez et al., 2008), autism (e.g., Kandalaft et al., 2013), and ADHD (Wang & Reid, 2011).

Although there is quite a bit of work around perceptual differences and sensory sensitivities in neurodivergent populations overall, a lot of the work discussed in this book is very much based around the initial inception of the project and associated studies, which are mostly related to

S. Savickaite, *Exploring Neurodiversity Through Virtual Reality*, https://doi.org/10.1007/978-3-032-19636-1_2

autistic perceptual differences. Autistic perceptual differences are also very varied and include research on concepts such as automatic imitation, eye contact, social responsiveness, or other autonomic variations in sensory perception (Kapp, 2025); however, I will focus predominantly on visual perceptual differences.

In this chapter, I will examine fundamental hypotheses related to visual processing variations in autistic people, with a special emphasis on local–global processing style preferences. Kapp (2025) provides a contemporary summary of sensory characteristics in autism if you wish to explore this topic further. Much of the groundwork for the VR free-drawing exercises described in this book comes from studies into global and local processing abnormalities in autistic people, as well as people with higher levels of autistic traits. Understanding this theoretical foundation is important because it informs further conversations about sketching methods in VR and how they might be employed with other neurodivergent populations.

In this chapter several neurodivergent conditions are discussed. Some are covered in more detail here, others will be explored later in the book. Some are outside of the scope of this piece of work. I provide key definitions here of the conditions that are relevant only for this current body of work.

Autism is a neurodevelopmental condition characterized by differences in social communication, sensory processing, and patterns of behaviors or interests.

ADHD (Attention-Deficit Hyperactivity Disorder) is a neurodevelopmental condition involving persistent patterns of inattention, hyperactivity, and/or impulsivity that affect daily functioning.

Synesthesia is a perceptual trait in which stimulation of one sensory or cognitive pathway involuntarily triggers experiences in another.

Aphantasia is the inability or greatly reduced ability to form voluntary mental visual imagery.

Hyperphantasia is the ability to generate exceptionally vivid and detailed voluntary mental imagery.

Although this book emphasizes the importance of neurodiversity, it does not assume that it is restricted to autism, ADHD, or a subset of disorders. Neurodivergence is a large, complicated spectrum that cannot be adequately described in a small volume. However, due to the scope of the book I will keep the primary focus on autistic perception, with extensions to conditions that are typically associated with autism.

Autism and Perceptual Differences

Autism is a neurodevelopmental condition defined by difficulties in social interactions, sensory processing, and repetitive behavior (APA, 2013). Autism is presently estimated to affect 1–2% of Western industrialized nations, including the United Kingdom (Baird et al., 2006). Autism research has generally disregarded the sensory world experienced by autistic people, focusing instead on understanding and supporting the condition's behavioral symptoms (Robertson & Baron-Cohen, 2017). Despite this, there is a considerable body of evidence suggesting autistic people have an unusual pattern of visual processing (Fleischmann & Fleischmann, 2012; Simmons et al., 2009), which may even explain the more well-recognized behavioral differences (Happé & Ronald, 2008). As a result, studying how autistic people interpret visual information is critical if we want to obtain a better understanding of their perceptual experiences and, ultimately, give more appropriate support (Bogdashina, 2016).

Although the concept of atypical perception in autism is widely accepted, the nature of the changes is controversial, and attempting to reconcile the multiple findings reported over the years may result in a jumbled and confusing image. Inconsistent and mixed findings can be linked to a range of methodological difficulties and inaccurate theoretical assumptions, including variability between clinical and non-clinical groups, publication bias, and a lack of experimental rigor (Simmons & Todorova, 2018).

Autistic people's brains appear to process previously encountered sensory stimuli as "new." This could be related to both unimodal perceptual strengths (e.g., visual and auditory modalities) and lower integration (Heffler & Oestreicher, 2016). It could be part of a larger trend of reduced perceptual narrowing in autistic people (Hadad & Yashar, 2022), which necessitates multisensory integration for often encountered stimuli (Lewkowicz & Ghazanfar, 2009). Instead of perceptual narrowing accelerating late in the first year (Lewkowicz, 2014), autistic infants' differences in processing more of their surroundings as uncertain may overwhelm and distress them, resulting in difficulties with self-regulation and a reduced social approach (Garon et al., 2016). Sensory and motor differences are generally obvious to autistic people, although they are frequently disregarded by others. Variations in sensorimotor learning, instinctual imitation, eye contact, sensory perception, and growing interests can all have an impact on behavior and communication.

In support of this viewpoint, the only assessment of autistic traits produced in equal partnership with the autistic community recently identified heightened sensory processing and a penchant for repetitive action as the only widely recognized features of autism (Ratto et al., 2023). Similarly, autistic adults' viewpoints have influenced modern understandings of autism, which are based on a particular sensorium—a way of experiencing perception in general—that includes a strong yearning for relationships. However, the creation of these relationships is frequently hampered by others' incorrect interpretations of autistic needs (Milton & Green, 2024). These findings suggest that autistic development may follow a different trajectory beginning early in life as a result of sensory and motor abnormalities.

Autistic people have frequently been observed to exhibit hypo- (under-reactivity to sensory stimuli) and hypersensitivity ("overload" of sensory stimuli), as well as "sensory seeking" behaviors (Bogdashina, 2016; Schauder & Bennetto, 2016). Self-report accounts of autistic people clearly demonstrate that their worldview differs from that of neurotypicals (Grandin & Duffy, 2008; Fleischmann & Fleischmann, 2012). "Sensory overload" is frequently mentioned as one of the key elements of autistic perceptual experience, in which daily sensory stimuli accumulates and becomes overpowering (Robertson & Simmons, 2015). "Fragmented world" is another element of perception in which autistic people report perceiving the world as separate fragments rather than the unified overall picture that neurotypicals appear to perceive (Frith, 2003).

"Fragmented World" and Autobiographical Accounts

This book focuses on the sensory features of autism, namely, autobiographical recollections of the "fragmented world" and sensory overload. In her book Nobody Nowhere (1992), Donna Williams recalls these experiences: "*My bed was surrounded and completely encompassed by small dots that I called stars, like some kind of mystical glass coffin. I've since discovered that they're air particles, but my vision was so acute that they frequently created a hypnotic foreground, with the rest of "the world" drifting away"* (p. 10).

Naoki Higashida, a minimally verbal autistic writer, has written extensively on his inner perceptual world in his book The Reason I Jump. He defined sensory overload as "*... a room with twenty radios, all turned to different stations, blaring out voices and music... suddenly sensory input from your environment is flooding in as well, unfiltered in quality and overwhelming in quantity... Colors and patterns swim and compete for your attention*" (p. 2). Naoki Higashida also mentions variances in processing patterns found in autistic people, explaining how "*...the details jump straight out at us first of all, and then only gradually, detail by detail, does the whole image sort of float up into focus*" (p 92). Finally, he discusses how many non-verbal or slightly verbal autistic people may have a rich interior world that is difficult to articulate: "*...to live my life as a human being, nothing is more important than being able to express myself*" (p 20).

In addition to written stories, there are various examples of how visual arts and new technologies have been used to help autistic people communicate themselves. Prof Yukie Nagai of the University of Tokyo's Cognitive Developmental Robotics group developed an Augmented Reality (AR) display in an attempt to simulate the sensory overload that autistic people frequently experience. The tool allows neurotypical persons to imagine what it could be like to have abnormal and hypersensitive perception (Qin et al., 2014).

We were also inspired by amazing autistic persons, such as Temple Grandin, who described her experiences as "*seeing in pictures.*" We also looked at the work of Stephen Wiltshire, an outstanding savant with detail-oriented memory and artistic aptitude, and Giles Trehin, a French autistic artist who creates meticulous line drawings of landscapes and structures. Another example of a detail-oriented artist is Peter Howson, who has been raising autism awareness and discussing how his diagnosis has influenced his paintings. Anna Berry is an artist that creates extensive and sophisticated works that address many seminal social issues. It is amazing how many autistic artists favor a detail-oriented style. Nadia Chomyn, characterized as "*the autistic child who could draw like Picasso,*" is another example of remarkable talent. Nadia bypassed the scribbling and doodling phase seen in neurotypical youngsters, producing sophisticated and proficient drawings as early as the age of three. Nadia battled with autism, frequently requiring assistance getting dressed and with daily chores.

However, art allowed her to express some of her inner perceptual world. These are just a few examples of remarkable perception in autism, which frequently manifests itself in art as self-expression and can extend to the therapeutic domain. According to Happé (1999), savant abilities in recognized domains such as music, painting, calculation, and memory are ten times more common in autistic people than in others with psychological disorders, occurring in around one out of every ten autistic people.

Furthermore, the question of whether autistic people have greater visuospatial ability relative to neurotypical people has been disputed for decades and continues to draw academics' interest. Embedded figures and mental rotation are among the visuospatial tasks most likely to reveal differences between autistic and neurotypical adults; however, the results vary due to methodological discrepancies between research. Such disparities are also evident when evaluating the cognitive profiles of neurotypical people in respect to their autistic features (Conson et al., 2022).

Key Theories

The underlying mechanisms of autistic visuospatial processing abilities are unknown, and recent research has yielded inconsistent and often contradictory findings (Kim et al., 2020). According to the findings, autistic children have an intact meta-cognitive ability to organize stimuli, but they prefer to focus on and replicate the components that interest them the most. Over the last few decades, a rising corpus of research has revealed novel skills in higher-level visuospatial processing (Allen & Courchesne, 2001; Keehn et al., 2010; Simmons et al., 2009). One such talent is the ability to recognize local elements of a stimuli in a larger perspective. Certain visuospatial attention skills, such as shape recognition in complicated designs, have been shown to improve in autistic persons. Studies have also regularly found variations in autistic people's prolonged and concentrated attention, which has been considered as a differentiating hallmark of later autism diagnosis (Chien et al., 2015).

Three separate (but not mutually exclusive) hypotheses about local/global processing in autism have been offered. Autistic people are thought to have limited global processing (Frith & Happé, 1994; Happé & Booth, 2008), enhanced local processing (Mottron et al., 2006; Plaisted et al., 2003), and a default preference to focus on local perceptual information (Plaisted et al., 1999). The evidence for each of these hypotheses, however, is frequently inconsistent.

Shah and Frith (1983) initially described atypical perceptual organization in autism. They later proposed the Weak Central Coherence (WCC) theory (Frith, 1989; Shah & Frith, 1993) to explain autistic people's exceptional performance in a variety of visuospatial tasks, including the embedded figures task, block design task, and apparent resistance to some visual illusions (Frith & Happé, 1994). WCC implies that autistic people have a higher local processing style, in which aspects of the object are perceived rapidly and frequently "pop out" of the context. Shah and Frith (1983, 1993) found that autistic youngsters have a local bias and fail to obtain global information. Thus, the researchers argued that local and global processing are independent and driven by two distinct systems.

The issue is that the WCC hypothesis is a difficult idea. Frith uses the term "central" to describe processes that extract overall meaning from a variety of data inputs (Frith, 1989). If these processes are genuinely "central," WCC may be anticipated to influence various levels of processing, from perception (typically referred to as "lower" levels) to conception (commonly referred to as "higher" levels). The challenge is determining what the central processes are. They could, for example, be the mechanisms responsible for creating a mental model or schema (Johnson-Laird, 1983). Alternatively, they could be attentional control processes that select goal-relevant input and suppress irrelevant input. However, it is unclear how changes in these processes affect central coherence at the perceptual level. Perceptual WCC might be caused by varied or weaker Gestalt processes, which are in charge of integrating the constituent components of a stimulus into a global whole. And, if this is the case, the term "central" is redundant, because Gestalt processes are often viewed as innate principles of perceptual organization (Cooper et al., 2015). Perhaps the contrast between "central" in perception and cognition should be emphasized further. Both cognitive science and popular psychology have historically supported the distinction between perception and cognition. There is little agreement on how to draw the line between the two (Phillips, 2019). As a result, Happé and Frith (2020) have dropped the "central" idea from the WCC theory.

In the early 2000s, Mottron and colleagues introduced the Enhanced Perceptual Functioning (EPF) idea. EPF provides an alternate hypothesis in which autistic people have enhanced low-level awareness, whereas global perception is discretionary. They discovered a local preference in autistic individuals and a lack of automatic global information extraction, implying that autistic participants prefer, but are not restricted to, a local processing style (Van der Hallen et al., 2015). Studies in which individuals are explicitly instructed to report the global or local level of hierarchical stimuli (e.g., "report the large letter" for stimuli shaped like a large letter) give evidence for altered global processing. According to these findings, autistic children and adults have less global precedent than ordinarily developing groups (Behrmann et al., 2006; Rinehart et al., 2001; Wang et al., 2007). Other research, employing the same tasks, have indicated that autistic children and adults perform similarly to typical controls (Hayward et al., 2012; Iarocci et al., 2006; Ozonoff & McEvoy, 1994; Plaisted et al., 1999; Scherf et al., 2007). When compared to typically developing people, autistic children and adults performed better (Perreault et al., 2011), worse (Nakano, 2010), and similarly (Vandenbroucke et al., 2008) on a variety of cognitive tasks that require global processing. Disagreements in these findings are most likely attributable to disparities in participant age (children vs. adults), phenotypic heterogeneity within autism, and the diverse stimuli used in these investigations.

Plaisted et al. (1999) also observed that autistic children performed comparably to typically developing children in a "selective attention" task, which required them to attend globally in one block of trials and locally in another. In a "divided" attention task in which participants were directed to monitor both global and local levels, autistic children outperformed typically developing children in terms of local objectives. Hayward et al. (2012) reproduced the conclusion that autistic individuals and typical controls performed similarly on the selective attention test but found no evidence of a larger local bias in the split attention task for the autistic group.

Finally, the Executive Dysfunction (ED) theory, proposed by Ozonoff et al. (1991), addresses executive function differences in autism. Autistic people performed differently than controls on various Executive Function (EF) tasks including working memory and reasoning (Minshew et al., 1997). The Executive Dysfunction Theory connects atypical frontal lobe function to autism, implying that EF differences in autism may be linked to atypical frontal lobe development, possibly through variations in synaptic connections, pruning, or myelination (Hill, 2004). This notion was reinforced by Luna et al. (2007), who identified fronto-parietal circuitry abnormalities as a possible reason of varying Working Memory performance on neuropsychological tasks in autism. They also stated that, although controls appeared to achieve prefrontal brain development around the age of 19, autistic participants did not reach maturity until the age of 25. Furthermore, autistic people have recently been shown to have poorer spatial integration skills (Cardillo et al., 2020). Several hypotheses have been proposed to explain the mixed results in visuospatial working memory (Brinkert, & Remington, 2020; Verte et al., 2006), implying that task demands, such as memory loading or attentional control, and memory (spatial simultaneous or sequential), may influence performance. What is unknown is whether an individual's greater perceptual capacity is related to sensory sensitivities (Brinkert & Remington, 2020). Autism has already been associated with improved visual perception (Bayliss & Kritikos, 2011). Increased perceptual load capacity may enhance distraction susceptibility when executing a task with low perceptual load, resulting in task-irrelevant processing (Brinkert & Remington, 2020). As previously indicated, it is unknown how perceptual bottom-up and cognitive bottom-down processes interact in these types of complicated tasks.

These theoretical frameworks have been studied for many years, but no unified consensus has been established, and research in this area is still extremely controversial. According to Van Der Hallen et al.'s (2015) meta-analysis of 56 studies involving 1000 autistic participants, the main issue is typically the studies themselves. They frequently differ in terms of participant demographics, sample size, stimuli, and task demands. Furthermore, the distinction between local and global processing is often ambiguous (Happé & Booth, 2008; Simmons & Todorova, 2018). There is also evidence of publication bias, and the tests utilized may not be focusing on the right parts of perceptual organization (Van der Hallen et al., 2015). It is also argued that autistic differences in visual processing, when compared to typically developing individuals, may have been exaggerated (Van der Hallen et al., 2015), and that many sensory difficulties are visible in a large proportion of the general population (Robertson & Simmons, 2015). Overall, the conflicting findings relating local and global processing preferences for both autistic and non-autistic populations have yet to be reconciled (Muth et al., 2014; Van der Hallen et al., 2015). Recently, researchers developed a dimensional model of autism (Fletcher-Watson & Happé, 2019). This paradigm implies that autistic features are distributed uniformly over a spectrum in both autistic and non-autistic populations. As a result, investigating the general population is a realistic strategy to get more insight into the visual processing patterns used by people with varied degrees of autistic features. The fluidity of the boundaries between various neurodevelopmental conditions' "categories" is still being contested, and many symptoms assigned to one diagnosable "disorder" may exist in varied degrees of severity in several others (Mammarella et al., 2022).

Attention-Deficit Hyperactivity Disorder (ADHD)

ADHD is a neurodevelopmental disorder defined by inattention, hyperactivity, and impulsivity (APA, 2013). ADHD symptoms, like autism, have been seen in the general population (Lubke et al., 2009). Some ADHD symptoms have been linked to autism (Panagiotidi, Overton, & Stafford, 2018), with 38.5–40.2% of autistic cases meeting ADHD criteria (Rong et al., 2021). The DSM-5 (APA, 2013) allows for the simultaneous diagnosis of both conditions due to their similar genetic origins (Epstein et al., 2010) and executive dysfunction (Rommelse et al., 2011). When autism and ADHD co-occur, they frequently interact. Antshel and Hier discovered that individuals with ADHD who have also been diagnosed with autism exhibit more severe ADHD symptoms. Individuals with ADHD have also been observed to perform differently on activities that require global processing (Cohen & Kalanthroff, 2019; Song & Hakoda, 2015), exhibiting comparable tendencies to autistic people.

According to Song and Hakoda's (2015) findings, children with ADHD displayed a reduced preference for global processing, which contradicts DSM-5 (APA, 2013) criteria that highlight failure to pay attention to detail. Pehlivanidis et al. (2020) suggest that the link between ADHD and autism could simply be due to different adaptive mechanisms. For example, autistic individuals frequently prefer to focus on details, such as number sequences, when sensorily overwhelmed, whereas individuals with ADHD may demonstrate local preference because breaking difficult tasks into smaller parts may help them organize their cognitive processes. Currently, the DSM-5 states that symptoms of inattention in people with ADHD may be a result of their difficulty completely attending and focusing on minor elements of their perceptual environment. This remark contradicts current data, indicating that the ADHD diagnosis criteria may need to be updated. Furthermore, new research suggests that autism and ADHD may have similar general visual processing styles, which could explain the overlap of symptoms (e.g., behavioral issues, difficulties with social interaction, particularly in a neurotypical setting). Currently, the amount of this overlap is unknown (Groom et al., 2010) and requires further exploration.

ADHD, like other neurodevelopmental conditions, has a wide range of symptom profiles, cognitive profiles, neurobiological and hereditary characteristics. Individuals with ADHD perform worse than controls in multiple domains, including inhibition, working memory, memory span, processing speed, arousal, temporal information processing, response variability, and motivational processes (Barkley, 1997; Engelhardt et al., 2008). However, the findings of neuropsychological differences have relatively moderate effect sizes; not all people with the disorders exhibit these differences, and each individual has a unique profile of such variances. Coghill et al. (2017) investigated six cognitive domains: inhibitory control, memory, delay aversion, decision-making, temporal processing, and response variability, and found that ADHD children performed badly at the group level in all domains when compared to neurotypical children. However, only 75% of these encountered difficulties, none had issues in all domains, and just 10% experienced problems in four or more domains. These data indicate that these categories are generally independent of one another, supporting the presence of distinct routes to ADHD. These data further support the view that ADHD is a heterogeneous disorder in terms of cognitive functioning, clinical symptoms, and differences, which is similar to the heterogeneity issue in autism.

ADHD and autism have substantial phenotypic and etiological parallels (Antshel & Russo, 2019; Johnston et al., 2013). Attentional and executive problems, behavioral disorders, and impaired social skills are all prevalent characteristics (Antshel & Russo, 2019; Bramham et al., 2009; Craig et al., 2015; Johnston et al., 2013). However, research has found that the manifestation and etiology of these areas differ between the two circumstances (Bramham et al., 2009; Mikami et al., 2019; Salley et al., 2015). For example, studies on young people have shown that communication and social interaction differences are related to negative behavior (e.g., impulsive speech and intrusiveness) in ADHD, whereas there is an absence of positive behavior (e.g., social approach and eye contact) in autism, which is thought to be due to not knowing "what to do" (Mikami et al., 2019). Meanwhile, research has increasingly shown that, despite their overlap, ADHD and autism are distinct conditions (Craig et al., 2015; Lau-Zhu et al., 2019), but their co-occurrence is common (Murray, 2010), including in adults (Johnson et al., 2005; Ohnishi et al., 2019).

Ozonoff and Jensen (1999) and Sergeant et al. (2003) stated that autism and ADHD each have their own individual "fingerprint" of executive function differences, and that future research should focus on identifying these patterns. Since then, research on the executive functioning profile of autistic children with ADHD has been broken down into numerous unitary components, including planning, working memory, flexibility, and inhibition (Verte et al., 2006). Autistic people with ADHD experience a variety and intensity of issues in several discrete domains of executive function. However, as Pehlivanidis et al. (2020) highlight, the area of attentional organization in autism and ADHD shares similar characteristics.

Autistic children, for example, have shown more significant disparities in attention shifting (Corbett et al., 2009; Courchesne et al., 1994). One example is their difficulties with the local–global processing task, which assesses spatial attention. This task necessitates decision-making based on inputs having both local and global properties. Autistic children may struggle with such activities due to their inflexibility in attention switching, as indicated by their difficulty shifting from attending to local details to global elements rather than vice versa. Aside from issues with cognitive flexibility, autistic children frequently struggle with planning. There is a considerable body of data indicating subclinical autistic features are common in the general population (Austin, 2005), and that they are continually dispersed (Constantino & Todd, 2003). Although clinical diagnoses are categorical, ADHD can also be seen dimensionally, with inattentive and hyperactive-impulsive symptoms occurring continually in the general population (Rodriguez & Baylis, 2007).

Dimensionality in autism has long been recognized. Evidence that relatives of autistic people frequently exhibit autism-like traits to varying degrees (Constantino et al., 2007) has given rise to the concept of a "broader phenotype" of autism. Furthermore, there is evidence that these characteristics are not only prevalent in the general population (Constantino & Todd, 2003), but are also distributed in a continuous manner (Hoekstra et al., 2008) with several co-occurring conditions, such as alexithymia (Barros et al., 2022), synesthesia (Dance et al., 2021; van Leeuwen et al., 2019; van Leeuwen et al., 2020; Ward & Simner, 2022), aphantasia (Dance et al., 2021), and many others.

The idea that autism's behavioral characteristics may extend beyond diagnosed autism is a relatively new concept (Happé & Frith, 2020); however, it is replicated in many other conditions such as ADHD. Instruments such as the Autism Spectrum Quotient (AQ) helped to broaden the autism phenotypic to the general population (although the questionnaire is being used in research much less these days due to over emphasis on male autistic phenotype). In the last ten years, there has been a significant increase in the number of autism research that has included non-diagnosed persons and investigated correlations of increased autistic features in general population samples. Approaching autism and ADHD through trait analysis and the nature of heterogeneity has recently revealed that some self-report measures, such as the AQ and other emerging questionnaires (such as CATI (English et al., 2025)), may reveal how various cognitive and perceptual domains in these conditions (or traits) overlap. Furthermore, with the involvement of the neurodivergent community and an increase in the use of qualitative measurements, we have been able to gain a better understanding of how autism and ADHD features (or diagnoses) are related.

Monotropism and Alternative Perspective on Perceptual Differences

Monotropism can be regarded in two ways: as a hypothesis of autism and as a trait that describes a certain pattern of attention allocation. As a theory, it proposes that many autistic differences stem from how attention is distributed, mainly focused on a few highly specific interests rather than wider spread, offering a unifying lens on behaviors and experiences that other cognitive accounts struggle to explain together (e.g., the intensity and centrality of "special interests," difficulties switching tasks, and the comfort of predictable attractors) (Murray et al., 2005). Monotropism is a feature that emphasizes lived, moment-to-moment "attention tunnels," in which whatever is currently gripping interest captures cognitive resources and being dragged out of that state is uncomfortable and slow (Murray, 2021). This framing is consistent with the discussions on perceptual diversity and the "same environment, different experience" motif. If attention and motivation are concentrated in a narrow band of interests, sensory input outside that tunnel will receive less anticipatory scaffolding, whereas stimuli inside it can be processed with striking depth and affective charge (Murray et al., 2005). That distribution helps to explain why controllability, predictability, and time to shift attention are so important in autistic comfort and performance; it also corresponds to accounts of aphantasia/hyperphantasia (top-down imagery precision) and conditions such as misophonia or visual snow (input channels that demand priority) but does not incorporate them into autism.

Monotropism provides a theoretical justification for the strong engagement, flow, and relaxing quality that we frequently experience when technologies fit a participant's interests and offer control over sensory statistics. A monotropic learner benefits from interest-led, low-collision environments that limit forced context switching while maximizing deep exploration, which is exactly what an infinite VR canvas with reversible actions, changeable ambience, and multi-perspective viewing can provide (more on this in later chapters). The theory also supports our methodological position: because drawings are frequently the most natural communicative medium within someone's attention tunnel, we should treat them as primary evidence rather than mere prompts or illustrations, and develop protocols that keep image + talk + action traces aligned (Murray, 2021; Murray et al., 2005).

Ultimately, people differ and monotropism (or any of theories presented) is unlikely to describe all variations of perceptual differences; however, discussing alternative lenses may be useful consideration for some of the elements of these differences. Monotropism provides a strong, practice-changing insight: if we fail to understand the intensity and aim of autistic passions, we misread behaviors and design inappropriate contexts and research (Murray, 2021; Murray et al., 2005). Including this lens in our mixed-methods work—VR drawing, multimodal displays, and analysis of drawn artifacts—helps to bridge previously siloed literatures and fills a real gap: clear, transparent protocols for presenting and analyzing drawings when they are the primary communicative channel for some neurodivergent participants.

Perceptual Differences and Neurodivergence

Contemporary theories of autistic perception increasingly define discrepancies as variances in the brain's weighting and organization of sensory input, rather than deficiencies. The Weak Central Coherence (WCC) theory (Frith & Happé, 1994) proposes a bias toward local detail processing over global integration. This has been used to explain autistic tendency to pay close attention to minor details and trends. The Enhanced Perceptual Functioning (EPF) concept (Mottron et al., 2006) expands on this idea, claiming that autistic people have superior low-level perceptual discrimination and rely on perceptual regions even during complicated cognitive activities. The visual search and embedded figure paradigms provide empirical support for both theories (Bertone et al., 2005; Dakin & Frith,

2005). More recently, predictive processing accounts (Pellicano & Burr, 2012; Lawson et al., 2014; Palmer et al., 2017) have reframed autism as involving atypical weighting of sensory evidence and prior expectations, often referred to as "flatter" priors or altered precision weighting, which can lead to hypersensitivity and a preference for controllable, low-uncertainty environments. As discussed earlier, monotropism (Murray et al., 2005; Lawson, 2025) views autistic attention as intensely concentrated on a small number of interests at a time, resulting in rich engagement but problems with quick context change. Together, these theories demonstrate that perception is not static or uniform; it is influenced by cognitive preferences, sensory integration, and individual brain tuning.

Expanding this lens to incorporate other perceptual circumstances reveals an even more diverse range of human variation. Aphantasia, or the absence or significant reduction of voluntary visual imagery, represents the bottom end of the imagery continuum. Individuals with aphantasia frequently use verbal or conceptual strategies for creative or memory activities (Zeman et al., 2015; Dawes et al., 2020). Hyperphantasia, on the other hand, is defined by extremely vivid imagery, which is frequently accompanied by powerful emotional and sensory associations (Dance et al., 2021). These extremes influence how people approach art, design, and even problem solving: hyperphantasic individuals may easily imagine compositions, whereas those with aphantasia may rely on tangible references or digital tools like 3D modeling and VR to externalize mental imagery. Such discrepancies are reminiscent of autistic perceptual variability, in which internal visualization, attention to detail, and imagination may be distributed atypically.

Synesthesia provides another doorway into perceptual variability. In grapheme-color synesthesia, letters or numbers produce constant color experiences, although in other variations, noises, tastes, or even personalities can cause visual impressions (Ward & Simner, 2020). Neuroimaging studies indicate that cross-activation between sensory regions and unusual connection patterns explain for these consistent cross-modal correspondences (Hubbard et al., 2011). Synesthesia is typically associated with increased memory for visual details and artistic creativity (Simner et al., 2009). Synesthesia, which has long been romanticized in talks of "artistic minds," reveals how perceptual systems can combine modalities to form unique aesthetic experiences—phenomena that are consistent with EPF explanations of autism that emphasize perceptual richness and local accuracy.

Visual Snow Syndrome (VSS) is a distinct form of perceptual syndrome that appears as a continuous overlay of dynamic "static" across the visual field, followed by afterimages, photophobia, and decreased night vision (Puledda & Goadsby, 2020). VSS is hypothesized to be associated with hyperexcitability in the visual cortex as well as disruption of thalamocortical rhythms. Although upsetting for some, the condition demonstrates how neuronal gain and cortical excitability influence subjective visual worlds. When compared to autism, VSS demonstrates how affected sensory filtering, whether due to cortical noise or predictive imbalance, can influence one's feeling of stability and contrast sensitivity, both of which are essential for sensory comfort.

Another example of neurodivergent perceptual differences is a developmental prosopagnosia (DP), a lifetime problem recognizing faces in the absence of brain injury, affects approximately 2–3% of the population (Susilo & Duchaine, 2013). Individuals with DP frequently use alternate tactics to identify persons, such as voice, clothes, or context signals (Dalrymple & Palermo, 2016). Neuroimaging reveals abnormal function in the fusiform face area and anterior temporal cortex (Behrmann & Avidan, 2005). DP is a prominent example of domain-specific perceptual specialization: while face processing is compromised, broad object recognition is frequently preserved. This is consistent with the pattern of "islets of ability" reported in autism, enhanced or reduced performance depending on the perceptual domain, and supports EPF's emphasis on specialization over impairment.

Misophonia, characterized by acute emotional reactions (anger, anxiety, disgust) to specific sounds like chewing or breathing, is another example of sensory-emotional processing. According to several studies, there is increased connection between auditory cortices and the anterior insula, implying that ordinary sounds are salient and effect considerably faster than in typical listeners (Kumar et al., 2017; Schröder et al., 2013). The consequent desire for environmental control is analogous to autistic sensory sensitivities, in which predictability and controllability frequently dictate comfort. Misophonia also demonstrates the "precision-weighting" imbalance suggested by predictive coding models, in which specific sensory channels dominate the perceptual hierarchy.

These instances demonstrate a key principle: perceptual reality is built separately by the sensory system's weighting, connection, and interpretive priors. Predictive coding (Friston, 2010; Palmer et al., 2017) is a theoretical framework that positions autism and associated perceptual problems on a continuum of differences in prior precision and sensory input. Aphantasia has less top-down prediction (imagery), while VSS has an excess of bottom-up sensory noise, misophonia has increased affective precision on specific stimuli, and synesthesia has hyperconnectivity between modalities. Collectively, these situations contribute to a better understanding of autistic perception by demonstrating how disparities in neuronal growth and connection produce diverse cognitive styles.

Chapter Conclusion

This chapter has mapped the major theoretical accounts used to explain neurodivergent differences in perception and cognition, focusing on autistic visual processing and the enduring local–global debate in perceptual organization, while showing why inconsistent findings and methodological variation have kept the field unsettled. By critically positioning frameworks such as Weak Central Coherence, Enhanced Perceptual Functioning, executive dysfunction, predictive processing/precision weighting, and monotropism, it has highlighted a shift from behavioral description toward mechanistic explanation—alongside the limits of any single account as a universal explanation for heterogeneous lived experience. Extending the neurodiversity frame to conditions such as aphantasia and hyperphantasia, synesthesia, visual snow syndrome, developmental prosopagnosia, and misophonia, the chapter argued that perceptual worlds are constructed through distinctive combinations of sensory weighting, priors, connectivity, and affective salience.

References

Allen, G., & Courchesne, E. (2001). Attention function and dysfunction in autism. *Frontiers in Bioscience, 6*(1), 105–119.

American Psychiatric Association. (2013). *Diagnostic and statistical manual of mental disorders* (5th edn). https://doi.org/10.1176/appi.books.9780890425596

Antshel, K. M., & Russo, N. (2019). Autism spectrum disorders and ADHD: Overlapping phenomenology, diagnostic issues, and treatment considerations. *Current Psychiatry Reports, 21*(5), 34.

Austin, E. J. (2005). Personality correlates of the broader autism phenotype as assessed by the Autism Spectrum Quotient (AQ). *Personality and Individual Differences, 38*(2), 451–460.

Baird, G., Simonoff, E., Pickles, A., Chandler, S., Loucas, T., Meldrum, D., & Charman, T. (2006). Prevalence of disorders of the autism spectrum in a population cohort of children in South Thames: The Special Needs and Autism Project (SNAP). *The Lancet, 368*(9531), 210–215.

Barkley, R. A. (1997). Behavioral inhibition, sustained attention, and executive functions: Constructing a unifying theory of ADHD. *Psychological Bulletin, 121*(1), 65.

Barros, F., Figueiredo, C., & Soares, S. C. (2022). Autism traits dimensionality and multivariate relationship with alexithymia and anxiety in the general population. *Research in Developmental Disabilities, 131*, 104361.

Bayliss, A. P., & Kritikos, A. (2011). Brief report: Perceptual load and the autism spectrum in typically developed individuals. *Journal of Autism and Developmental Disorders, 41*(11), 1573–1578.

Behrmann, M., & Avidan, G. (2005). Congenital prosopagnosia: Face-blind from birth. *Trends in Cognitive Sciences, 9*(4), 180–187. https://doi.org/10.1016/j.tics.2005.02.011

Behrmann, M., Thomas, C., & Humphreys, K. (2006). Seeing it differently: Visual processing in autism. *Trends in Cognitive Sciences, 10*(6), 258–264.

Bertone, A., Mottron, L., Jelenic, P., & Faubert, J. (2005). Enhanced and diminished visuo-spatial information processing in autism depends on stimulus complexity. *Brain, 128*(10), 2430–2441. https://doi.org/10.1093/brain/awh561

Bogdashina, O. (2016). *Sensory perceptual issues in autism and asperger syndrome: Different sensory experiences-different perceptual worlds.* Jessica Kingsley Publishers.

Bramham, J., Ambery, F., Young, S., Morris, R., Russell, A., Xenitidis, K., et al. (2009). Executive functioning differences between adults with attention deficit hyperactivity disorder and autistic spectrum disorder in initiation, planning and strategy formation. *Autism, 13*(3), 245–264.

Brinkert, J., & Remington, A. (2020). Making sense of the perceptual capacities in autistic and non-autistic adults. *Autism, 24*(7), 1795–1804.

Cardillo, R., Vio, C., & Mammarella, I. C. (2020). A comparison of local-global visuospatial processing in autism spectrum disorder, nonverbal learning disability, ADHD and typical development. *Research in Developmental Disabilities, 103*, 103682.

Chien, Y. L., Gau, S. F., Shang, C. Y., Chiu, Y. N., Tsai, W. C., & Wu, Y. Y. (2015). Visual memory and sustained attention impairment in youths with autism spectrum disorders. *Psychological Medicine, 45*(11), 2263–2273.

Coghill, D. R., Banaschewski, T., Soutullo, C., Cottingham, M. G., & Zuddas, A. (2017). Systematic review of quality of life and functional outcomes in randomized placebo-controlled studies of medications for attentiondeficit/hyperactivity disorder. *European Child & Adolescent Psychiatry, 26*(11), 1283–1307.

Cohen, E., & Kalanthroff, E. (2019). Visuospatial processing bias in ADHD: A potential artifact in the Wechsler Adult Intelligence Scale and the Rorschach Inkblots Test. *Psychological Assessment, 31*(5), 699.

Conson, M., Senese, V. P., Zappullo, I., Baiano, C., Warrier, V., Raimo, S., et al. (2022). The effect of autistic traits on disembedding and mental rotation in neurotypical women and men. *Scientific Reports, 12*(1), 4639.

Constantino, J. N., Lavesser, P. D., Zhang, Y. I., Abbacchi, A. M., Gray, T., & Todd, R. D. (2007). Rapid quantitative assessment of autistic social impairment by classroom teachers. *Journal of the American Academy of Child & Adolescent Psychiatry, 46*(12), 1668–1676.

Constantino, J. N., & Todd, R. D. (2003). Autistic traits in the general population: A twin study. *Archives of General Psychiatry, 60*(5), 524–530.

Cooper, R. A., Plaisted-Grant, K. C., Hannula, D. E., Ranganath, C., Baron-Cohen, S., & Simons, J. S. (2015). Impaired recollection of visual scene details in adults with autism spectrum conditions. *Journal of Abnormal Psychology, 124*(3), 565.

Corbett, B. A., Constantine, L. J., Hendren, R., Rocke, D., & Ozonoff, S. (2009). Examining executive functioning in children with autism spectrum disorder, attention deficit hyperactivity disorder and typical development. *Psychiatry Research, 166*(2–3), 210–222.

Courchesne, E., Townsend, J., Akshoomoff, N. A., Saitoh, O., Yeung-Courchesne, R., Lincoln, A. J., et al. (1994). Impairment in shifting attention in autistic and cerebellar patients. *Behavioral Neuroscience, 108*(5), 848.

Craig, F., Lamanna, A. L., Margari, F., Matera, E., Simone, M., & Margari, L. (2015). Overlap between autism spectrum disorders and attention deficit hyperactivity disorder: Searching for distinctive/common clinical features. *Autism research, 8*(3), 328–337.

Dakin, S., & Frith, U. (2005). Vagaries of visual perception in autism. *Neuron, 48*(3), 497–507. https://doi.org/10.1016/j.neuron.2005.10.018

Dalrymple, K. A., & Palermo, R. (2016). Guidelines for studying developmental prosopagnosia in adults and children. *WIREs Cognitive Science, 7*(1), 73–87. https://doi.org/10.1002/wcs.1374

Dance, C. J., Ward, J., & Simner, J. (2021). What is the link between mental imagery and sensory sensitivity? Insights from aphantasia. *Perception, 50*(9), 757–782.

Dawes, A. J., Keogh, R., Andrillon, T., & Pearson, J. (2020). A cognitive profile of multi-sensory imagery, memory and dreaming in aphantasia. *Scientific Reports, 10*, 10022. https://doi.org/10.1038/s41598-020-65705-7

Engelhardt, P. E., Nigg, J. T., Carr, L. A., & Ferreira, F. (2008). Cognitive inhibition and working memory in attention-deficit/hyperactivity disorder. *Journal of Abnormal Psychology, 117*(3), 591.

English, M. C., Poulsen, R. E., Maybery, M. T., McAlpine, D., Sowman, P. F., & Pellicano, E. (2025). Psychometric evaluation of the Comprehensive Autistic Trait Inventory in autistic and non-autistic adults. *Autism, 29*(12), 2955–2974.

Epstein, J. N., Langberg, J. M., Lichtenstein, P. K., Altaye, M., Brinkman, W. B., House, K., & Stark, L. J. (2010). Attention-deficit/hyperactivity disorder outcomes for children treated in community-based pediatric settings. *Archives of Pediatrics & Adolescent Medicine, 164*(2), 160–165.

Fleischmann, A., & Fleischmann, R. H. (2012). Advantages of an ADHD diagnosis in adulthood: Evidence from online narratives. *Qualitative Health Research, 22*(11), 1486–1496.

Fletcher-Watson, S., & Happé, F. (2019). *Autism: A new introduction to psychological theory and current debate.* Routledge.

Freeseman, L. J., Colombo, J., & Coldren, J. T. (1993). Individual differences in infant visual attention: Four-month-olds' discrimination and generalization of global and local stimulus properties. *Child Development, 64*(4), 1191–1203.

Friston, K. (2010). The free-energy principle: A unified brain theory? *Nature Reviews Neuroscience, 11*, 127–138. https://doi.org/10.1038/nrn2787

Frith, U. (1989). Autism and "theory of mind". In *Diagnosis and treatment of autism* (pp. 33–52). Springer US.

Frith, U. (2003). *Autism: Explaining the enigma.* Blackwell Publishing.

Frith, U., & Happé, F. (1994). Autism: Beyond "theory of mind". *Cognition, 50*(1–3), 115–132.

Garon, N., Zwaigenbaum, L., Bryson, S., Smith, I. M., Brian, J., Roncadin, C., et al. (2016). Temperament and its association with autism symptoms in a high-risk population. *Journal of Abnormal Child Psychology, 44*(4), 757–769.

Goldstein, E. B., & Brockmole, J. (2016). *Sensation and perception* (8. Baskı). Wadsworth Cengage Learning.

Grandin, T., & Duffy, K. (2008). *Developing talents: Careers for individuals with Asperger syndrome and high-functioning autism.* AAPC Publishing.

Groom, M. J., Scerif, G., Liddle, P. F., Batty, M. J., Liddle, E. B., Roberts, K. L., et al. (2010). Effects of motivation and medication on electrophysiological markers of response inhibition in children with attentiondeficit/hyperactivity disorder. *Biological Psychiatry, 67*(7), 624–631.

Hadad, B. S., & Yashar, A. (2022). Sensory perception in autism: What can we learn? *Annual Review of Vision Science, 8*, 239–264.

Happé, F. (1999). Autism: Cognitive deficit or cognitive style? *Trends in Cognitive Sciences, 3*(6), 216–222.

Happé, F., & Frith, U. (2020). Annual research review: Looking back to look forward–changes in the concept of autism and implications for future research. *Journal of Child Psychology and Psychiatry, 61*(3), 218–232.

Happé, F., & Ronald, A. (2008). The 'fractionable autism triad': A review of evidence from behavioural, genetic, cognitive and neural research. *Neuropsychology Review, 18*(4), 287–304. https://doi.org/10.1007/s11065-008-9076-8

Happé, F. G., & Booth, R. D. (2008). The power of the positive: Revisiting weak coherence in autism spectrum disorders. *The Quarterly Journal of Experimental Psychology, 61*(1), 50–63.

Hayward, D. A., Shore, D. I., Ristic, J., Kovshoff, H., Iarocci, G., Mottron, L., & Burack, J. A. (2012). Flexible visual processing in young adults with autism: The effects of implicit learning on a global–local task. *Journal of Autism and Developmental Disorders, 42*(11), 2383–2392.

Heffler, K. F., & Oestreicher, L. M. (2016). Causation model of autism: Audiovisual brain specialization in infancy competes with social brain networks. *Medical Hypotheses, 91*, 114–122.

Hill, E. L. (2004). Executive dysfunction in autism. *Trends in Cognitive Sciences, 8*(1), 26–32.

Hubbard, E. M., et al. (2011). The cross-activation theory at 10. *Journal of Neuropsychology, 5*(2), 152–177. https://doi.org/10.1111/j.1748-6653.2011.02014.x

Hoekstra, R. A., Bartels, M., Cath, D. C., & Boomsma, D. I. (2008). Factor structure, reliability and criterion validity of the Autism-Spectrum Quotient (AQ): A study in Dutch population and patient groups. *Journal of Autism and Developmental Disorders, 38*(8), 1555–1566.

Iarocci, G., Burack, J. A., Shore, D. I., Mottron, L., & Enns, J. T. (2006). Global–local visual processing in high functioning children with autism: Structural vs. implicit task biases: Iarocci et al. *Journal of Autism and Developmental Disorders, 36*(1), 117–129.

Johnson, S. C., Lowery, N., Kohler, C., & Turetsky, B. I. (2005). Global–local visual processing in schizophrenia: Evidence for an early visual processing deficit. *Biological Psychiatry, 58*(12), 937–946.

Johnson-Laird, P. N. (1983). *Mental models: Towards a cognitive science of language, inference, and consciousness* (vol 6). Harvard University Press.

Johnston, K., Dittner, A., Bramham, J., Murphy, C., Knight, A., & Russell, A. (2013). Attention deficit hyperactivity disorder symptoms in adults with autism spectrum disorders. *Autism Research, 6*(4), 225–236.

Kandalaft, M. R., Didehbani, N., Krawczyk, D. C., Allen, T. T., & Chapman, S. B. (2013). Virtual reality social cognition training for young adults with high-functioning autism. *Journal of Autism and Developmental Disorders, 43*(1), 34–44.

Kapp, S. K. (2025). Sensory–movement underpinnings of lifelong neurodivergence: Getting a grip on autism. *Frontiers in Integrative Neuroscience, 19*, 1489322.

Keehn, B., Lincoln, A. J., Müller, R. A., & Townsend, J. (2010). Attentional networks in children and adolescents with autism spectrum disorder. *Journal of Child Psychology and Psychiatry, 51*(11), 1251–1259.

Kim, S. Y., Song, D. Y., Kim, Y. A., Bong, G., Kim, J. M., Kim, J. H., & Yoo, H. J. (2020). How do children with autism spectrum disorder encode and reproduce visuospatial stimuli?: Investigation into visuospatial processing abilities and styles. *Psychiatry Investigation, 17*(11), 1105.

Kumar, S., et al. (2017). The brain basis for misophonia. *Current Biology, 27*(4), 527–533. https://doi.org/10.1016/j.cub.2016.12.048

Lau-Zhu, A., Lau, M. P., & McLoughlin, G. (2019). Mobile EEG in research on neurodevelopmental disorders: Opportunities and challenges. *Developmental Cognitive Neuroscience, 36*, 100635.

Lawson, R. P., Rees, G., & Friston, K. J. (2014). An aberrant precision account of autism. *Frontiers in Human Neuroscience, 8*, 302. https://doi.org/10.3389/fnhum.2014.00302

Lawson, W. B. (2025). Monotropism theory. In *Autism and being monotropic: What medical and other practitioners need to know* (pp. 17–27). Springer Nature Singapore.

Lewkowicz, D. J. (2014). Early experience and multisensory perceptual narrowing. *Developmental Psychobiology, 56*(2), 292–315.

Lewkowicz, D. J., & Ghazanfar, A. A. (2009). The emergence of multisensory systems through perceptual narrowing. *Trends in Cognitive Sciences, 13*(11), 470–478.

Li, W., Lai, T. M., Bohon, C., Loo, S. K., McCurdy, D., Strober, M., et al. (2015). Anorexia nervosa and body dysmorphic disorder are associated with abnormalities in processing visual information. *Psychological Medicine, 45*(10), 2111–2122.

Lopez, C., Tchanturia, K., Stahl, D., & Treasure, J. (2008). Central coherence in eating disorders: A systematic review. *Psychological Medicine, 38*(10), 1393–1404.

Lubke, G. H., Hudziak, J. J., Derks, E. M., van Bijsterveldt, T. C., & Boomsma, D. I. (2009). Maternal ratings of attention problems in ADHD: Evidence for the existence of a continuum. *Journal of the American Academy of Child & Adolescent Psychiatry, 48*(11), 1085–1093.

Luna, B., Doll, S. K., Hegedus, S. J., Minshew, N. J., & Sweeney, J. A. (2007). Maturation of executive function in autism. *Biological Psychiatry, 61*(4), 474–481.

Mammarella, I. C., Cardillo, R., & Semrud-Clikeman, M. (2022). Do comorbid symptoms discriminate between autism spectrum disorder, ADHD and nonverbal learning disability? *Research in Developmental Disabilities, 126*, 104242.

McKone, E., Davies, A. A., Fernando, D., Aalders, R., Leung, H., Wickramariyaratne, T., & Platow, M. J. (2010). Asia has the global advantage: Race and visual attention. *Vision Research, 50*(16), 1540–1549.

Mikami, K., Inomata, S., Onishi, Y., Orihashi, Y., Yamamoto, K., & Matsumoto, H. (2019). Gender differences in the suicide attempts of adolescents in emergency departments: Focusing on individuals with autism spectrum disorder. *Adolescent Psychiatry, 9*(3), 232–240.

Milton, D. E., & Green, J. (2024). Theorising autism. *Autism, 28*(4), 795–797.

Minshew, N. J., Goldstein, G., & Siegel, D. J. (1997). Neuropsychologic functioning in autism: Profile of a complex information processing disorder. *Journal of the International Neuropsychological Society, 3*(4), 303–316.

Mottron, L., Dawson, M., Soulières, I., Hubert, B., & Burack, J. (2006). Enhanced perceptual functioning in autism: An update, and eight principles of autistic perception. *Journal of Autism and Developmental Disorders, 36*(1), 27–43.

Murray, D. (2021). Monotropism: An interest-based account of autism. In *Encyclopedia of autism spectrum disorders* (pp. 2954–2956). Springer International Publishing.

Murray, D., Lesser, M., & Lawson, W. (2005). Attention, monotropism and the diagnostic criteria for autism. *Autism, 9*(2), 139–156.

Murray, M. J. (2010). Attention-deficit/hyperactivity disorder in the context of autism spectrum disorders. *Current Psychiatry Reports, 12*(5), 382–388.

Muth, A., Hönekopp, J., & Falter, C. M. (2014). Visuo-spatial performance in autism: A meta-analysis. *Journal of Autism and Developmental Disorders, 44*(12), 3245–3263.

Nakano, T., Tanaka, K., Endo, Y., Yamane, Y., Yamamoto, T., Nakano, Y., et al. (2010). Atypical gaze patterns in children and adults with autism spectrum disorders dissociated from developmental changes in gaze behaviour. *Proceedings of the Royal Society B: Biological Sciences, 277*(1696), 2935–2943.

Ohnishi, T., Kobayashi, H., Yajima, T., Koyama, T., & Noguchi, K. (2019). Psychiatric comorbidities in adult attention-deficit/hyperactivity disorder: Prevalence and patterns in the routine clinical setting. *Innovations in Clinical Neuroscience, 16*(9–10), 11.

Ozonoff, S., & Jensen, J. (1999). Brief report: Specific executive function profiles in three neurodevelopmental disorders. *Journal of Autism and Developmental Disorders, 29*(2), 171–177.

Ozonoff, S., & McEvoy, R. E. (1994). A longitudinal study of executive function and theory of mind development in autism. *Development and Psychopathology, 6*(3), 415–431.

Ozonoff, S., Pennington, B. F., & Rogers, S. J. (1991). Executive function deficits in high-functioning autistic individuals: Relationship to theory of mind. *Journal of Child Psychology and Psychiatry, 32*(7), 1081–1105.

Panagiotidi, M., Overton, P. G., & Stafford, T. (2018). The relationship between ADHD traits and sensory sensitivity in the general population. *Comprehensive Psychiatry, 80*, 179–185.

Pehlivanidis, A., Papanikolaou, K., Mantas, V., Kalantzi, E., Korobili, K., Xenaki, L. A., et al. (2020). Lifetime co-occurring psychiatric disorders in newly diagnosed adults with attention deficit hyperactivity disorder (ADHD) or/and autism spectrum disorder (ASD). *BMC Psychiatry, 20*(1), 423.

Perreault, A., Gurnsey, R., Dawson, M., Mottron, L., & Bertone, A. (2011). Increased sensitivity to mirror symmetry in autism. *PLoS One, 6*(4), e19519.

Phillips, B. (2019). The shifting border between perception and cognition. *Noûs, 53*(2), 316–346.

Palmer, C. J., Lawson, R. P., & Hohwy, J. (2017). Bayesian approaches to autism: Towards volatility, action, and behavior. *Psychological Bulletin, 143*(5), 521–542. https://doi.org/10.1037/bul0000097

Pellicano, E., & Burr, D. (2012). When the world becomes 'too real': A Bayesian explanation of autistic perception. *Trends in Cognitive Sciences, 16*(10), 504–510. https://doi.org/10.1016/j.tics.2012.08.009

Plaisted, K., Saksida, L., Alcántara, J., & Weisblatt, E. (2003). Towards an understanding of the mechanisms of weak central coherence effects: Experiments in visual configural learning and auditory perception. *Philosophical Transactions of the Royal Society of London. Series B: Biological Sciences, 358*(1430), 375–386.

Plaisted, K., Swettenham, J., & Rees, L. (1999). Children with autism show local precedence in a divided attention task and global precedence in a selective attention task. *The Journal of Child Psychology and Psychiatry and Allied Disciplines, 40*(5), 733–742.

Puledda, F., & Goadsby, P. J. (2020). Visual snow syndrome: A clinical and phenotypical description of 1,100 cases. *Neurology, 94*(6), e564–e574. https://doi.org/10.1212/WNL.0000000000008909

Qin, S., Nagai, Y., Kumagaya, S., Ayaya, S., & Asada, M. (2014, October). Autism simulator employing augmented reality: A prototype. In *4th International Conference on Development and Learning and on Epigenetic Robotics* (pp. 155–156). IEEE.

Ratto, A. B., Bascom, J., daVanport, S., Strang, J. F., Anthony, L. G., Verbalis, A., et al. (2023). Centering the inner experience of autism: Development of the self-assessment of autistic traits. *Autism in Adulthood, 5*(1), 93–105.

Rinehart, N. J., Bradshaw, J. L., Brereton, A. V., & Tonge, B. J. (2001). Movement preparation in high-functioning autism and Asperger disorder: A serial choice reaction time task involving motor reprogramming. *Journal of Autism and Developmental Disorders, 31*(1), 79–88.

Robertson, A. E., & Simmons, D. R. (2015). The sensory experiences of adults with autism spectrum disorder: A qualitative analysis. *Perception, 44*(5), 569–586.

Robertson, C. E., & Baron-Cohen, S. (2017). Sensory perception in autism. *Nature Reviews Neuroscience, 18*(11), 671–684.

Rodriguez, P. D., & Baylis, G. C. (2007). Activation of brain attention systems in individuals with symptoms of ADHD. *Behavioural Neurology, 18*(2), 115–130.

Rommelse, N. N., Geurts, H. M., Franke, B., Buitelaar, J. K., & Hartman, C. A. (2011). A review on cognitive and brain endophenotypes that may be common in autism spectrum disorder and attention-deficit/hyperactivity disorder and facilitate the search for pleiotropic genes. *Neuroscience & Biobehavioral Reviews, 35*(6), 1363–1396.

Rong, Y., Yang, C. J., Jin, Y., & Wang, Y. (2021). Prevalence of attention-deficit/hyperactivity disorder in individuals with autism spectrum disorder: A meta-analysis. *Research in Autism Spectrum Disorders, 83*, 101759.

Sadler-Smith, E. (2011). The intuitive style: Relationships with local/global and verbal/visual styles, gender, and superstitious reasoning. *Learning and Individual Differences, 21*(3), 263–270.

Salley, B., Gabrielli, J., Smith, C. M., & Braun, M. (2015). Do communication and social interaction skills differ across youth diagnosed with autism spectrum disorder, attention-deficit/hyperactivity disorder, or dual diagnosis? *Research in Autism Spectrum Disorders, 20*, 58–66.

Schauder, K. B., & Bennetto, L. (2016). Toward an interdisciplinary understanding of sensory dysfunction in autism spectrum disorder: An integration of the neural and symptom literatures. *Frontiers in Neuroscience, 10*, 268. https://doi.org/10.3389/fnins.2016.00268

Scherf, K. S., Behrmann, M., Humphreys, K., & Luna, B. (2007). Visual category-selectivity for faces, places and objects emerges along different developmental trajectories. *Developmental Science, 10*(4), F15–F30.

Schröder, A., Vulink, N., & Denys, D. (2013). Misophonia: Diagnostic criteria for a new psychiatric disorder. *PloS one, 8*(1), e54706.

Sergeant, J. A., Geurts, H., Huijbregts, S., Scheres, A., & Oosterlaan, J. (2003). The top and the bottom of ADHD: A neuropsychological perspective. *Neuroscience & Biobehavioral Reviews, 27*(7), 583–592.

Shah, A., & Frith, U. (1983). An islet of ability in autistic children: A research note. *Journal of Child Psychology and Psychiatry, 24*(4), 613–620.

Shah, A., & Frith, U. (1993). Why do autistic individuals show superior performance on the block design task? *Journal of Child Psychology and Psychiatry, 34*(8), 1351–1364.

Simmons, D. R., & Todorova, G. K. (2018). Local versus global processing in autism: Special section editorial. *Journal of Autism and Developmental Disorders, 48*(4), 1338–1340.

Simmons, D. R., et al. (2009). Vision in autism spectrum disorders. *Vision Research, 49*(22), 2705–2739. https://doi.org/10.1016/j.visres.2009.08.005

Simner, J., et al. (2009). (Synesthesia & memory review cited in your text.)

Song, Y., & Hakoda, Y. (2015). Lack of global precedence and global-to-local interference without local processing deficit: A robust finding in children with attention-deficit/hyperactivity disorder under different visual angles of the Navon task. *Neuropsychology, 29*(6), 888.

Susilo, T., & Duchaine, B. (2013). Advances in developmental prosopagnosia research. *Current Opinion in Neurobiology, 23*(3), 423–429. https://doi.org/10.1016/j.conb.2012.12.011

Van Leeuwen, T. M., Van Petersen, E., Burghoorn, F., Dingemanse, M., & Van Lier, R. (2019). Autistic traits in synaesthesia: Atypical sensory sensitivity and enhanced perception of details. *Philosophical Transactions of the Royal Society B: Biological Sciences, 374*, 1787.

Van Leeuwen, T. M., Neufeld, J., Hughes, J., & Ward, J. (2020). Synaesthesia and autism: Different developmental outcomes from overlapping mechanisms? *Cognitive Neuropsychology, 37*(7–8), 433–449.

Van der Hallen, R., Evers, K., Brewaeys, K., Van den Noortgate, W., & Wagemans, J. (2015). Global processing takes time: A meta-analysis on local–global visual processing in ASD. *Psychological Bulletin, 141*(3), 549–573. https://doi.org/10.1037/bul0000004

Vandenbroucke, M. W., Scholte, H. S., van Engeland, H., Lamme, V. A., & Kemner, C. (2008). A neural substrate for atypical low-level visual processing in autism spectrum disorder. *Brain, 131*(4), 1013–1024.

Verté, S., Geurts, H. M., Roeyers, H., Oosterlaan, J., & Sergeant, J. A. (2006). Executive Functioning in Children with an Autism Spectrum Disorder: Can We Differentiate Within the Spectrum? Verté, Geurts, Roeyers, Oosterlaan, and Sergeant. *Journal of Autism and Developmental Disorders, 36*(3), 351–372.

Wagemans, J., et al. (2012). A century of Gestalt psychology in visual perception: I. Perceptual grouping and figure–ground organization. *Psychological Bulletin, 138*(6), 1172–1217. https://doi.org/10.1037/a0029333

Wang, A. T., Lee, S. S., Sigman, M., & Dapretto, M. (2007). Reading affect in the face and voice: Neural correlates of interpreting communicative intent in children and adolescents with autism spectrum disorders. *Archives of General Psychiatry, 64*(6), 698–708.

Wang, M., & Reid, D. (2011). Virtual reality in pediatric neurorehabilitation: Attention deficit hyperactivity disorder, autism and cerebral palsy. *Neuroepidemiology, 36*(1), 2–18.

Ward, J., & Simner, J. (2020). Synesthesia: The current state of the field. In *Multisensory perception* (pp. 283–300). Academic Press. https://www.sciencedirect.com/science/chapter/edited-volume/abs/pii/B9780128124925000139

Ward, J., & Simner, J. (2022). How do different types of synesthesia cluster together? *Implications for causal mechanisms. Perception, 51*(2), 91–113.

Yovel, I., Revelle, W., & Mineka, S. (2005). Who sees trees before forest? The obsessive-compulsive style of visual attention. *Psychological Science, 16*(2), 123–129.

Zeman, A., Dewar, M., & Della Sala, S. (2015). Lives without imagery—Congenital aphantasia. *Cortex, 73*, 378–380. https://doi.org/10.1016/j.cortex.2015.05.019

CHAPTER 3

Beyond the Lab: Virtual reality as a Bridge Between Control and Experience

There is an increasing corpus of work analyzing the relationship between technical advancements and autism study. Since the start of the so-called technological revolution in the 1980s and 1990s, researchers have been encouraged to figure out how to best deploy new technologies. These trends can also be observed in autism studies. One of the earliest studies on the impact of modern technology breakthroughs on autism was published in the 1980s (e.g., Lovaas, 1987), coinciding with the introduction of personal computers. Since then, the quantity of published research articles on technology has grown dramatically. As the world has become more technologically advanced, research has attempted to keep pace.

In these modern technology times, it is becoming increasingly beneficial for research to match with social technological improvements (deLeyer-Tiarks et al., 2023). We are currently using technology for more entertainment and education than ever before. It is becoming obvious that autistic individuals not only understand but also enjoy technology. For example, when engaging with robots, autistic children have displayed prosocial behaviors (e.g., keeping eye contact, shared attention, imitation) that may not be noticed when dealing with humans (Robins et al., 2004). As a result, the data validates and encourages the continuous development of technological aids for autistic persons (deLeyer-Tiarks et al., 2023; Fletcher-Watson et al., 2016), including immersive technology like Virtual reality (VR).

S. Savickaite, *Exploring Neurodiversity Through Virtual Reality*,
https://doi.org/10.1007/978-3-032-19636-1_3

Virtual reality (VR) is as challenging to characterize as the experience itself (Fig. 3.1). VR systems are a complex combination of technology and human perception. VR is frequently defined as an artificial environment controlled (at least partially) by user interactions and perceived through computer-generated sensory signals (such as sights and sounds). A more simple definition of virtual reality is an artificial environment created by a computer and accessed through a display, most commonly a Head-Mounted Display (HMD) (Mandal, 2013). A head-mounted display (HMD) is a set of lenses with display screens attached. These are arranged in such a way that unique images are displayed to each eye, creating the fascinating illusion of a three-dimensional scene surrounding the user. A VR system often involves one or more input devices (such as controllers, gloves, or motion trackers) as well as cutting-edge visuals (Newbutt et al., 2020). HMDs frequently contain headphones that provide stereophonic sound, enhancing the sensation of immersion.

Virtual reality (VR) refers to a variety of technologies, such as virtual worlds (VW), massive multiplayer online role-playing games (MMORPGs), virtual (collaborative) environments, cave automatic virtual environments

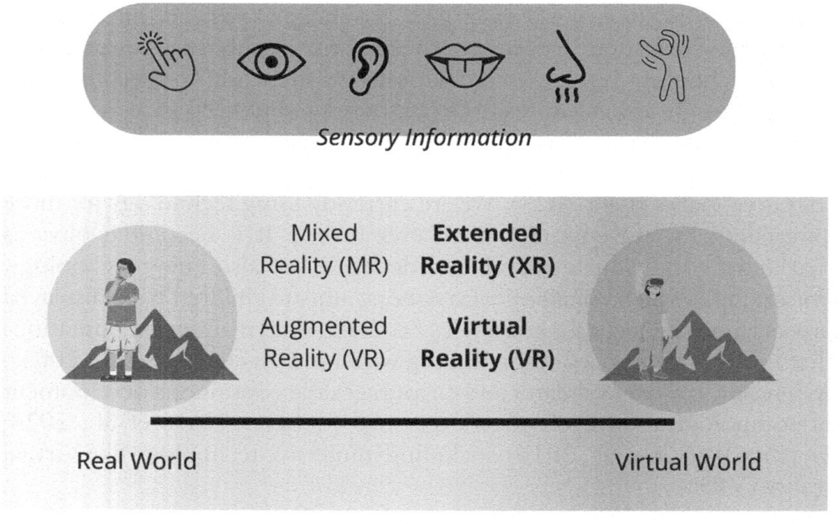

Fig. 3.1 This figure illustrates how sensory information supports experiences across the reality–virtuality continuum

(CAVE), static VR (using smartphones), and head-mounted displays (HMDs) (Newbutt et al., 2020). In the 1980s, Jaron Lanier created the phrase "Virtual reality" or "VR." Following an early surge in the 1980s and 1990s, the use of Virtual reality quickly declined due to restricted technological availability and expensive costs. Engineering, aeronautics, and visual perception were the primary areas of research (Sheridan, 1992; Robinett & Rolland, 1992). However, in 2014, Facebook (now Meta) purchased start-up company Oculus (BBC, 2014), ushering in a new era of virtual reality. The technology has gotten cheaper and more accessible. This has led to an increased interest in immersive technologies, such as augmented reality (AR) and mixed reality (MR).

The capabilities of virtual reality systems vary substantially depending on the device's capability and the quality of the three-dimensional world created. However, all VR systems have three common characteristics: immersion, interaction, and a sense of presence (Alcañiz Raya et al., 2020). Presence is usually assumed implicitly in immersive systems, to the point that the terms "immersion" and "presence" are commonly used interchangeably (Cummings & Bailenson, 2016). Furthermore, VR is frequently stated as simply "a computer-generated environment" (Pan & Hamilton, 2018). As Slater (2018) points out, a VR system must include a computer-generated world, ideally one that perceptually surrounds the participant. To understand "immersion," we should consider it as an objective property of a system, and higher or lower immersion as the extent to which a VR system can support natural sensorimotor contingencies for perception (O'Regan & Noë, 2001). Thus, a system that allows you to "perceive" with your complete body (bending down to look behind something or reaching out) would provide a greater level of immersion than one that merely allows you to stare at a small or limited display (Slater, 2018). Whereas "presence" is sometimes defined as the "belief" of being there in a virtual environment (Slater, 2018), presence does not involve believing; rather, it relates to creating the illusion of being there even when you are not. This is a visual illusion, not a cognitive one. This is the true power of VR, and, like many illusions, knowing it is an illusion does not change your perception or response to it (Slater, 2018).

Immersive VR research can investigate and identify mechanisms that underpin everyday perception more effectively than traditional laboratory tests. This is significant because psychology as a science requires generalizability to real-life situations. Even when immersive VR is used, the ecological validity of behavioral studies is not guaranteed (Vasser & Aru,

2020). While VR enables experimenters to create accurate duplicates of reality, it also allows researchers to change and violate the fundamental rules that control our environment in order to get new insights into the workings of the human mind. As the consumer VR content industry has grown in recent years, the basic criteria used thus far may be insufficient to fully reflect the intricacies of psychology and experimental VR paradigms (Vasser & Aru, 2020).

Dorothy Strickland published one of the first accounts of virtual reality in autism in 1997. Many empirical investigations have since recognized virtual reality as an essential therapeutic tool (Kandalaft et al., 2013; Wang & Reid, 2011). VR was offered as a useful tool, characterized by controllable stimuli, allowing for safe alteration of the environment, consisting largely of a visual and audio world, and with the potential for personalized scenarios (Strickland, 1997). Stimuli might be presented gradually and regulated, and given the frequent attentional variations in autism, an organized and customizable setting could help individuals retain their focus. Furthermore, participants may interact with the objects around them while aware that they were in a simulated environment. Computer-based treatments and interventions have also been demonstrated to be effective for autistic people (Strickland, 1997; Maskey et al., 2014).

So far, most VR research has used the head-mounted display (HMD) as the main way to get into virtual worlds. Ivan Sutherland's (1968) HMD (one of the first ones reported) created the sense of three-dimensional motion via the kinetic depth effect (Green, 1961). Psychologists Wallach and O'Connell (1953) first observed this effect by projecting the shadow of a revolving wire object onto a screen, leading participants to infer a 360-degree form from the moving shadow, thereby creating an illusion of rotation. Computer vision scientists Aloimonos and Brown (1989) built on this work by creating computational algorithms that explain how people update perceptual cues by regularizing optic flow. This is the perception of apparent motion from unchanging data in a scene relative to the observer's position (Marr & Vaina, 1982). This computational modeling of vision enhanced comprehension of stereoscopic perception in virtual environments (Aloimonos & Huang, 1990). These improvements happened at the same time as the release of HMDs that were lighter, cheaper, and sharper (Lanier, 2017). As human-computer interaction became more common, developmental psychology (Calvert & Tan, 1994), perceptual psychology (Gentilucci et al., 1994), and social psychology (Shapiro & McDonald, 1992) all became interested in VR as a research tool.

Perceptual psychologists, especially, were interested in VR research in the 1990s. They used non-mobile HMDs that were connected to rendering computers and transmitted audio through earbuds (Fox et al., 2009; Kalawsky, 1993; Loomis et al., 1999). Later advances made things more mobile. For example, real-time trackers, body and hand coordinates in space (Delaney & Biocca, 1995). Burdea and Coiffet (2003) suggested gloves and force-feedback systems to make things feel more real. These advancements created novel opportunities for the investigation of perceptual cues and multisensory integration. For example, Rothbaum et al. (1995a, 1995b) employed virtual reality exposure treatment to examine visuo-vestibular integration in acrophobia, whereas Warren et al. (2001) investigated optic flow and gait (Warren et al., 2001). Subsequently, Pine et al. (2002) investigated spatial cognition in virtual reality in conjunction with neuroimaging (see Bohil et al., 2011).

Improvements in rendering fidelity made ecological validity better, while multimodal tracking and visuotactile input gave researchers a way to examine artistic production in VR (Peli, 1990). However, VR's aesthetic uses did not catch on (Loomis et al., 1999). The HMD market started to go down in the middle of the 1990s (see Blascovich et al., 2002). By the 2000s, virtual reality in experimental psychology had virtually vanished (Slater & Sanchez-Vives, 2016). Nonetheless, cognitive neuroscience sustained modest yet promising VR initiatives, especially in therapeutic contexts. Rose et al. (2005) shown that VR interactivity is helpful for cognitive assessment and rehabilitation in patients with brain injuries, hence endorsing its application in cognitive remediation (e.g., Crosbie et al., 2007; Merians et al., 2002; Rizzo et al., 2005; Sveistrup, 2004). Nonetheless, Slater (2018) determined that the substantial expenses associated with HMDs and computing gear hindered widespread acceptance within the field of psychology.

Virtual reality (VR) can provide a comprehensive assessment of cognitive spatial processing skills in diverse populations (Connors et al., 2014; Bennett et al., 2018; Malihi et al., 2020). Adjorlu and colleagues conducted several studies on how autistic children utilize VR applications and HMDs (Adjorlu et al., 2017; Adjorlu & Serafin, 2019a, 2019b). They largely concentrated on daily skill development, such as grocery shopping, crossing the street, money management, and social skills. Their findings on learning outcomes, less disruptive behavior and social anxiety, and collaborative learning in inclusive classrooms are very encouraging. Furthermore, Newbutt et al. (2020) reported that for autistic students,

HMDs were enjoyable, physically and visually comfortable, and simple to use. Parong and Mayer (2020) argued that video games could help people enhance their cognitive, social, and academic skills.

These strands collectively depict a merging narrative: Virtual reality (VR) serves as a potent experimental instrument to investigate perception and interaction among diverse neurotypes, while firsthand narratives and rights-based methodologies highlight the necessity of prioritizing agency, lived experience, and ecological context. Instead of seeing inner speech, sensory processing, or gaze perception as fixed standards, a neurodiversity paradigm asks us to look at how social and technological settings can help people feel included and show how different perceptions can be.

Virtual Reality and Art

Artistic practices have long been acknowledged as effective means for enhancing health, self-expression, and communication (World Health Organization, 2019). Art therapy is frequently situated inside therapeutic settings, wherein therapist-facilitated creative practices enhance mental health and emotional regulation (Malchiodi, 2011). However, art can also serve as a broader medium for sharing experiences and rendering internal moods perceptible to others. Drawing, for example, offers an accessible medium for communication that externalizes perception, memory, and emotion, allowing participants to express complex experiences that may be challenging to define orally. This is particularly pertinent for neurodivergent populations, as conventional interview techniques may inadequately reflect their lived experiences.

Recent research has examined how emerging technologies, such as virtual reality, can enhance these principles by creating immersive settings that facilitate artistic activities, including drawing, free from conventional material limitations (Kaimal et al., 2016; Shamri Zeevi, 2021). VR-based art practices have been utilized to alleviate stress, foster self-acceptance, and facilitate health-related education (Meijers et al., 2022; Lee et al., 2023). Even outside of clinical or therapeutic settings, the main advantage of drawing is that it can be a co-constructed record of experience that captures emotional and perceptual details in a way that is both very personal and easy to communicate. In this way, drawing is a mix of art, communication, and health. It can help with therapy, but more significantly, it is a flexible and inclusive medium that helps people of different neurotypes, cultures, and ways of communicating understand each other. Shi and Wang (2024) contend that the incorporation of art into communicative practice signifies a transition from an exclusive emphasis on treatment to a focus on participation, discussion, and experiential sharing.

Recent advancements in virtual reality (VR) have broadened the scope of art-related practices, such as drawing, by facilitating immersive and interactive environments for creative expression. Tilt Brush (now OpenBrush) and other VR-based painting apps let people draw and paint in three-dimensional space, making worlds that go beyond what traditional media can do. These platforms can facilitate group experiences; for instance, through acoustic response modes, numerous people can cooperate within a shared VR sketching environment, promoting connection and mutual comprehension (Hacmun et al., 2021; Haeyen & Noorthoorn, 2021). VR has been used to replicate culturally significant activities, such as ceramic modeling, offering digital tools that integrate health education with customs and identity (Capece et al., 2023). These apps demonstrate the utility of VR-based artistic activities for communication and experience sharing among diverse groups. Interactive VR drawing activities have been incorporated into neurorehabilitation programs for children, enhancing the ecological validity of therapies and fostering participation (Goharinejad et al., 2022; Zangiacomi et al., 2022). For older individuals, VR-based screening and drawing tools have aided in the early identification of cognitive decline while promoting accessible health communication (Skurla et al., 2022). The capacity for creative expression at home with VR drawing and painting tools enhances engagement and offers novel avenues for health awareness and self-expression (Barroso et al., 2022).

From an experiential standpoint, VR amplifies the aesthetic attributes of drawing and art-making by enveloping users in settings that enhance both perception and production. Aesthetic experience is characterized as heightened, immersive, and particularly meaningful (Parrish, 2009), with VR contextualizing sketching and art-making within this paradigm. In this way, it gives participants a sense of control and presence, turning artistic production into a strong way to communicate about health, reflect on oneself, and make meaning (Sajnani et al., 2020; Tao et al., 2021). Shi and Wang (2024) assert that VR drawing and artistic practices provide not only therapeutic advantages but also function as novel instruments for discourse and collective experience. Health communication, conceptualized as a reciprocal exchange, necessitates shared systems of signs and expressions to cultivate understanding and empathy (Malikhao, 2020).

VR-based drawing activities facilitate this by diminishing communication obstacles, especially for populations that may find traditional spoken techniques challenging. VR-based art promotes inclusivity, balances power dynamics between facilitators and participants, and facilitates narrative construction in ways that conventional communication approaches may not accomplish (Haeyen & Noorthoorn, 2021; Gillibrand et al., 2023).

As costs go down and tools get better, virtual reality (VR) is crossing more and more disciplinary lines. It is now much more than just a way to "show off." In arts-based practice and study, VR serves as a versatile medium for communication, investigation, and creative expression, which can also be modified, when suitable, to therapeutic objectives. Recent research reframes immersive media not just as "digital art" for aesthetic purposes, but as a medium for involvement, reflection, and meaning-making that can enhance contexts related to well-being while staying true to artistic approaches and inquiries (Hadjipanayi et al., 2023).

One of the main reasons VR can do these things is that it can make people feel like they are really there and immersed in the experience. Immersion is how well a system supports normal sensory dependencies. Presence is the feeling of "being there" that comes after that. When a virtual brush or pen lines up with a user's grip and movement, and when a first-person virtual body maps to the user's real motions in real time, participants often say they feel like they own the virtual limb or body. This embodied setup is important because it makes people operate in VR the same way they would in real life, which makes creative exploration more natural and self-directed (Slater & Sanchez-Vives, 2016). The emphasis here is on producing visual art in immersive VR as an artistic activity that can also be utilized, when appropriate, for therapeutic objectives. This is similar to formal art therapy, which is conducted by a therapist and focuses on the triangular relationship between the participant, the facilitator, and the artwork. On the other hand, arts-based practice uses drawing to explore questions, share experiences, and support reflection, with therapy seen as an option use instead of the default.

VR opens up new ways to express yourself. Participants can create entire environments, make drawings as big as buildings or as small as they need to see tiny details, and even go "inside" their own work. These features are hard to copy with physical media: being able to look at a piece from many angles encourages thinking, rethinking, and trying again. For some individuals, especially those who cannot move around much or do not have easy access to a studio, motion mappings can be adjusted such that small movements form big strokes, giving them back control over gesture and scale. Portable headphones also let people practice outside of studios or clinics, letting them create at home or in bed and taking them to places that feel tranquil or inspiring.

The data trail of VR is just as crucial for study as its ability to engage the participants. Researchers can see the process, not just the results, because every brushstroke, movement, and decision can be recorded and played back. The capacity to erase a session, scrutinize sequencing, or return pivotal periods facilitates mixed-methods study that integrates qualitative interpretation with temporal, path, and interaction data. For participants, replay facilitates meta-reflection: observing one's own creation from a brief distance frequently reveals implicit strategies, emotional shifts, or areas of conflict that are challenging to describe in the present moment (Hadjipanayi et al., 2023).

Another strength is engagement. The fun and inquisitive nature of VR often boosts motivation and lowers performance anxiety. Many people, especially "digital natives," feel more comfortable trying new things in a medium where mistakes can be fixed, supplies are endless, and the risk is low. Setting clear creative goals (such as finishing a scenario or turning a 2D sketch into a 3D shape) can help structure sessions and keep people focused. The option to mix making with background sounds or guided prompts can also help with focus and mood control.

There are certain things to think about when it comes to these benefits. Current headsets cannot entirely replicate the tactile qualities of paper, paint, or clay. Haptics are becoming better, but is still not fully integrated with most of the mainstream headsets. Another problem is that facilitators need to know a lot about technology. To plan VR sessions that are inclusive, ethical, and productive, they need to know how to use technology, how to onboard people well, and how to give people other options (like desktop or AR) if they get ill, tired, or uncomfortable with head-mounted displays. Access and cost are still important, even though consumer systems are getting cheaper.

These concerns are not arguments against VR, but reminders that technology should support rather than dictate the practice. A careful approach prioritizes task-appropriate design, accessibility, and triangulation with other media. In some contexts, augmented reality can strengthen co-presence and shared attention, while collaborative social VR can recreate a sense of creative togetherness during remote work. Ultimately, the aim is consistent: to use immersion, embodiment, and flexible virtual space to enable conversation, reflection, and shared inquiry.

When you put all of these things together, you get a picture of VR as a versatile art form that adds new spatial, temporal, and analytical possibilities. It can enhance engagement, expand involvement, and render the process transparent—benefits for artists, educators, and researchers alike. These same affordances can be used for therapeutic purposes when the situation calls for it, but the main strength is still the same: VR's ability to let people make, explore, and understand through embodied, situated, and revisitable experiences (Hadjipanayi et al., 2023; Slater & Sanchez-Vives, 2016; Savickaite, 2024).

Full procedural framework—STUDIO—is available in the Appendix. It provides a structured yet flexible approach for implementing arts-based research within virtual reality environments. Building on the methodological foundations outlined in Savickaite (2024), it translates the key theoretical principles of participatory, exploratory, and creative inquiry into a practical, stepwise protocol. The framework's name—STUDIO—symbolizes both the creative and collaborative space in which arts-based VR research takes place and the six core stages guiding its implementation: Skills & Readiness, Theoretical Grounding, Upholding Data Integrity, Design Development, Involvement & Recruitment, and Oversight & Safety. Together, these stages support researchers in moving from conceptualization to ethical and methodological rigor, while maintaining participant-centered, reflective practice. The STUDIO framework thus serves as a bridge between the arts-based and immersive methodologies discussed in Savickaite's work and their application across diverse research contexts, providing a foundation for consistency, transparency, and creativity in experimental design.

Chapter Conclusion

This chapter has argued that virtual reality occupies a productive space between experimental control and lived experience, offering psychology a means to study perception, interaction, and communication in ways that are both systematic and ecologically meaningful. Tracing VR's development from early laboratory-based applications to contemporary immersive systems, the chapter highlighted how immersion, interaction, and presence enable researchers to move beyond static, reductionist paradigms while retaining methodological rigor.

By focusing on arts-based practices, especially immersive 3D drawing, the chapter further reframed VR as a participatory medium that supports non-linguistic expression, agency, and shared meaning-making. The capacity to externalize perceptual and emotional experience, alongside the generation of rich process-level data, positions VR art-making as a powerful mixed-methods approach that bridges subjective experience and empirical analysis. At the same time, the chapter acknowledged practical and ethical constraints, emphasizing that VR should be deployed thoughtfully, with attention to accessibility, training, and triangulation rather than as a universal solution.

References

Adjorlu, A., Duedahl, A., Nielsen, G., & Serafin, S. (2017). Daily living skills training in virtual reality to help children with autism spectrum disorder in a real shopping scenario. *2017 IEEE International Symposium on Mixed and Augmented Reality (ISMAR-Adjunct)*, 294–302. https://doi.org/10.1109/ISMAR-Adjunct.2017.93

Adjorlu, A., & Serafin, S. (2019a, March). Teachers' Views on how to use Virtual Reality to Instruct Children and Adolescents Diagnosed with Autism Spectrum Disorder. In *In 2019 IEEE Conference on Virtual Reality and 3D User Interfaces (VR)* (pp. 1439–1442). IEEE.

Adjorlu, A., & Serafin, S. (2019b). Virtual Reality (VR) for children diagnosed with autism spectrum disorder (ASD): Interventions to train social and everyday living skills. In *Virtual and augmented reality in mental health treatment* (pp. 159–175). IGI Global Scientific Publishing.

Alcañiz Raya, M., Chicchi Giglioli, I. A., Marín-Morales, J., Higuera-Trujillo, J. L., Olmos, E., Minissi, M. E., et al. (2020). Application of supervised machine learning for behavioral biomarkers of autism spectrum disorder based on electrodermal activity and virtual reality. *Frontiers in Human Neuroscience, 14*, 90.

Aloimonos, J., & Brown, C. M. (1989). On the kinetic depth effect. *Biological Cybernetics, 60*(6), 445–455.

Aloimonos, J., & Huang, L. (1990). Motion–boundary illusions and their regularization. Proceedings of the Royal Society of London. *Series B: Biological Sciences, 242*(1304), 75–81.

Barroso, A. C., Rai, H. K., Sousa, L., Orrell, M., & Schneider, J. (2022). Participatory visual arts activities for people with dementia: A review. In *Improving the lives of people with dementia through technology* (pp. 100–126). Routledge.

BBC News. (2014, March 26). Facebook buys virtual reality headset start-up for $2bn. https://www.bbc.co.uk/news/business-26742625

Bennett, C. L., Brady, E., & Branham, S. M. (2018, October). Interdependence as a frame for assistive technology research and design. In *Proceedings of the 20th International ACM Sigaccess Conference on Computers and Accessibility* (pp. 161–173).

Blascovich, J., Loomis, J., Beall, A. C., Swinth, K. R., Hoyt, C. L., & Bailenson, J. N. (2002). Immersive virtual environment technology as a methodological tool for social psychology. *Psychological Inquiry, 13*(2), 103–124.

Bohil, C. J., Alicea, B., & Biocca, F. A. (2011). Virtual reality in neuroscience research and therapy. *Nature Reviews Neuroscience, 12*, 752–762. https://doi.org/10.1038/nrn3122

Burdea, G. C., & Coiffet, P. (2003). *Virtual reality technology*. John Wiley & Sons.

Calvert, S. L., & Tan, S. L. (1994). Impact of virtual reality on young adults' physiological arousal and aggressive thoughts: Interaction versus observation. *Journal of Applied Developmental Psychology, 15*(1), 125–139.

Capece, N., Gatto, C., Manfredi, G., Gilio, G., Nuzzo, B. L., De Paolis, L. T., & Erra, U. (2023, September). Enhancing art therapy with virtual reality and hand gesture recognition: A case study in pottery modeling. In *International Conference on Extended Reality* (pp. 210–226). Springer Nature Switzerland.

Connors, E. C., Chrastil, E. R., Sánchez, J., & Merabet, L. B. (2014). Virtual environments for the transfer of navigation skills in the blind: A comparison of directed instruction vs. video game based learning approaches. *Frontiers in Human Neuroscience, 8*, 223.

Crosbie, J. H., Lennon, S., Basford, J. R., & McDonough, S. M. (2007). Virtual reality in stroke rehabilitation: Still more virtual than real. *Disability and Rehabilitation, 29*(14), 1139–1146.

Cummings, J. J., & Bailenson, J. N. (2016). How immersive is enough? A meta-analysis of the effect of immersive technology on user presence. *Media Psychology, 19*(2), 272–309.

Delaney, B., & Biocca, F. (1995). *Immersive virtual reality technology. Communication in the age of virtual reality* (pp. 57–124). Lawrence Erlbaum Associates, Inc.

deLeyer-Tiarks, J. M., Li, M. G., Levine-Schmitt, M., Andrade, B., Bray, M. A., & Peters, E. (2023). Advancing autism technology. *Psychology in the Schools, 60*(2), 495–506.

Fletcher-Watson, S., Petrou, A., Scott-Barrett, J., Dicks, P., Graham, C., O'Hare, A., et al. (2016). A trial of an iPad™ intervention targeting social communication skills in children with autism. *Autism, 20*(7), 771–782.

Fox, J., Bailenson, J., & Binney, J. (2009). Virtual experiences, physical behaviors: The effect of presence on imitation of an eating avatar. *Presence: Teleoperators and Virtual Environments, 18*(4), 294–303.

Gentilucci, M., Toni, I., Chieffi, S., & Pavesi, G. (1994). The role of proprioception in the control of prehension movements: a kinematic study in a peripherally deafferented patient and in normal subjects. *Experimental Brain Research, 99*(3), 483–500.

Gillibrand, S., Hine, P., Conyers, R., Gravestock, J., Walsh, C., McAvoy, A., & Sanders, C. (2023). "Take a walk in someone else's shoes": The role of participatory arts for health research development and training. *Research Involvement and Engagement, 9*(1), 40.

Goharinejad, S., Goharinejad, S., Hajesmaeel-Gohari, S., & Bahaadinbeigy, K. (2022). The usefulness of virtual, augmented, and mixed reality technologies in the diagnosis and treatment of attention deficit hyperactivity disorder in children: An overview of relevant studies. *BMC Psychiatry, 22*(1), 4.

Green, D. M. (1961). Detection of auditory sinusoids of uncertain frequency. *The Journal of the Acoustical Society of America, 33*(7), 897–903.

Hacmun, I., Regev, D., & Salomon, R. (2021). Artistic creation in virtual reality for art therapy: A qualitative study with expert art therapists. *The Arts in Psychotherapy, 72*, 101745.

Hadjipanayi, C., Banakou, D., & Michael-Grigoriou, D. (2023). Art as therapy in virtual reality: A scoping review. *Frontiers in Virtual Reality, 4*, 1065863.

Haeyen, S., & Noorthoorn, E. (2021). Validity of the self-expression and emotion regulation in art therapy scale (SERATS). *Plos One, 16*(3), e0248315.

Kaimal, G., Ray, K., & Muniz, J. (2016). Reduction of cortisol levels and participants' responses following art making. *Art Therapy, 33*(2), 74–80.

Kalawsky, R. (1993). *The science of virtual reality and virtual environments.* Addison-Wesley Longman Publishing Co., Inc..

Kandalaft, M. R., Didehbani, N., Krawczyk, D. C., Allen, T. T., & Chapman, S. B. (2013). Virtual reality social cognition training for young adults with highfunctioning autism. *Journal of Autism and Developmental Disorders, 43*(1), 34–44.

Lanier, J. (2017). *Dawn of the new everything: Encounters with reality and virtual reality.* Henry Holt.

Lee, J., Wu, D. Y., Lin, J. H., Kim, J., & Ahn, S. J. (2023). Using time travel in virtual reality (VR) to increase efficacy perceptions of influenza vaccination. *Journal of Computer-Mediated Communication, 28*(3), zmad010.

Loomis, J. M., Blascovich, J. J., & Beall, A. C. (1999). Immersive virtual environment technology as a basic research tool in psychology. *Behavior Research Methods, Instruments, & Computers, 31*(4), 557–564.

Lovaas, O. I. (1987). Behavioral treatment and normal educational and intellectual functioning in young autistic children. *Journal of Consulting and Clinical Psychology, 55*(1), 3–9. https://doi.org/10.1037/0022-006X.55.1.3

Mandal, S. (2013). Brief introduction of virtual reality & its challenges. *International Journal of Scientific & Engineering Research, 4*(4), 304–309.

Malchiodi, C. A. (Ed.). (2011). *Handbook of art therapy*. Guilford Press.

Malihi, M., Nguyen, J., Cardy, R. E., Eldon, S., Petta, C., & Kushki, A. (2020). Evaluating the safety and usability of head-mounted virtual reality compared to monitor-displayed video for children with autism spectrum disorder. *Autism, 24*(7), 1924–1929.

Malikhao, P. (2020). Health communication: Approaches, strategies, and ways to sustainability on health or health for all. In *Handbook of communication for development and social change* (pp. 1015–1037). Springer Singapore.

Marr, D., & Vaina, L. (1982). Representation and recognition of the movements of shapes. *Proceedings of the Royal Society of London. Series B. Biological Sciences, 214*(1197), 501–524.

Maskey, M., Lowry, J., Rodgers, J., McConachie, H., & Parr, J. R. (2014). Reducing specific phobia/fear in young people with autism spectrum disorders (ASDs) through a virtual reality environment intervention. *PLOS ONE, 9*(7), e100374. https://doi.org/10.1371/journal.pone.0100374

Meijers, M. H., Smit, E. S., de Wildt, K., Karvonen, S. G., van der Plas, D., & van der Laan, L. N. (2022). Stimulating sustainable food choices using virtual reality: Taking an environmental vs health communication perspective on enhancing response efficacy beliefs. *Environmental Communication, 16*(1), 1–22.

Merians, A. S., Jack, D., Boian, R., Tremaine, M., Burdea, G. C., Adamovich, S. V., et al. (2002). Virtual reality–augmented rehabilitation for patients following stroke. *Physical Therapy, 82*(9), 898–915.

Newbutt, N., Bradley, R., & Conley, I. (2020). Using virtual reality head-mounted displays in schools with autistic children: Views, experiences, and future directions. *Cyberpsychology, Behavior, and Social Networking, 23*(1), 22–33. https://doi.org/10.1089/cyber.2019.0206

O'Regan, J. K., & Noë, A. (2001). A sensorimotor account of vision and visual consciousness. *Behavioral and Brain Sciences, 24*(5), 939–1031. https://doi.org/10.1017/S0140525X01000115

Pan, X., & Hamilton, A. F.de C (2018). Why and how to use virtual reality to study human social interaction: The challenges of exploring a new research landscape. *British Journal of Psychology, 109*(3), 395–417. https://doi.org/10.1111/bjop.12290

Parong, J., & Mayer, R. E. (2020). Cognitive and affective processes for learning science in immersive virtual reality. *Journal of Computer Assisted Learning, 36*(6), 1014–1030. https://doi.org/10.1111/jcal.12482

Parrish, P. E. (2009). Aesthetic principles for instructional design. *Educational Technology Research and Development, 57*(4), 511–528.

Peli, E. (1990). Visual issues in the use of a head-mounted monocular display. *Optical Engineering, 29*(8), 883–892.

Pine, D. S., Grun, J., Maguire, E. A., Burgess, N., Zarahn, E., Koda, V., et al. (2002). Neurodevelopmental aspects of spatial navigation: A virtual reality fMRI study. *Neuroimage, 15*(2), 396–406.

Rizzo, A. A., Kim, G. J., Yeh, S. C., Thiebaux, M., Hwang, J., & Buckwalter, J. G. (2005, July). Development of a benchmarking scenario for testing 3D user interface devices and interaction methods. In *Proceedings of the 11th International Conference on Human Computer Interaction, Las Vegas, Nevada, USA*.

Robinett, W., & Rolland, J. P. (1992). A computational model for the stereoscopic optics of a head mounted display. *Presence: Teleoperators & Virtual Environments, 1*(1), 45–62.

Robins, B., Dickerson, P., Stribling, P., & Dautenhahn, K. (2004). Robot-mediated joint attention in children with autism. *Interaction Studies, 5*(2), 161–198. https://doi.org/10.1075/is.5.2.02rob

Rose, F. D., Brooks, B. M., & Rizzo, A. A. (2005). Virtual reality in brain damage rehabilitation. *Cyberpsychology & Behavior, 8*(3), 241–262.

Rothbaum, B. O., Hodges, L., Kooper, R., Opdyke, D., Williford, J. S., & North, M. (1995a). Effectiveness of computer-generated (virtual reality) graded exposure in the treatment of acrophobia. *American Journal of Psychiatry, 152*(4), 626–628. https://doi.org/10.1176/ajp.152.4.626

Rothbaum, B. O., Hodges, L. F., Kooper, R., Opdyke, D., Williford, J. S., & North, M. (1995b). Virtual reality graded exposure in the treatment of acrophobia: A case report. *Behavior Therapy, 26*(3), 547–554.

Shapiro, M. A., & McDonald, D. G. (1992). I'm not a real doctor, but I play one in virtual reality: Implications of virtual reality for judgments about reality. *Journal of Communication., 42*(4), 94–114.

Sajnani, N., Mayor, C., & Tillberg-Webb, H. (2020). Aesthetic presence: The role of the arts in the education of creative arts therapists in the classroom and online. *The Arts in Psychotherapy, 69*, 101668.

Savickaite, S. (2024). Using Virtual Reality to explore individual differences in perception due to neurodiversity (Doctoral dissertation, University of Glasgow).

Shamri Zeevi, L. (2021). Making art therapy virtual: Integrating virtual reality into art therapy with adolescents. *Frontiers in Psychology, 12*, 584943.

Sheridan, T. B. (1992). Musings on telepresence and virtual presence. *Presence Teleoperators Virtual Environments, 1*(1), 120–125.

Shi, Z., & Wang, Y. (2024). Enhancing health communication through virtual reality-based art therapy: An opinion. *Frontiers in Psychology, 15*, 1438172.

Skurla, M. D., Rahman, A. T., Salcone, S., Mathias, L., Shah, B., Forester, B. P., & Vahia, I. V. (2022). Virtual reality and mental health in older adults: A systematic review. *International Psychogeriatrics, 34*(2), 143–155.

Slater, M. (2018). Immersion and the illusion of presence in virtual reality. *British Journal of Psychology, 109*(3), 431–433.

Slater, M., & Sanchez-Vives, M. V. (2016). Enhancing our lives with immersive virtual reality. *Frontiers in Robotics and AI, 3*, 74. https://doi.org/10.3389/frobt.2016.00074

Strickland, D. (1997). Virtual reality for the treatment of autism. Virtual reality in neuro-psycho-physiology. *Cognitive, Clinical and Methodological Issues in Assessment and Rehabilitation, 44*, 81.

Sutherland, I. E. (1968). A head-mounted three dimensional display. In *Proceedings of the Fall Joint Computer Conference*, 757–764. https://doi.org/10.1145/1476589.1476686.

Sveistrup, H. (2004). Motor rehabilitation using virtual reality. *Journal of Neuroengineering and Rehabilitation, 1*(1), 10.

Tao, G., Garrett, B., Taverner, T., Cordingley, E., & Sun, C. (2021). Immersive virtual reality health games: A narrative review of game design. *Journal of NeuroEngineering and Rehabilitation, 18*(1), 31.

Vasser, M., & Aru, J. (2020). Guidelines for immersive virtual reality in psychological research. *Current Opinion in Psychology, 36*, 71–76. https://doi.org/10.1016/j.copsyc.2020.04.010

Wallach, H., & O'Connell, D. N. (1953). The kinetic depth effect. *Journal of Experimental Psychology, 45*(4), 205–217. https://doi.org/10.1037/h0056880

Wang, M., & Reid, D. (2011). Virtual reality in pediatric neurorehabilitation: Attention deficit hyperactivity disorder, autism and cerebral palsy. *Neuroepidemiology, 36*(1), 2–18.

Warren, W. H., Kay, B. A., Zosh, W. D., Duchon, A. P., & Sahuc, S. (2001). Optic flow is used to control human walking. *Nature Neuroscience, 4*(2), 213–216. https://doi.org/10.1038/84054

World Health Organization. (2019). WHO guideline: Recommendations on digital interventions for health system strengthening: Web supplement 2: Summary of findings and GRADE tables (No. WHO/RHR/19.7). World Health Organization.

Zangiacomi, A., Flori, V., Greci, L., Scaglione, A., Arlati, S., & Bernardelli, G. (2022). An immersive virtual reality-based application for treating ADHD: A remote evaluation of acceptance and usability. *Digital Health, 8*, 20552076221143242.

CHAPTER 4

Lines of Perception: VR Drawing as Method and Expression

Recent studies progressively highlight the significant influence of art on the human brain, especially concerning well-being. Creativity is not just about making art; it is also about being able to make something new, find unexpected solutions, and feel free from limits. Picasso's remark that "every child is an artist" highlights how important is creative play in childhood and that sometimes that is lost in adulthood. Re-engaging with creativity reinstates an early sense of freedom, play, and exploration, providing a conduit to mental health and identity development (Richard et al., 2023).

Drawing as a means of expression will be discussed in this chapter and some key terms need to be clarified first.
Creativity is the ability to generate original and valuable ideas, solutions, or expressions.
Arts-based methods are research or practice approaches that use artistic processes, such as drawing or storytelling, to explore, generate, or communicate knowledge.
Art therapy is a therapeutic practice that uses artistic creation to support emotional expression, insight, and well-being.
Aesthetics is the philosophical study of beauty, artistic experience, and the nature of sensory perception.

S. Savickaite, *Exploring Neurodiversity Through Virtual Reality*, https://doi.org/10.1007/978-3-032-19636-1_4

Creativity is a manifestation of "life force," facilitating human growth, emotional articulation, and interpersonal connection. It helps people break out of rigid ways of thinking, adjust to change, and deal with trauma or uncertainty. Creativity is not only an aesthetic luxury but an essential component for human flourishing, serving as a "bubble of peace" that anchors humans in the present moment, alleviates stress, and promotes mental well-being. From this perspective, creativity serves as both a therapeutic asset and a profoundly human mechanism for facilitating meaning and transformation (Richard et al., 2023).

Richard et al. (2023) assert that creativity and artistic involvement are vital components of human well-being, characterizing them as both restorative and transformative. They criticize the prevalence of rational and cognitive ways of cognition, observing that the "artistic brain" has gone inactive in modern culture. Creativity, on the other hand, brings people back to their intuition, feelings, and imagination, which are all things that help people grow and stay strong. Historical evidence corroborates this, since skills like stitching were employed therapeutically with traumatized soldiers during the world wars to facilitate psychological rehabilitation.

In the past, art history and neuroscience worked independently; art history focused on aesthetic judgment, cultural significance, and interpretation, while neuroscience examined brain structure and function. Zeki's initial research (1999, 2007) demonstrated that visually captivating paintings might activate brain pleasure centers in a manner akin to the recognition of a cherished individual. Recent studies indicate that art activates the prefrontal cortex, a crucial area for meaning-making and sensory interpretation, hence connecting artistic experience with cognitive processing and emotional regulation. This connection is particularly significant for neurodivergent individuals. For instance, autistic individuals frequently have strengths in pattern recognition, memory, and, in certain instances, creative talent, hence contesting deficit-oriented perspectives on neurodiversity.

The idea of a "neurotribe" (Silverman, 2015) has changed the way people talk about neurological diversity. It sees neurodivergent persons, like those on the autistic spectrum, as part of communities with their own unique traits, strengths, and ways of seeing and feeling things, rather than just as people with "problems". From an art-and-mental-health standpoint, this necessitates customized strategies: inclusive art shows adapted for diverse neurotypes, collaboration with neurodivergent artists, and what some refer to as "success enablers" instead of mere accommodations. These tactics help neurodivergent people find their "neurotribe," learn more about themselves, and improve their quality of life through art-based activities.

Aesthetics

The notion of aesthetics has undergone significant transformation from its classical philosophical origins, where philosophers like Aristotle, Plato, Augustine, and Aquinas linked beauty to symmetry, harmony, or divine connection, to a more expansive interpretation that now includes psychology and sensory-emotional processes. Modern narratives characterize aesthetic experience as both an uncommon, exalted condition and as a prevalent, emotionally charged engagement with the world (Silvia, 2012). Beardsley (1979) elaborated on aesthetics as the ability of an element to produce experiences distinguished by aesthetic quality.

When applied to autism, these theories pose significant inquiries regarding the formation of aesthetic experiences through sensory processing, cognition, interests, and social interaction. As autistic people see and engage with the world in their own unique ways, using their own sensory and linguistic modes can be seen as a type of indigenous knowledge. This framing recognizes autism as a distinct perspective that shapes the creation and perception of aesthetic meaning, while also acknowledging the diversity within autistic group.

Detail-oriented processing and enhanced pattern recognition, characteristics frequently linked with autistic cognition, may result in a more complex and nuanced interpretation of sensory stimuli (Hartman et al., 2023). A neurotypical spectator may find something like the pattern of a ceiling border unimportant, whereas an autistic person may find it very beautiful. This demonstrates the significant influence of sensory profiles on aesthetic judgments and reaffirms the focus on bodily and emotional sensations: aesthetic appreciation manifests as a subjective fact, contingent upon each individual's sensory-emotional profile.

In general, looking at autistic aesthetics via the prism of indigenous knowledge gives us a way to see how real and deep these experiences are. Autistic aesthetic worlds emphasize the multiplicity and relativity of beauty, rooted in sensory and emotional diversity, instead of evaluating them by neurotypical criteria.

Empathy and Art-Based Encounters

Nilson (2025) contextualizes the discourse on empathy and autism within the contentious history of theory of mind (Premack & Woodruff, 1978; Baron-Cohen, 1997, 2000). The prevailing "mind-blindness" and "extreme male brain" theories have historically portrayed autistic individuals as lacking empathy, implying an incapacity to comprehend the mental states of others (Frith, 2001; Happé, 2015). Recent critiques indicate that issues in theory of mind are not universal nor exclusive to autism (Gernsbacher & Yergeau, 2019; Quesque & Rossetti, 2020). Milton's (2012) double empathy dilemma represents a substantial conceptual transformation, redefining autistic-neurotypical miscommunication as a reciprocal challenge rather than a singular deficiency. Subsequent research corroborates this assertion, revealing that interactions among autistic individuals are frequently more fluid and effective than those between different neurotypes (Crompton et al., 2020a, 2020b).

The double empathy paradigm elucidates the social ramifications of marginalization: autistic individuals frequently "camouflage" in neurotypical environments, a behavior associated with increased anxiety, sadness, and suicidality (Pryke-Hobbes et al., 2023). Misrepresentations of autistic individuals in research, often articulated in terms of deficits, intensify marginalization and obliterate autistic viewpoints from both academia and society (Milton, 2014; Chown et al., 2017). Cultivating authentic empathy among neurotypes may facilitate more equal participation and utilise the strengths of autistic individuals, as illustrated by figures like Temple Grandin (Grandin, 2009).

In this context, visual art is proposed as a viable method to connect cognitive spaces. Autistic individuals possess unique perceptual and sensory profiles, including heightened attention to detail, sensitivity to symmetry, and monotropism (Frith, 1989; Happé & Frith, 2006; Murray et al., 2005), which influence their aesthetic engagement. Studies indicate that autistic individuals frequently concentrate on the technical or tangible aspects of artworks, whereas neurotypical individuals are more inclined to focus on interpersonal or emotional elements (Roth, 2020; Brosnan & Ashwin, 2023). Even if some people say they have "impaired" aesthetic sensitivity (Mazza et al., 2020), first-person narratives show how art can make people feel deeply and even help them understand others (Coelho et al., 2025).

Nilson's studies indicate that art serves as a common focal point, fostering "cognitive overlap" between autistic and neurotypical persons (Williams et al., 2021). According to Sperber and Wilson's (1986) theory of relevance, shared experiences like co-viewing and talking about art let people see things from one other's point of view, which builds empathy through joint attention and conversation. This process may function via predictive coding mechanisms: empathy entails formulating predictions regarding others' feelings based on clues and past information (Lockwood et al., 2015). Due to the distinct cognitive contexts experienced by autistic and neurotypical persons, predictive accuracy diminishes across neurotypes, resulting in the double empathy dilemma. Art-based encounters, on the other hand, offer a structured environment that can enhance prediction accuracy and, as a result, foster mutual empathy (Rapaport & Sowman, 2024; Qela et al., 2025).

Neurodiversity and Alternative Research Methods

The concept of neurodiversity communicates multiple messages. To begin, there is no single way for a brain to be normal, because the brain can be wired and grow in a variety of ways. Second, more ethical, non-stigmatizing vocabulary and concepts for thinking about persons who are different and/or disabled are needed. Third, we need a paradigm that does not pathologize and overemphasize what the person struggles with, but rather takes a more balanced approach, focusing equally on what the person can do. Finally, genetic or other sorts of biological variation are inextricably linked to a person's identity, sense of self, and personhood, and should be treated with the same regard as any other form of diversity, including gender.

Since Leo Kanner's first description of autism in 1943, significant research has been performed to examine the disorder from a variety of perspectives. What professionals in the field have rarely considered is the perspective of the "native experts"—autistic people themselves. Despite the fact that many autistic persons have attempted to convey their thoughts and insights, these efforts have mainly gone ignored by experts, for a variety of reasons, including the fact that their views and insights appear unorthodox to the majority (Courchesne et al., 2022).

Autism is a way of life for autistic individuals. It pervades everything; it colors every experience, sensation, perception, idea, and emotion—all part of life. Autistic people frequently do not respond in the way that non-autistic people expect them to because of differences in perception and communication systems. Most studies on sensory differences in autism do not include autistic people's ideas and viewpoints on these differences. Bob Morris et al. (1999) describes this as "the original error" of the investigations, referring to the attempt to reconstruct the "autistic world" using non-autistic people's methods and perceptions. To avoid this, autistic people's own narratives and communications should be treated as the major source of knowledge. Recently, research charities like Autistica have embraced the new era of stakeholder and self-advocacy-led research. Non-autistic academics were challenged by new participatory research models to interact with autistic persons at various stages of the study process, from developing crucial questions to creating methodologies, recruiting participants, interpreting findings, dissemination, and public involvement (Happé & Frith, 2020).

Person-Centered Research and Power Imbalances

Participant-centered (Person-centric/centered) research has lately emerged as one of the best models for studying neurodiversity. Person-centered research is based on three major principles: attention and dialogue, empowerment and engagement, and critical reflexivity (Jacobs et al., 2017). Attentiveness is the ability to perceive oneself, people, surroundings, and their interrelationships as human. It necessitates the ability to be contextually aware, listen, observe, and sympathetically interpret what we hear and see. Person-centered practice and research seek to empower individuals and groups by promoting self-awareness and self-esteem, capacity development, and (individual or collective) action. Critical reflexivity is essential in research to understand how power connections are formed and maintained, as well as who benefits from them. Gender, race, socioeconomic status, age, and other societal power dynamics interact with the research environment and relationships. Concerns about the researcher's assumed power led to a focus on reflexivity to reframe power dynamics between participants and researchers (Finlay and Gough, 2008). For example, researchers should be conscious of their own viewpoints and interests and actively position themselves inside the research (Jacobs et al., 2017).

Recognizing the power imbalance (Fig. 4.1) between researchers and community partners is a crucial principle of person-centered research (Gaventa & Cornwall, 2015; Nelson & Wright, 1995). According to

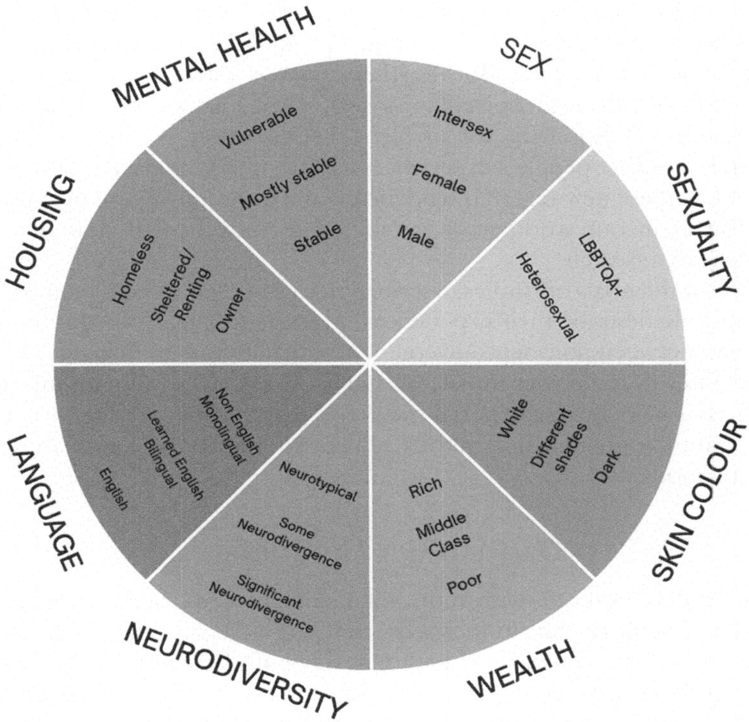

Fig. 4.1 This figure presents a wheel of intersecting identity and social factors that shape individual lived experience

Arnstein's (1969) participation ladder, power fluctuates across different sorts of participation: no power (e.g., therapy), tokenism (e.g., consultation), and shared power (e.g., collaboration). Increased interest in methodologies such as citizen science, crowdsourcing, co-production, participant-led research, and community-based participatory research indicates a change toward power balance in research (Wallerstein et al., 2017).

Research is frequently viewed as a researcher-participant co-production of knowledge in which the lines between researcher and participant are blurred and control over representation is more distributed. The researchers' goal is to reduce the distance and separation between the researcher and the participant (Karnieli-Miller et al., 2009). Researchers and participants are inextricably linked to the final product because of their distinct contributions to a project. Both partners may feel a strong sense of involvement: individuals feel involved as a result of the analysis of their personal experiences. Researchers are involved because they conduct extensive research on other people's experiences and want to comprehend them. As a result of these new research tendencies, and in order to minimize power imbalances in our work, we have shifted to mixed methodologies and exploratory research.

One of the goals of studies described in this book is to help neurodivergent people describe their experiences. There is frequently a communication gap between non-neurodivergent researchers and participants, which contributes to the power imbalance stated. Creating new communication methods can help researchers bridge the gap between self-report measures, autobiographical narratives addressed previously, and lab-based investigations.

Drawing and Art Therapy

Humans communicate with more than simply words. Some experiences may be difficult to explain in words, resulting in a challenge to create an authentic expressive voice. The complexities of ideas and feelings might often be buried, resulting in a superficial interpretation of these experiences by others. Using drawings to describe these thoughts and feelings can help achieve more nuanced communication, capturing the complexities of experiences more precisely. Using creative, arts-based research methodologies invites participants to think on, discuss, and express their own experiences. Drawing has primarily been employed in therapeutic practices (Oster & Crone, 2004; Guillemin, 2004) and research with children (Zhang et al., 2021). Real-world events, feelings, experiences, or occurrences can be represented non-verbally utilizing visual arts and sketching, making them more easily comprehended by both the creator and others. It can also transmit something that is difficult to express verbally, such as a sensation, intuition, or concept. Images, unlike spoken utterances, can deepen associations with a phenomenon and promote reflective awareness. By merging these methodologies into data collecting, we hope to gain a greater understanding of people's experiences and inner lives. Each individual can contribute their own unique experiences, memories, and world to the connection by using the drawings as a starting point for dialog. The artwork serves as a vehicle for both knowledge of the world and people, as well as the artist's personal mental expression. Thus, art has an ontological advantage in that it provides a wide range of meanings and can be understood in a variety of ways. However, as with earlier discussions on power imbalance, researchers should be conscious of how interpretation methods are carried out and reflect appropriately on their practice.

An artistic experience is defined as the interactions of a person, a community, and art. We constantly perceive the environment through our senses and then filter this information through our imagination. We shape our own experiences and share them with others via communication. This is a conversation between our internal and external worlds. The approach of analyzing drawings involves cultural visual analysis, which typically includes picture content analysis (Bal, 2009; Rose, 2014). The analysis can be regarded as a comprehensive reading with interpretation cycles (Orland-Barak & Maskit, 2017). In cultural visual analysis, "image" refers to an idea or mental representation. Losing sense of time and space while creating art may be a highly healing experience in and of itself, which is one of the driving concepts of art therapy (Betts, 2013). This delightful feeling of combining relaxation and strong focus is referred to as "flow" by Mihaly Csikszentmihalyi (1990) and "deep play" by Diane Ackerman (1999). Shaping artistic work in a therapeutic environment can help to widen and deepen the process of investigation, leading to new questions and awareness (Atkins & Duggins Williams, 2007).

Drawing has mostly been utilized in developmental studies in psychology to track how people's minds grow. Historically, children's performance on various drawing assessments has been used as a metric for "normative" visuospatial development (Chappell & Steitz, 1993; Shah & Frith, 1983). This enduring connection between drawing and development has been associated with the notion of autistic savant syndrome—the correlation of neurodevelopmental variation with extraordinary ability (Treffert, 2009). Baron-Cohen et al. (1993) observed that drawings by autistic children exhibited an atypical level of visual realism in comparison to their non-autistic counterparts. O'Connor and Hermelin (1988) showed that advanced sketching skills in autistic children were not related to intellect.

The link between autistic people who are good at seeing things and their preference for "visual thinking" has become well known in popular culture, thanks to the work of artists like Nadia Chomyn, Jessica Park, and

Stephen Wiltshire, as well as first-person accounts by famous autistic people like Temple Grandin (2009). The weak central coherence model of cognition agrees with the thinking in pictures hypothesis that Kunda and Goel (2011) tested in real life. This theory argues that people with autism have a cognitive bias toward processing that focuses on details and the surrounding environment (Happé & Frith, 2006; Shah & Frith, 1993). A tendency for local processing has been correlated with enhanced drawing abilities in non-autistic youngsters (Drake et al., 2010). In a similar vein, art students exhibiting diminished central coherence—reconceptualized as heightened perceptual sensitivity—surpassed both non-artistic counterparts and fellow art students in observational drawing assessments (Chamberlain et al., 2013).

Chamberlain et al. (2019, 2021) conducted a longitudinal study that offered the most compelling evidence to date indicating that although artists' perceptual styles initially resemble those found in autism, they diverge with time as artists cultivate distinct perceptual strategies through training (Chamberlain & Wagemans, 2015). Artists exhibited enhancements in executive function, task switching, mental rotation, and disembedding objects, while elevated autistic symptoms correlated with improvements mainly in disembedding and mental rotation tasks (Conson et al., 2022). Although the current study does not explicitly compare autistic and non-autistic individuals, the findings indicate that comprehension of perceptual differences may enhance the development of creative applications in virtual reality, including VR-based art therapy (Winkel, 2022).

The Think Aloud Method and Drawing

Participants in the Think Aloud approach think aloud while performing a task or recall their thoughts soon after finishing it (Eccles & Arsal, 2017). The argument here is based on a representational perspective of language, which holds that elicited verbal reports can accurately reflect cognitions. In contrast, many qualitative researchers argue that language is constitutive and that word meaning is relationally and socially created.

Concerns about the credibility of self-reported thoughts have long existed. According to Nisbett and Wilson's (1977) survey of social psychology studies, people commonly make erroneous accounts about their cognitions due to a lack of conscious access. When a person is asked to report on their cognitions but is unable to do so, they typically rely on implicit cognition theories, which are fundamental beliefs about how the world works, to deliver their answer. The issue with implicit theories is that they frequently have little to do with the individual's real cognitive processes. Ericsson and Simon (1980) hypothesized, however, that people can make correct reports on their cognitions under particular elicitation settings. During continuous action, information in short-term memory is only present for a few seconds; as new information arrives, previous knowledge is erased. Unless information recalled in short-term memory is also remembered in long-term memory, the primary strategy for collecting verbalization is to question participants about their thoughts while they are executing a task, a technique known as concurrent reporting.

Combining sketching with interviewing (sometimes dubbed graphic or visual elicitation) is a great approach to get neurodivergent people to talk about their experiences in a more honest way. Traditional, verbal-only interviews favor linear, vocally mediated stories and may unintentionally put participants at a disadvantage if they prefer to communicate in more visual, sensory, or non-linear ways (Milton, 2012; Fletcher-Watson et al., 2019). Visual elicitation externalizes experience and alleviates verbal and working memory demands, allowing participants to construct representations at their own pace and in their preferred modalities (Crilly et al., 2006; Harper, 2002). These benefits correspond with enduring evidence indicating that numerous autistic individuals process information distinctively (e.g., heightened local/detail focus; atypical sensory weighting), potentially rendering static, text-intensive formats less accessible (Happé & Frith, 2006; Robertson & Baron-Cohen, 2017; Van der Hallen et al., 2015).

Illustration also serves as a framework that facilitates meaning-making throughout the interview. Drawing timelines, mapping procedures, and sketching significant surroundings serve as "external memory" that aids in organizing story structure and triggering episodic detail (Paivio, 1991; Mayer, 2009). In autism research, visual supports are a well-recognized accommodation that enhances understanding and engagement (Knight et al., 2015). When researchers collaboratively create visuals (keywords, icons, timelines), they establish common reference points that mitigate pragmatic and inferential demands—specifically, the interactional pressures associated with the double empathy problem (Milton, 2012; Crompton et al., 2020b).

Illustrative interviewing is firmly situated within the phenomenological and participatory paradigms in anthropology and psychology, emphasizing first-person significance and the collaborative construction of data

(Pink, 2015; Prosser & Loxley, 2008). Visual and graphic methods provide participants more control over the flow, pace, and shape of representation of the issue. This is an important ethical goal in neurodiversity-aligned research (Chapman & Veit, 2021; Fletcher-Watson et al., 2019). They are especially appropriate for sensory-first narratives: numerous autistic individuals articulate experiences in vividly perceptual terms (texture, rhythm, boundedness), which are more readily demonstrated than conveyed verbally (Alderson-Day & Fernyhough, 2015). Illustrative artifacts can be repeatedly examined and changed during the session, which is very important because it makes the data more reliable and less likely to be misinterpreted.

Sketching and talking to each other helps people with different neurotypes understand each other better in interviews. Joint attention to a common visual object reduces disparities in the "cognitive environment" and facilitates more precise inferences regarding each other's meanings (Crompton et al., 2020a; Quesque & Rossetti, 2020). Research employing photo/visual elicitation regularly demonstrates more profound and candid revelation, particularly with sensitive or challenging themes to articulate, compared to verbal-only formats (Harper, 2002; Aldridge, 2014). For neurodivergent participants, this distinction can delineate between a transcript that records superficial behavior and one that reflects contextualized sense-making.

Virtual Reality, Art Therapy, and Lived Experiences

Art therapy is a way to express yourself that can help both autistic and non-autistic people feel better (Richardson, 2022). American psychiatrist Margaret Naumburg is credited with its modern development. She was the first to employ it in the 1940s. Naumburg's work was based on older ideas about using art to look at differences within ourselves. It came after Cesare Lombroso's studies of art made by people with psychosis (Schopbach, 1967) and Auguste Marie's 1905 public showing of art made by asylum patients at the Musée de la folie (Museum of Madness). Scottish artist Joyce Laing also fought for creativity in long-term psychiatric facilities in the 1960s. She promoted art therapy as a way to help people recover and showed how useful it might be for those with schizophrenia and manic depression (Philo & Andrews, 2017; McGeachan & Philo, 2023). Laing's most well-known job was at HMP Barlinnie's Special Unit, where she helped prisoners like Jimmy Boyle and Hugh Collins, who later became famous sculptors (Carrell & Laing, 1982).

However, similar to the creations of inherently gifted autistic artists, the artwork produced by psychiatric patients and inmates frequently faced challenges in gaining recognition beyond mere voyeuristic fascination with difference. Often classified as art brut or outsider art (Cardinal, 2020; Roth, 2020), this type of work is mostly distinguished by the fact that the people who made it did not have any professional training. The inclination to categorize work as either "outsider" or "trained" highlights the necessity of viewing artistic ability as a continuum of expertise. This conceptualization aligns with known research on artists' perceptual organization—the equilibrium between global (holistic) and local (detail-oriented) processing (Wagemans et al., 2012)—and is particularly pertinent to sketching in VR, where a scarcity of visual experts currently exists.

Hadjipanayi et al. (2023) examined various recent research that have attempted to give art therapy in virtual reality (e.g., Hacmun et al., 2021; Haeyen et al., 2021; Kaimal et al., 2020; Shamri Zeevi, 2021). Hacmun et al. (2018) posited that VR art therapy provides three principal clinical benefits: the production of immersive three-dimensional artworks; the ability to alter virtual environments to meet therapeutic objectives; and the immersive nature of VR, which can enhance presence—the sensation of "being there" in the virtual realm (Riva, 2009; Riva & Waterworth, 2014). Their assertion that presence in virtual reality can facilitate dynamic personality transformation is bold and inadequately substantiated. It is important to note that the iGroup Presence Questionnaire (Schubert et al., 2001) and the ITC-Sense of Presence Inventory (Lessiter et al., 2001) are both validated measures of presence, but they were not used. Instead, their 2021 study included qualitative assessments of a single session in Tilt Brush with seven art therapists, rather than clients.

Additional data referenced by Hacmun et al. (2018) originates from studies on visuotactile synchronization and virtual body illusions; however, these results are only tangentially related to art therapy. Art therapy does not necessitate the embodiment of another individual. It is instead based on the triangle formed by the artist, the artwork, and the therapist. This makes it hard to see how body ownership illusions could be useful in VR art therapy. Most of the VR art therapy research have used Tilt Brush (now OpenBrush; Icosa Foundation, 2021), as Hadjipanayi et al. (2023) point out. Hacmun et al. (2021) characterized VR art therapy as offering a first-person perspective on artistic creativity that reflects interior sensations without necessitating the incorporation of an alternative body.

There have also been a number of qualitative studies that looked at how people felt about VR art therapy. People with personality disorders who were interviewed by Haeyen et al. (2021) said that using Tilt Brush made them feel free and safe, but they also stressed how important it was for the therapist to be there in person. One participant, "David," said that the surroundings could feel lonely without the therapist's voice. On the other hand, Shamri Zeevi (2021) discovered that VR art therapy was especially advantageous for adolescents with social anxiety, as the lack of a therapist in the virtual environment diminished self-consciousness regarding errors. Kaimal et al. (2020), examining a non-clinical sample ($n = 17$), found that participants appreciated the imaginative play and physical engagement of VR art-making, in contrast to the sitting and static characteristics of conventional art therapy.

These findings highlight possible advantages while simultaneously revealing significant limitations. For instance, the people who took part in Kaimal et al.'s (2020) study said that VR art therapy might be harder for people with cognitive impairments, visuo-vestibular problems, or phobias like acrophobia and claustrophobia. Another obstacle is the learning curve necessary to become proficient with VR tools, which diverge markedly from real-world physics. So, in addition to studying how people perceive things differently, future research should also look into how previous training in painting affects how people feel immersed, present, and engaged when drawing in VR.

A Personalized Approach to Artistic Creation and Perception in Virtual Reality

Before we can completely appreciate how useful and reproducible VR is for art therapy, we need to figure out some of the main difficulties that are holding us back. The most evident information deficiency pertains to the influence of stable personality traits on varied cognitive and behavioral outcomes in a virtual environment. In the field of human-computer interaction, Wang et al. (2024) and Zhang et al. (2022) broaden the notion of individual differences to encompass not only stable personality traits but also demographic factors and technological proficiency. An individual differences method can elucidate the influence of stable qualities on perception (Williams et al., 2008).

By looking at individual differences, researchers can use tools like the Autism-Spectrum Quotient (AQ50; Baron-Cohen et al., 2001), the Glasgow Sensory Questionnaire (GSQ; Robertson & Simmons, 2013), and presence inventories to compare how a virtual environment's simulated perceptual cues compare to real-world experiences. Prior research has elucidated gender and individual disparities in behavioral inhibition during tactile perception in virtual reality (Harjunen et al., 2017) and the influence of trait anxiety on visual processing within a virtual environment engineered to provoke acrophobia (Krupić et al., 2021).

These results augment prior research in vision science. Bryant (1982) was one of the first to comment on personality differences in how people navigate in the actual world. Czerwinski et al. (2002) later added to this by showing that there are gender disparities in how people navigate in virtual settings. It is important to note that perceptual cues in virtual reality do not necessarily correspond exactly to real-world processing. For instance, Rzepka et al. (2023) discovered that individuals in virtual settings frequently overlook binocular cues when assessing distance and scale, instead depending on heuristics related to familiar item dimensions. Clinical populations display distinctive perceptual profiles: individuals with schizophrenia demonstrate specific audiovisual processing differences (Sorkin & Zwolan, 2008), whereas a review by Dehghan et al. (2022) indicated that individuals with obsessive-compulsive disorder experience intensified negative responses and increased emotional arousal to visual stimuli in virtual reality.

Examining the intersections between artistic and autistic perceptual styles, especially in the experience of actual and virtual environments, is essential for comprehending art and perception in virtual reality. Examining fundamental sensory variances frequently associated with autism, Jones et al. (2003) found two types of sensitivity: hypersensitivity, which is being overly reactive to stimuli no matter how strong they are, and hyposensitivity, which is being less conscious of sensory input. For example, Bogdashina (2003) talks about how adults with autism cover their eyes when they are in strong light as an example of visual hypersensitivity. The GSQ, which is based on self-reported experiences from autistic adults (Robertson & Simmons, 2013), can be used to measure these kinds of sensory disparities. Koirala et al. (2021) employed eye-tracking in VR to look at how autistic and non-autistic teens reacted to visuotactile stimuli while doing a maze activity. Autistic subjects exhibited heightened aversion to visual distractions, indicative of visual hypersensitivity, while simultaneously displaying tactile hyposensitivity, as seen by a pronounced inclination to lift a ball from the maze to assess its weight. While these findings have limited generalizability, they indicate that more investigation into sensory sensitivities, possibly prevalent among artistic individuals, is necessary.

Savickaite et al. (2022) looked at how autistic and ADHD features affected performance on a VR test that required sketching a complex figure from memory after a delay. They observed no distinctions between global (big-picture) and local (detail-oriented) processing, even among subjects exhibiting elevated autistic symptoms as assessed by the AQ50 (Baron-Cohen et al., 2001). But scores on the attention-to-detail subscale indicated better memory and organization of figures. This outcome in VR aligned with results obtained from the identical task conducted on a two-dimensional tablet external to VR (Savickaite et al., 2022). These findings indicate that individual characteristics, in addition to autistic features, influence perceptual variation. Within this context, the current example aimed to investigate the interaction between artistic training and perceptual variations in VR drawing. No previous studies have looked at how artistic talent and perceptual differences in VR work together.

Our study included 22 adults (5 males and 17 women; Mean age = 29.00, SD = 6.07). In June 2023, recruitment took place in Glasgow through posters and social media. To be eligible, volunteers had to be at least 18 years old, speak English fluently, and not have any neurological disorders. Nineteen participants said they wore glasses or contact lenses, and 18 said they had used VR before. Participants were classified as artistic ($n = 7$), somewhat artistic ($n = 9$), or non-artistic ($n = 6$) based on their self-reported artistic skills.

After giving their permission, participants used the VR art program OpenBrush (HTC Vive Pro 2 HMD) to finish six drawing prompts (tree, house, person, self-portrait, dream, cherished memory), while the researcher did unstructured interviews at the same time. Sessions went as long as 70 minutes. Participants then completed four questionnaires: the Autism-Spectrum Quotient (AQ50), Glasgow Sensory Questionnaire (GSQ), iGroup Presence Questionnaire (IPQ), and ITC-Sense of Presence Inventory (ITC-SOPI). The data were examined through a mixed-methods sequential exploratory strategy, combining descriptive quantitative analysis with qualitative thematic analysis.

Quantitative Results

An examination of questionnaire data revealed that participants exhibited elevated autistic features on the AQ50 (M = 21.09, SD = 9.00) in contrast to the general population mean (16.94; Ruzich et al., 2015). A few of subjects achieved scores beyond the clinical threshold of 26. Participants on the GSQ indicated greater hypersensitivity (M = 31.77, SD = 10.69) compared to hyposensitivity (M = 26.18, SD = 10.53), implying a pronounced inclination toward overstimulation rather than under-sensing.

Presence measures yielded mixed results. Participants reported relatively high levels of spatial presence (M = 3.44, SD = 1.49) but lower levels of participation (M = 2.57, SD = 1.49), general presence (M = 2.00, SD = 2.45), and realism (M = 1.97, SD = 1.68) on the IPQ. The ITC-SOPI also showed high levels of involvement (M = 1.08, SD = 0.50) and spatial presence (M = 0.47, SD = 0.30). However, it showed lower levels of ecological validity (M = −0.18, SD = 0.79) and negative impacts (M = −0.86, SD = 0.73). Overall, these results indicate that participants typically sensed immersion and presence in VR; nevertheless, they felt decreased realism, and most did not report major unfavorable effects.

Qualitative Results

We identified four main themes and one subtheme emerging from the data. The first theme, *drawing beyond physics*, included the subtheme *feeling by seeing*, which highlighted how participants perceived sensory input through visual means. The second theme, *perfecting creative outputs*, reflected participants' efforts to refine and improve their artistic creations. The third theme, *storyboarding a narrative*, captured how participants structured their drawings to convey stories or sequences. Finally, the fourth theme, *breaking the virtual fourth wall*, described moments where participants reflected on the artificiality of the virtual environment and their interactions within it.

Drawing Beyond Physics

We developed this main theme from participants' attempts—sometimes successful—to transfer two-dimensional drawing into the virtual environment without being constrained by the laws of physics or linear perspective found in the real world. For example, P14 (artistic, aged 26) commented: "*It feels really weird to just like being able to do this and going through the the tree, yeah.*"

P14's observation highlights a conflict between their artistic training and the experience of envisioning an organic, solid tree in VR, resembling a physical sculpture. At the same time, P14 reflected that passing through the tree—appearing concrete yet lacking physical boundaries—disrupted immersion ("*it feels really weird*"). The visual realism of the tree, suggestive of opacity restricting motion, conflicted with the absence of real-world physics. This demonstrates how proprioceptive accuracy in VR is challenged when objects that look solid can be penetrated, revealing their transparency. Likewise, P16 (somewhat artistic, aged 24) reflected on the contrast between two- and three-dimensional drawing: "*It's a different beast, isn't it? Because I want- I want to keep my tree becoming taller.*"

In this case, P16 embraces the unnatural laws of VR physics. The novel experience of growing a tree in real time is quickly assimilated into their understanding of how to act when freed from two-dimensional constraints. Thus, the release from physical laws in VR distinguishes the experience from real-world artistic training by creating new expectations for spatial and motion perception. Additionally, some participants reflected on how the spatial organization of drawings allowed movement without relying on linear perspective. P17 (somewhat artistic, aged 30) noted such a discontinuity from real-world art: "*I feel like I'm having trouble connecting the drawing together, but in a way it makes it look more interesting because it's just popping out at you.*"

P17 (Fig. 4.2) demonstrates less confidence in transferring two-dimensional knowledge into VR, noting their figure's lack of continuity. However, this concern is tempered by the unexpected effect of uneven lines extending into the x-axis ("*popping out at you*") of a Cartesian coordinate system. This surprising three-dimensional quality of perspective alters what constitutes ideal viewing. Similarly, P06 (somewhat artistic, aged 29) described experiencing movement after illustrating a path without traditional action lines or blurring: "*Yeah, but yeah, kind of abstract, but also like in surface where you know, I'm just trying to reach somewhere, somewhere very far.*" Here, P06 conveys a sense of navigating both an internal ("*kind of abstract*") and external ("*but also like in surface*") limitless terrain in VR. Despite the physical restrictions of the lab's walls, P06 is still able to reach "*somewhere very far,*" without relying on illusions crafted by the virtual environment's composition. In contrast, P07

"In a way it makes it look more interesting" (P17, somewhat artistic)

Fig. 4.2 Screenshot of a 3D drawing created by Participant 17 during the VR session

(non-artistic, aged 40) perceived two-dimensional limitations, likening the task to drawing on a flat surface: "*So it feels a bit like I'm painting a wall rather than writing in 2D though, like if I was home decorating.*" P07 interprets immersion in OpenBrush as being confined within a room, where movement is restricted by the solidity of a "*wall.*" This familiar surface allows the participant to translate creativity into a practical context (painting a wall) without engaging with the rules of artistic training.

Feeling by Seeing

The subtheme *Feeling by seeing* captures how artistic and somewhat artistic participants translated visual textures into imagined tactile sensations. For example, P09 (artistic, aged 24) reflected on the ease of experimenting with textures in VR: "*Switching between brushes so easily and making that now possible, and the artwork and this eventually can just be really printed.*"

P09 envisions the potential of rendering a 360-degree, three-dimensional drawing as a tangible object, though without directly referencing its texture. Similarly, P01 (somewhat artistic, aged 24) imagined the materiality of their creation, noting: "*I tried to make the colour as close to a brick colour as possible, but that's not happening because I'm finding it a bit hard to mix colours in the yeah wheel again.*" Despite challenges in achieving a brick-like hue, P01 employed an impasto technique, layering brushstrokes thickly to replicate the coarse surface of brick, much like a painter might evoke dimensionality on canvas. They further explained that this overlapping style "*makes me feel uhh like the house will be more solid with strokes like that.*"

Overall, artistic and somewhat artistic participants employed distinct strategies to convey perceptual realism in their drawings, aligning with the creation of visuotactile illusions. Some artistic participants achieved their aims of tactile realism by selecting textural brushes. For example, to depict a tree, P02 (somewhat artistic, aged 34) chose a brush that visually and texturally resembled bark, remarking: "*It just looks like, yeah, like a wood.*"

In response to the same prompt, P14 (artistic, aged 26) described the sensation of dew on wet leaves: "*It's like a type of soft that feels slippery … It's just like slick.*" This suggests that OpenBrush's pixel-rendered, three-dimensional brushes can effectively evoke sensory illusions without relying on the traditional lines, shading, and spatial techniques of two-dimensional artistic training. Distinctively, P20 (artistic, aged 30) likened the use of HMD controllers to papier-mâché, explaining: "*So paper with again you'd have like your hands were dunking in the pocket and like wiping it around.*"

This comparison illustrates how P20 experienced the controllers as extensions of their hands. Unlike other participants, P20 did not attribute textural sensations to any brush, aligning with the absence of haptic feedback in OpenBrush. Instead, the act of using the controllers simulated the process of working with glue and paper.

Perfecting Creative Outputs

Many artistic participants expressed reduced confidence when drawing in OpenBrush, describing the experience as learning an entirely new visual grammar. From these reflections, the researcher identified a second theme: *perfecting creative outputs.* For example, P08 (Fig. 4.3) (artistic, aged 24) highlighted the perceived gap between sculpting and drawing in three dimensions, remarking: "*If it was like like a training, like, doing sculptures, like in the real world, like the 3D World, like, I would see, like much better.*"

This discrepancy between "*the real world*" and "*the 3D World*" appears to be mediated by comparisons to sculpting, which participants viewed as a transferable skill for OpenBrush—though one requiring greater manual

"Doing sculptures, like in the real world, like the 3D world (P08, artistic)

Fig. 4.3 Screenshot of a 3D drawing created by Participant 08 during the VR session

dexterity to anticipate where drawings would emerge in space. Similarly, P11 (artistic, aged 30) expressed frustration with the challenge of drawing in VR:

> *I'm just wondering how I'm going to draw in 3D because it's a thing to model or sculpt, but right this is. Well, if I was sculpting in real life I would stop by the base because OK that makes no sense, so maybe I could have started by the- by the leaves, but*

Since both P08 and P11 had artistic training, their references to the challenge of anchoring a sculpture to a base are unsurprising. In VR, however, this constraint is removed, allowing for creative departures from traditional methods. As P11 observed, "*so maybe I could have started by the- by the leaves,*" suggesting that anti-gravity feats are achievable in VR without adhering to the conventions of formal artistic training, thereby broadening creative possibilities.

In contrast, participants who self-identified as non-artistic expressed greater satisfaction with their creations. For example, P12 (non-artistic, aged 23) reflected positively on their Magic Kingdom castle: "*I think this is perfect like I don't, yeah, it doesn't necessarily look like Disneyland, but I think it looks really like magical.*"

For P12 (Fig. 4.4), achieving an exact likeness—"*doesn't necessarily look like Disneyland*"—was less important than evoking the memory itself. Similarly, P18 (non-artistic, aged 24) demonstrated a personal sense of closure by using the snapshot tool in OpenBrush to capture each drawing once satisfied, stating, "*I don't know; it's like marking it as finished.*"

Despite the artificial study environment, P18 chose to preserve their otherwise impermanent creations, suggesting that the final outcome ("*marking it as finished*") held greater importance than the creative process itself. Furthermore, by taking snapshots, P18 may have sought to rebalance the power dynamic between researcher and participant, asserting control over their own narrative before progressing to the next drawing.

Storyboarding a Narrative

The researcher identified a third theme based on how all participants constructed continuous visual narratives. For instance, P05 (somewhat artistic, aged 23) described carrying forward their artistic process as a comic artist:

> *Yeah, maybe that's the way I draw some storyboards in my project. When I doing some some like major project I use this kind of this style of drawing to express how people my observation of people how they work on the day.* (Figure 28)

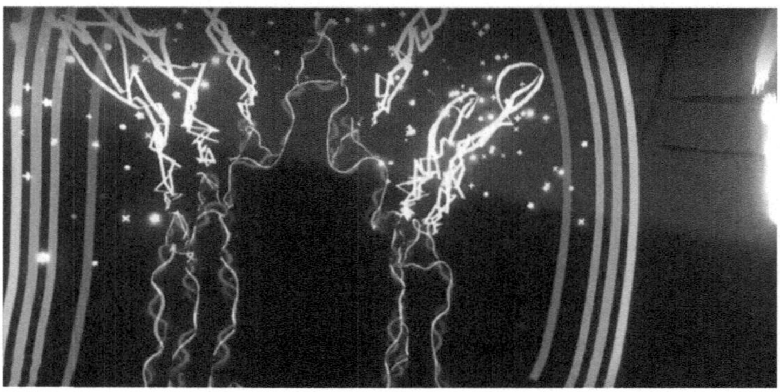

"It doesn't necessarily look like Disneyland, but I think it looks really like magical" (P12, non-artistic)

Fig. 4.4 Screenshot of a 3D drawing created by Participant 12 during the VR session

P05 experienced OpenBrush as aligning with their free-form storyboarding process for "*some like major project*," where early concepts are mapped out. Their observational approach to illustrating "*how they work on the day*" was carried over from two-dimensional media into VR. Similarly, P02 (somewhat artistic, aged 34) maintained narrative consistency by linking prompts together: "*For me to draw, I think the kind to me it's like in a flow, so that the house and then I think personally I can put those together.*"

P02 characterizes their drawings as having "*a flow*," akin to the way a viewer might experience an art exhibition in a museum. In contrast, P21 (somewhat artistic, aged 28) approached the task through a scientific lens, constructing their own narrative by drawing a flowchart. They explained: "*And I can make things easier. So when, especially when something when someone tell me their their, their experiment their project, easy to get lost.*"

P21's diagrammatic sequence of "*their experiment their project*" illustrates an effort to prioritize clarity and accessibility, taking into account the perspective of the viewer. Collectively, these examples highlight how artistic and somewhat artistic participants considered an audience, anticipating that viewers would engage with their storytelling through the virtual medium of OpenBrush. This emphasis on narrative cohesion also inspired innovation among some participants. For instance, P19 (artistic, aged 32) revised their drawings dynamically as they unfolded, remarking: "*Yeah, maybe I'll do this and then just kind of like animate, maybe I can hold on. I might reconsider, yeah.*"

This associative process enabled fluid shifts and developments in visual ideas with minimal revision. Additionally, P04 (non-artistic, aged 40) described sensing an intrinsic, almost self-propelling quality in their VR drawings, noting: "*I just I like the way that animates it sort of feels into itself, it just feels.*"

The perception of interconnectivity ("*it sort of feels into itself, it just feels*") is not attributed to P04's intentional control. Rather, the virtual environment itself seems to provide creative potential by linking forms and ideas. Through animated brushes and a 360-degree perspective, participants either intentionally sought or naturally experienced the emergence of unified artistic narratives.

Breaking the Virtual Fourth Wall

The researcher identified a fourth theme concerning how participants navigated their simultaneous awareness of both the virtual and real environments. For instance, at the end of the VR session, P22 (artistic, aged 29) reflected: "*Yeah, it's, it's weird like cause when I actually say that I'm like, oh, I'm here, but it's my it's like my head. It's just not really in the same room as my body.*" This account suggests a dissociative experience, in which the participant remained aware of the physical room while also engaging with the perceptual cues of OpenBrush. P22 elaborated further: "*It feels like lots of different planes of two dimensions, rather than what 3D actually feels like, which is like not differentiable.*"

By observing "*lots of different planes of two dimensions,*" P22 provided an account aligned with real-life perception, suggesting they may have been parsing individual visual cues rather than perceiving them as a unified whole. In contrast, P10 (non-artistic, aged 36) reflected on the artificiality of VR, stating: "*Yeah, it's it's kind of unlike being in a room with the light source in the centre or being outside with the sun in one place.*"

Here, P10 interprets value in drawing (light and darkness) as distinct from real-world lighting conditions, such as illumination from an overhead source. Importantly, the participant who reported the lowest level of experienced realism on the IPQ (Schubert et al., 2001) also expressed contextual unease. When asked to draw a person, P16 (somewhat artistic, aged 24) anticipated the unsettling possibility of disconnected limbs, stating: "*I feel a bit creeped out by the 3D effect.*" Unlike inanimate subjects such as trees or houses, the fragmented human form evoked a sinister quality. This discomfort may stem from the three-dimensional rendering of "*body parts,*" which appeared severed. P16 elaborated further: "*I feel that I cannot step too much into technology and into that disconnect between like the real and the, and I feel like it's a real person into this, so I feel some kind of strange like yeah, you're like, guilt about leaving them behind.*"

P16's (Fig. 4.5) emotional engagement with drawing is so strong that they establish a boundary ("*I cannot step too much into technology*"). Although they attempt to resist attributing human qualities to their art, they still acknowledge feeling "*strange.*" While P16 appears to recognize the artificial nature of VR, they nonetheless express "*guilt about leaving them behind.*" This response suggests a perception of VR drawings as animated or alive, blurring the boundary between the virtual and the real worlds.

"I feel like it's a real person into this, so I feel some kind of strange like year, you're like, guilt about leaving them behind" (P16, somewhat artistic)

Fig. 4.5 Screenshot of a 3D drawing created by Participant 16 during the VR session

Artistic Proficiency and Presence in Virtual Reality

Individuals with artistic expertise had greater engagement and ecological validity/naturalness on the ITC-SOPI (Lessiter et al., 2001), along with enhanced general presence, spatial presence, involvement, and perceived realism on the IPQ (Schubert et al., 2001), in contrast to non-artistic participants. They also reported fewer adverse effects (e.g., fatigue, headache, nausea), which are typically linked to virtual reality cybersickness (Woo et al., 2023). One elucidation for these patterns resides in the notion of mastery.

Bandura (1977, 1997) characterized mastery as the individual perception of fulfillment and achievement subsequent to enhancement in a certain domain, whereas Ryff (1989) conceptualized environmental mastery as a facet of well-being. In virtual reality situations, mastery correlates with favorable learning experiences via enhanced competence and flexibility (Aksel Stenberdt & Makransky, 2023). Likewise, Kaimal et al. (2020) discovered that art therapists employing Tilt Brush reported experiences of mastery and flow subsequent to the translation of two-dimensional artistic talents into virtual reality. Mastery in virtual reality—successfully completing tasks and responding to unforeseen changes—has been correlated with increased presence (Miller & Reid, 2003; Riva et al., 2004). Presence, broadly defined as the cognitive sense of "being there" in a virtual environment (Schubert et al., 1999), arises when individuals perceive environmental features as realistic, resulting in coherence between real and virtual spaces (Barfield & Hendrix, 1995; Hendrix & Barfield, 1996; Kim & Biocca, 1997). This is in line with what the current study found: the creative individuals said the virtual environement felt more realistic.

Ren et al. propose that creative persons, including trained visual artists, exhibit greater exterior attention to visual stimuli rather than internal focus on their thoughts, thereby facilitating prolonged involvement in virtual reality. The majority of participants opting not to remove their drawings may indicate prolonged attention and immersion. The sequential hierarchy of vocal cues employed in this study (tree, house, person, self-portrait, dream, and pleasant memory) may have contributed to a progression of creative mastery in virtual reality (Maskey et al., 2014, 2019).

Also, mastery is linked to experiential learning, which is the process of learning skills by doing them (Pellas et al., 2021). VR makes this even more true because sketching while moving breaches the constraints of the real world. For example, drawings could be walked through, defied gravity, and made people feel like they were moving in a realistic way (e.g., ducking beneath drawings to escape looming effects; Rolin et al., 2018). Artistic and somewhat artistic participants may have attained enhanced presence and realism via the development of skills and creative mastery, distinguishing their experiences from those of non-artistic participants.

Flow and Adverse Effects

Previous studies indicate that mastery and presence are significantly associated with diminished external awareness of the actual world during virtual reality experiences (Plechatá et al., 2022; Yeh et al., 2019). In the current study, qualitative narratives aligned with flow encompassed artistic and semi-artistic participants documenting realistic VR drawings (first topic) and visuotactile sensory illusions (subtheme). Flow also seemed to keep participants interested when their drawings were part of a tale, as if their drawings were in the same universe (third and fourth themes). On the other hand, breaks in flow may assist explain why both artists and non-artists say they feel disoriented because of strange things about the visual display (fifth theme).

Csikszentmihalyi (1975) initially characterized flow as a state of heightened focus wherein individuals become oblivious to themselves and temporal constraints. A primary prerequisite for achieving flow is the alignment between one's skills and the demands of the activity; excessively hard activities, perceived as a loss of control over the environment, hinder flow (Csikszentmihalyi, 1990). This growth through skill-set matching is similar to the idea of mastery. In this study, creative participants may have encountered ability discrepancies when transitioning their two-dimensional training to three-dimensional VR drawing, resulting in more stringent assessments of their outputs. Conversely, non-artistic participants, devoid of this foundational ability, may have encountered delight and a perceived enhancement of new skills rather than a sense of mismatch.

VR study has shown that there is a strong link between matching skills, expertise, and flow. For example, Lemmens and von Münchhausen (2023) demonstrated that enjoyment and skill alignment promoted flow, hence improving performance in a VR rhythm game. In a similar vein, Tan et al. (2022) found that elevated flow levels in Tilt Brush, assessed using the Long Flow State Scale: General (FSS-2-General; Jackson & Marsh, 1996), exhibited a good correlation ($r = 0.61$) with all dimensions of the IPQ (Schubert et al., 2001). Consequently, it is probable that artistic and semi-artistic individuals in our study experienced both immersion—a less intense state of focus (Richesin et al., 2021)—and flow. However, the novelty of VR sketching may have increased sensory engagement, complicating the differentiation between flow and elevated task satisfaction (Jackson & Csikszentmihalyi, 1999). Indeed, the argument that flow is often confounded with strong task participation remains a constraint of its construct validity (Abuhamdeh, 2020). Nonetheless, previous research on VR art therapy substantiates the explanatory significance of flow and competence in comprehending individual variances in immersion and presence.

Flow might also explain why all groups have minimal amounts of negative impacts. Tan et al. (2022) discovered a moderate negative correlation ($r = -0.58$) between flow in Tilt Brush and state anxiety as measured by the State-Trait Anxiety Inventory (STAI; Spielberger et al., 1983). Since state anxiety induces physiological reactions like increased heart rate and perspiration (Cohen & Bodner, 2019), its correlation with VR sickness indicates a common mechanism. Biasutti and Antonini Philippe (2023) assert that emotive, cognitive, and physiological interruptions impede flow in the arts. In the current study, the documented sensory variations among artistic participants may have protected them from creativity- and performance-related worries, thereby maintaining flow (Antonini Philippe et al., 2022). Participants engaged in artistic creation in auditory but not visual contact with the researcher, so removing visual stimuli that could potentially increase self-awareness. This absence of external visual attention may have diminished feelings of performance and creative anxiety (Barbot & Carrasco, 2018).

Neurocognitive disparities also manifested. Artistic individuals obtained lower scores on the AQ50 (Baron-Cohen et al., 2001) and exhibited the least hyper- and hyposensitivity on the GSQ (Robertson & Simmons, 2013). Conversely, four out of six non-artistic individuals exceeded the AQ50 threshold (>26; Zeisel et al., 2023). Since elevated autistic features correlate with diminished attentional control (Hendry et al., 2020), this may have constrained flow in non-artists. Attentional control, an essential condition for flow (Csikszentmihalyi & Nakamura, 2010), was evidenced by the creative participants' reduced scores on the AQ50 attention switching subscale. This conclusion corroborates with research indicating that trained painters exhibit enhanced top-down attentional regulation (Chamberlain et al., 2019; Nodine et al., 1993), facilitating adaptable transitions between general VR stimuli and specific drawing details (Chamberlain & Wagemans, 2015). This kind of flexible attention could explain why creative participants felt a steady flow and more realism.

Naturalistic sensory processing was also a factor. Kilteni et al. (2015) contend that naturalistic visual settings facilitate sensory integration. Artistic participants, who exhibited the lowest hypersensitivity levels, may have experienced less cognitive load from multisensory integration demands, facilitating enhanced vestibular control of balance and orientation (González-Franco & Lanier, 2017). Vestibular atypicalities are prevalent in autism (Robertson, 2012) and associated with reduced visual attention in both neurodiverse and neurotypical individuals (Rajagopalan et al., 2017). The capacity of artists to mitigate incoherent visuo-vestibular feedback (Medina et al., 2015) may elucidate their lower prevalence of VR sickness. Their perceptual tolerance may encompass intermittent delays between haptic input and visual output (Fan et al., 2023), so mitigating adverse effects.

Another reason is tactile engagement. Chittenden (2018) posited that artists are becoming more sensitive to haptic nuances owing to their frequent utilization of touch-screen technology for drawing, such as tablets and smartphones. Such experience with discontinuous feedback may have mitigated disorientation among artistic participants in VR (Fan et al., 2023). In general, less hypersensitivity, better attention management, and better perceptual adaptation probably helped artistic and somewhat creative individuals get into flow more easily and improve their skills (Banfield & Burgess, 2013).

Hyperfocus and the Evaluation of Three-Dimensional Art

A third reason why creative individuals rated their VR drawings more negatively is hyperfocus. Hyperfocus, frequently characterized as a state of heightened, detail-oriented concentration, resembles the local processing bias shown in autism (Ashinoff & Abu-Akel, 2021) and has also been documented in ADHD (Hupfeld et al., 2019) and bipolar disorder (Lobban et al., 2012). Although theoretically linked to flow, hyperfocus is increasingly recognized as a separate cognitive process (Dupuis et al., 2022; Grotewiel et al., 2023). In the current study, artistic and semi-artistic participants exhibited elevated scores on the AQ50 attention-to-detail subscale (Baron-Cohen et al., 2001), a facet associated with Baron-Cohen et al.'s (2009) hyper-systemizing theory, which conceptualizes autistic cognition as fundamentally rooted in pattern recognition and rule-governed processing. Autistic performance artists have identified hyperfocus and attention to detail as beneficial attributes in creative endeavors (Buckley et al., 2021). Nonetheless, hyperfocus might function as a double-edged blade, exacerbating perfectionistic inclinations. In this scenario, artistic participants may have reached a hyperfocused state while seeking to apply the principles of two-dimensional art (e.g., perspective) to the unfamiliar three-dimensional medium of VR sketching.

In line with this understanding, artists' VR outputs often contravened the grammatical norms of object placement typically observed in two-dimensional practices (Võ & Wolfe, 2013). Previous research indicates that syntactic violations in art are evaluated more severely than semantic or global inconsistencies (Markey et al., 2019). Consequently, the increased focus on detail exhibited by artistic participants may have contributed to the persistence of local inconsistencies, resulting in dissatisfaction with their drawings (Bimler et al., 2019; Zabelina & Beeman, 2013).

Conversely, non-artistic participants exhibited diminished self-criticism. Most of them scored above the AQ50 clinical cut-off for autistic features (>26; Baron-Cohen et al., 2001; Sapey-Triomphe et al., 2018), which is interesting. Research indicates that persons with autism may interpret artistic stimuli more readily, as the predictable characteristics of aesthetic information present a less cognitive load compared to social stimuli (Coelho et al., 2025). Empirical research suggests that individuals with autism are less likely to render harshly negative evaluations of artistic quality in comparison to their non-autistic counterparts (Brosnan & Ashwin, 2023). In this study, the interview format may have exacerbated this phenomenon: non-artistic participants exhibiting elevated autistic traits may have depended more on logical, deliberative reasoning to elucidate their creative choices, resulting in more neutral or positive assessments of their outputs, whereas artistic participants seemed to react more instinctively with negative self-criticism. This explanation corresponds with the dual process hypothesis of autism, which differentiates between deliberative and intuitive thinking (Ashwin & Brosnan, 2019).

Considering personality variables yields further insights. Individuals without artistic backgrounds achieved the highest scores in imagination, a characteristic that has a negative correlation with conscientiousness (Wakabayashi et al., 2006). Low conscientiousness is linked to a greater appreciation of abstract or modern art styles (Chamorro-Premuzic & Furnman, 2004; Furnham & Walker, 2001a; Gotz & Gotz, 1974). This means that non-artistic participants' positive evaluations of VR drawings may show that they like the abstract, non-representational forms that OpenBrush offers. Their elevated hyposensitivity scores on the GSQ (Robertson & Simmons, 2013) correspond with sensation-seeking tendencies, which have shown a positive correlation with a preference for abstract and pop art (Furnham & Walker, 2001b).

Conversely, artistic and semi-artistic participants' education in classical, representational traditions may have fostered expectations of canonical visual grammar that were at odds with the nontraditional spatiality of VR sketching. These expectations, along with an excessive concentration on local minutiae, probably made their negative self-judgments even stronger. When taken collectively, the disparities in hyperfocus, cognitive style, sensory sensitivity, and personality factors seem to have caused the different ways that artistic and non-artistic people evaluated things in this study.

Hacmun, Regev, and Salomon (2018) conducted a study examining the experiences of creating and viewing art in virtual reality, utilizing semi-structured interviews with seasoned art therapists following practical engagement with tools such as Tilt Brush/OpenBrush (seven experts; theme analysis). Four themes emerged: (1) the lived user experience of VR art-making; (2) distinctive properties of the VR "material" (immersion, 3D space, infinite scale, dynamic/animated strokes, freedom from gravity and mess, easy revision/undo); (3) the VR setting as a studio that can be rearranged around the maker; and (4) perceived relevance for practice. These discoveries, although originally intended for therapeutic purposes, clearly correlate with scientific applications of drawing to express perception: virtual reality enables individuals to spatialize internal sensations, overlay motion and texture onto form, and situate events "around" or "within" the body—capabilities that two-dimensional media find challenging to represent. People can also go within the drawing and move around it, turning private feelings that are hard to put into words into things that can be shared and explored. There were some practical concerns, such the learning curve, occasional cybersickness, limited tactile resistance, access and training demands, but the experts still thought VR drawing had a lot of potential because it allows for embodied, scaled, and revisable visualization of experience. In summary, the study advocates for the utilization of VR sketching as a research tool for the non-verbal communication of perceptual realities, as it provides immediacy, movement, spatial positioning, and co-presence that enable participants to "show" rather than "tell" their perceptions (Hacmun et al., 2021).

Kaimal et al. (2020) executed a pilot study investigating the potential of drawing in virtual reality, contextualizing it within art therapy while yielding insights that extend well beyond that framework. Participants took part in immersive sketching sessions, some of which included a scent stimulus, and they created both visual art and written thoughts on their experiences. Although the authors noted small therapeutic effects, including decreases in negative affect in the presence of fragrance, the most pertinent discoveries for the current discourse are to the utilization of VR for the creation and sharing of visuals that resonate with individuals' internal perceptual experiences. Participants illustrated natural landscapes, personal symbols, recollections, and fantastical components, showcasing that virtual sketching can externalize private, often unfathomable experiences in a manner that is comprehensible to others (Kaimal et al., 2020).

The study emphasizes how VR facilitates the ability to "show rather than tell," a significant advantage when examining perceptual disparities or circumstances that defy straightforward language expression. The immersive nature of VR encouraged playful experimentation, with participants characterizing their experiences as enjoyable, delightful, and soothing. They also said that there was a learning curve and that they sometimes got lost, which reminds us that while using these tools for research, it is important to be comfortable and learn how to use them. These observations highlight the significance of design concerns in the implementation of VR sketching as a means of eliciting and conveying perceptual experience.

The function of cross-sensory input is of special importance. The incorporation of olfactory signals, originally implemented for therapeutic purposes, serves as a methodological illustration of how VR sketching might be structured to investigate cross-modal perception. This aligns with synesthetic-oriented methodologies, which aim to investigate the interaction among many sensory modalities and individual interpretations thereof. Kaimal et al. (2020) advocate for additional research comparing VR drawing to conventional media and evaluating various forms of sensory augmentation, indicating explicit pathways for the application of VR in perceptual research.

This study ultimately shows that VR drawing is a viable and captivating medium, enabling participants to create rich, meaningful visuals connected to memory, imagination, and subjective perception. VR sketching is recognized as a potent research instrument for examining how individuals perceive, organize, and articulate their perceptual experiences. It is a useful method in the larger field of participatory and synesthetic design since it may combine sensory stimuli, encourage fun exploration, and make private experiences public.

Chapter Conclusion

Emerging creative technologies, such as virtual reality (VR), provide new potential for neurodivergent expression and self-regulation. VR sketching platforms (such as OpenBrush or Tilt Brush) offer an endless, three-dimensional canvas, embodied engagement, and the ability to modify sensory load in real time. These affordances are strongly related to autistic and other neurodivergent perceptual needs: stimulus controllability, action reversibility, and the ability to explore from many perspectives (Kaimal et al., 2020; Hacmun et al., 2021).

VR art-making has also been linked to relaxation, flow, and decreased anxiety in both neurotypical and clinical populations (Kaimal et al., 2020).

The technology enables what Murray et al. (2005) refer to as monotropism: focused, immersive interaction inside a safe, restricted perceptual environment. Furthermore, the option to "undo" or reset the environment directly addresses the unpredictability that frequently exacerbates sensory overload in autism (Robertson & Simmons, 2013). As a result, VR may serve as both a research tool for understanding perceptual variety and an inclusive creative platform that supports a wide range of sensory profiles.

References

Abuhamdeh, S. (2020). Investigating the "flow" experience: Key conceptual and operational issues. *Frontiers in Psychology, 11*, 158.

Ackerman, P. L. (1999). Traits and knowledge as determinants of learning and individual differences: Putting it all together. In P. L. Ackerman, P. C. Kyllonen, & R. D. Roberts (Eds.), *Learning and individual differences: Process, trait, and content determinants* (pp. 437–462). American Psychological Association. https://doi.org/10.1037/10315-019

Alderson-Day, B., & Fernyhough, C. (2015). Inner speech: Development, cognitive functions, phenomenology, and neurobiology. *Psychological Bulletin, 141*(5), 931.

Aldridge, J. (2014). Working with vulnerable groups in social research: Dilemmas by default and design. *Qualitative Research, 14*(1), 112–130.

Antonini Philippe, R., Kosirnik, C., Ortuño, E., & Biasutti, M. (2022). Flow and music performance: Professional musicians and music students' views. *Psychology of Music, 50*(4), 1023–1038.

Arnstein, S. R. (1969). A ladder of citizen participation. *Journal of the American Institute of Planners, 35*(4), 216–224. https://doi.org/10.1080/01944366908977225

Ashinoff, B. K., & Abu-Akel, A. (2021). Hyperfocus: The forgotten frontier of attention. *Psychological Research, 85*(1), 1–19. https://doi.org/10.1007/s00426-019-01245-8

Ashwin, C., & Brosnan, M. (2019). The dual process theory of autism. In K. Morsanyi & R. Byrne (Eds.), *Thinking, reasoning, and decision making in autism*. Routledge.

Atkins, S. S., & Williams, L. D. (2007). *Sourcebook in expressive arts therapy*. Parkway Publishers, Inc.

Bal, M. (2009). Working with concepts. *European Journal of English Studies, 13*(1), 13–23.

Bandura, A. (1977). Self-efficacy: Toward a unifying theory of behavioral change. *Psychological Review, 84*(2), 191–215. https://doi.org/10.1037/0033-295X.84.2.191

Bandura, A. (1997). *Self-efficacy: The exercise of control.* W. H. Freeman.
Banfield, J., & Burgess, M. (2013). A phenomenology of artistic doing: Flow as embodied knowing in 2D and 3D professional artists. *Journal of Phenomenological Psychology, 44*(1), 60–91.
Barbot, A., & Carrasco, M. (2018). Emotion and anxiety potentiate the way attention alters visual appearance. *Scientific Reports, 8*, 5938. https://doi.org/10.1038/s41598-018-23686-8
Barfield, W., & Hendrix, C. (1995). The effect of update rate on the sense of presence within virtual environments. *Virtual Reality, 1*(1), 3–15.
Baron-Cohen, S. (1997). *Mindblindness: An essay on autism and theory of mind.* MIT press.
Baron-Cohen, S. (2000). Theory of mind and autism: A fifteen year review. In *Understanding other minds: Perspectives from developmental cognitive neuroscience*, 2(3–20), 102. Oxford: University Press.
Baron-Cohen, S., Wheelwright, S., Skinner, R., Martin, J., & Clubley, E. (2001). The Autism-Spectrum Quotient (AQ). *Journal of Autism and Developmental Disorders, 31*(1), 5–17. https://doi.org/10.1023/A:1005653411471
Baron-Cohen, S., Ashwin, E., Ashwin, C., Tavassoli, T., & Chakrabarti, B. (2009). Talent in autism: Hyper-systemizing, hyper-attention to detail and sensory hypersensitivity. *Philosophical Transactions of the Royal Society B, 364*(1522), 1377–1383. https://doi.org/10.1098/rstb.2008.0337
Baron-Cohen, S., Spitz, A., & Cross, P. (1993). Do children with autism recognise surprise? *A research note. Cognition & Emotion, 7*(6), 507–516.
Beardsley, M. C. (1979, August). In defense of aesthetic value. In *Proceedings and Addresses of the American Philosophical Association* (Vol. 52, No. 6, pp. 723–749). American Philosophical Association.
Betts, D. (2013). A review of the principles for culturally appropriate art therapy assessment tools. *Art Therapy, 30*(3), 98–106.
Biasutti, M., & Antonini Philippe, R. (2023). Editorial: I got flow! The flow state in music and artistic sport contexts. *Frontiers in Psychology, 14*, 1138638. https://doi.org/10.3389/fpsyg.2023.1138638
Bimler, D., Snellock, M., & Paramei, G. (2019). Art expertise in construing meaning of representational and abstract artworks. *Acta Psychologica, 192*, 11–22. https://doi.org/10.1016/j.actpsy.2018.10.012
Bogdashina, O. (2003). *Sensory perceptual issues in autism and Asperger syndrome.* Jessica Kingsley.
Brosnan, M., & Ashwin, C. (2023). Thinking, fast and slow on the autism spectrum. *Autism, 27*(5), 1245–1255.
Brosnan, M., & Ashwin, C. (2023). Differences in art appreciation in autism: A measure of reduced intuitive processing. *Journal of Autism and Developmental Disorders, 53*(3), 1218–1228.

Bryant, K. J. (1982). Personality correlates of sense of direction and geographic orientation. *Journal of Personality and Social Psychology, 43*(6), 1318–1324. https://doi.org/10.1037/0022-3514.43.6.1318

Buckley, E., Pellicano, E., & Remington, A. (2021). Experiences of autistic performing arts professionals. *Journal of Autism and Developmental Disorders, 51*(1), 45–59. https://doi.org/10.1007/s10803-020-04517-0

Cardinal, R. (2020). Outsider Art. Kunst und Krankenhaus: Interdisziplinäre Zusammenarbeit und Perspektivwechsel in Gesundheitsförderung und Prävention, 37. https://doi.org/10.17433/978-3-17-036381-6.

Carrell, C., & Laing, J. (1982). *The special unit: Its evolution through its art.* Third Eye Centre.

Chamberlain, R., McManus, I. C., Riley, H., Rankin, Q., & Brunswick, N. (2013). Local processing enhancements associated with superior observational drawing are due to enhanced perceptual functioning, not weak central coherence. *The Quarterly Journal of Experimental Psychology, 66*(7), 1448–1466.

Chamberlain, R., Drake, J. E., Kozbelt, A., Hickman, R., Siev, J., & Wagemans, J. (2019). Artists as experts in visual cognition: An update. *Psychology of Aesthetics, Creativity, and the Arts, 13*(1), 58.

Chamberlain, R., & Wagemans, J. (2015). Visual arts training is linked to flexible attention to local and global levels of visual stimuli. *Acta Psychologica, 161*, 185–197.

Chamberlain, R., Kozbelt, A., Drake, J. E., & Wagemans, J. (2021). Learning to see by learning to draw: A longitudinal analysis of the relationship between representational drawing training and visuospatial skill. *Psychology of Aesthetics, Creativity, and the Arts, 15*(1), 76.

Chamorro-Premuzic, T., & Furnham, A. (2004). Art judgment: A measure related to both personality and intelligence? *Imagination, Cognition and Personality, 24*(1), 3–24.

Chapman, R., & Veit, W. (2021). The essence of autism: Fact or artefact? *Molecular Psychiatry, 26*(5), 1440–1441.

Chappell, P. A., & Steitz, J. A. (1993). Young children's human figure drawings and cognitive development. *Perceptual and Motor Skills, 76*(2), 611–617.

Chittenden, T. (2018). Tilt Brush painting: Chronotopic adventures in a physical-virtual threshold. *Journal of Contemporary Painting, 4*(2), 381–403.

Chown, N., Robinson, J., Beardon, L., Downing, J., Hughes, L., Leatherland, J., & MacGregor, D. (2017). A framework for participatory autism research. *Disability & Society, 32*(7), 935–959.

Coelho, F., Gonçalves, D., & Abreu, A. M. (2025). The impact of game-based interventions on adult cognition: A systematic review. *International Journal of Human–Computer Interaction, 41*(19), 12479–12514.

Cohen, S., & Bodner, E. (2019). The relationship between flow and music performance anxiety amongst professional classical orchestral musicians. *Psychology of Music, 47*(3), 420–435.

Conson, M., Senese, V. P., Zappullo, I., Baiano, C., Warrier, V., Raimo, S., et al. (2022). The effect of autistic traits on disembedding and mental rotation in neurotypical women and men. *Scientific Reports, 12*(1), 4639.

Courchesne, V., Tesfaye, R., Mirenda, P., Nicholas, D., Mitchell, W., Singh, I., et al. (2022). Autism Voices: A novel method to access firstperson perspective of autistic youth. *Autism, 26*(5), 1123–1136.

Crilly, N., Blackwell, A. F., & Clarkson, P. J. (2006). Graphic elicitation: Using research diagrams as interview stimuli. *Qualitative Research, 6*(3), 341–366. https://doi.org/10.1177/1468794106065007

Crompton, C. J., Hallett, S., Ropar, D., Flynn, E. G., & Fletcher-Watson, S. (2020a). 'I never realised everybody felt as happy as I do when I am around autistic people': A thematic analysis of autistic adults' relationships. *Frontiers in Psychology, 11*, 586171. https://doi.org/10.3389/fpsyg.2020.586171

Crompton, C. J., Ropar, D., Evans-Williams, C. V. M., Flynn, E. G., & Fletcher-Watson, S. (2020b). Autistic peer-to-peer information transfer is highly effective. *Autism, 24*(7), 1704–1712. https://doi.org/10.1177/1362361320919286

Csikszentmihalyi, M. (1975). *Beyond boredom and anxiety*. Jossey-Bass.

Csikszentmihalyi, M. (1990). *Flow: The psychology of optimal experience*. Harper & Row.

Csikszentmihalyi, M., & Nakamura, J. (2010). Effortless attention in everyday life: A systematic phenomenology. In B. Bruya (Ed.), *Effortless attention*. MIT Press.

Czerwinski, M., Tan, D. S., & Robertson, G. G. (2002, April). Women take a wider view. In *Proceedings of the SIGCHI conference on Human factors in computing systems* (pp. 195–202).

Dehghan, B., Saeidimehr, S., Sayyah, M., & Rahim, F. (2022). The effect of virtual reality on emotional response and symptoms provocation in patients with OCD: A systematic review and meta-analysis. *Frontiers in Psychiatry, 12*, 733584.

Drake, J. E., Redash, A., Coleman, K., Haimson, J., & Winner, E. (2010). 'Autistic'local processing bias also found in children gifted in realistic drawing. *Journal of Autism and Developmental Disorders, 40*(6), 762–773.

Dupuis, A., Mudiyanselage, P., Burton, C. L., Arnold, P. D., Crosbie, J., & Schachar, R. J. (2022). Hyperfocus or flow? Attentional strengths in autism spectrum disorder. *Frontiers in Psychiatry, 13*, 886692.

Eccles, D. W., & Arsal, G. (2017). The think aloud method: What is it and how do I use it? *Qualitative Research in Sport, Exercise and Health, 9*(4), 514–531.

Ericsson, K. A., & Simon, H. A. (1980). Verbal reports as data. *Psychological Review, 87*(3), 215–251. https://doi.org/10.1037/0033-295X.87.3.215

Fan, W., Guo, X., Feng, E., Lin, J., Wang, Y., Liang, J., et al. (2023). Digital twin-driven mixed reality framework for immersive teleoperation with haptic rendering. *IEEE Robotics and Automation Letters, 8*(12), 8494–8501.

Finlay, L., & Gough, B. (Eds.). (2008). *Reflexivity: A practical guide for researchers in health and social sciences.* John Wiley & Sons.

Fletcher-Watson, S., Adams, J., Brook, K., Charman, T., Crane, L., Cusack, J., et al. (2019). Making the future together: Shaping autism research through meaningful participation. *Autism, 23*(4), 943–953.

Frith, U. (1989). *Autism: Explaining the Enigma* (2nd ed.). Blackwell. 2003.

Frith, U. (2001). Mind blindness and the brain in autism. *Neuron, 32*(6), 969–979.

Furnham, A., & Walker, J. (2001a). Personality and judgements of abstract, pop art, and representational paintings. *European Journal of personality, 15*(1), 57–72.

Furnham, A., & Walker, J. (2001b). The influence of personality traits, previous experience of art, and demographic variables on artistic preference. *Personality and Individual Differences, 31*(6), 997–1017.

Gaventa, J., & Cornwall, A. (2015). Power and knowledge. In *The SAGE handbook of action research* (Vol. 3, pp. 465–471). Sage.

Gernsbacher, M. A., & Yergeau, M. (2019). Empirical failures of the claim that autistic people lack a theory of mind. *Archives of Scientific Psychology, 7*(1), 102.

Gonzalez-Franco, M., & Lanier, J. (2017). Model of illusions and virtual reality. *Frontiers in Psychology, 8*, 112.

Götz, K. O., & Götz, K. (1974). Color preferences of art students: Surface colors. *I. Perceptual and Motor Skills, 38*(3), 1103–1109.

Grandin, T. (2009). How does visual thinking work in the mind of a person with autism? A personal account. *Philosophical Transactions of the Royal Society B: Biological Sciences, 364*(1522), 1437–1442.

Grotewiel, M. M., Crenshaw, M. E., Dorsey, A., & Street, E. (2023). Experiences of hyperfocus and flow in college students with and without attention deficit hyperactivity disorder (ADHD). *Current Psychology, 42*(16), 13265–13275.

Guillemin, M. (2004). Understanding illness: Using drawings as a research method. *Qualitative Health Research, 14*(2), 272–289.

Hacmun, I., Regev, D., & Salomon, R. (2018). The principles of art therapy in virtual reality. *Frontiers in Psychology, 9*, 2082. https://doi.org/10.3389/fpsyg.2018.02082

Hacmun, I., Regev, D., & Salomon, R. (2021). Artistic creation in virtual reality for art therapy: A qualitative study with expert art therapists. *The Arts in Psychotherapy, 72*, 101745.

Hadjipanayi, E., Banakou, D., & Michael-Grigoriou, D. (2023). Virtual reality in art therapy: A systematic review. *Frontiers in Virtual reality, 4*, 1065863. https://doi.org/10.3389/frvir.2023.1065863

Haeyen, S., Jans, S., & Heijman, W. (2021). Virtual reality in art therapy: A pilot study. *The Arts in Psychotherapy, 76*, 101855. https://doi.org/10.1016/j.aip.2021.101855

Happé, F. R. (2015). Autism as a neurodevelopmental disorder of mind-reading. *Journal of the British Academy, 3*(1), 197–209.

Happé, F., & Frith, U. (2006). The weak coherence account: Detail-focused cognitive style in autism spectrum disorders. *Journal of Autism and Developmental Disorders, 36*(1), 5–25. https://doi.org/10.1007/s10803-005-0039-0

Happé, F., & Frith, U. (2020). Annual research review: Looking back to look forward–changes in the concept of autism and implications for future research. *Journal of Child Psychology and Psychiatry, 61*(3), 218–232.

Harper, D. (2002). Talking about pictures: A case for photo elicitation. *Visual Studies, 17*(1), 13–26.

Hartman, D., O'Donnell-Killen, T., Doyle, J. K., Kavanagh, M., Day, A., & Azevedo, J. (2023). *The adult autism assessment handbook: A neurodiversity affirmative approach.* Jessica Kingsley Publishers.

Harjunen, V. J., Ahmed, I., Jacucci, G., Ravaja, N., & Spapé, M. M. (2017). Manipulating bodily presence affects cross-modal spatial attention: A virtualreality-based ERP study. *Frontiers in Human Neuroscience, 11*, 79.

Hendrix, C., & Barfield, W. (1996). Presence within virtual environments as a function of visual display parameters. *Presence: Teleoperators & Virtual Environments, 5*(3), 274–289.

Hupfeld, K. E., Abagis, T. R., & Shah, P. (2019). Living "in the zone": Hyperfocus in adult ADHD. *ADHD Attention Deficit and Hyperactivity Disorders, 11*(2), 191–208.

Icosa Foundation. (2021). OpenBrush [Computer software]. https://openbrush.app/

Jackson, S. A., & Csikszentmihalyi, M. (1999). Flow in sports. Human Kinetics. https://books.google.co.uk/books?hl=en&lr=&id=Jak4A8rEZawC&oi=fnd&pg=PP8&dq=Jackson+and+Csikszentmihalyi+(1999)&ots=GyXDoz4o2T&sig=7fQKxBrwFoR8kp-IBGrfw8vY12Y#v=onepage&q&f=false

Jacobs, G., van Lieshout, F., Borg, M., & Ness, O. (2017). Being a person-centred researcher: Principles and methods for doing research in a personcentred way. In *Person-centred Healthcare Research* (pp. 51–60). Wiley.

Jones, R. S., Quigney, C., & Huws, J. C. (2003). First-hand accounts of sensory perceptual experiences in autism: A qualitative analysis. *Journal of Intellectual & Developmental Disability, 28*(2), 112–121.

Kaimal, G., Ray, K., & Muniz, J. (2020). Reduction of cortisol levels and participants' responses following art making with three different art materials. (Study using VR art-making context discussed in chapter). *Art Therapy, 37*(1), 16–24. https://doi.org/10.1080/07421656.2019.1659662

Karnieli-Miller, O., Strier, R., & Pessach, L. (2009). Power relations in qualitative research. *Qualitative Health Research, 19*(2), 279–289. https://doi.org/10.1177/1049732308329306

Kilteni, K., Maselli, A., Kording, K. P., & Slater, M. (2015). Over my fake body: Body ownership illusions for studying the multisensory basis of own-body perception. *Frontiers in Human Neuroscience, 9*, 141.

Kim, T., & Biocca, F. (1997). Telepresence via television: Two dimensions of telepresence may have different connections to memory and persuasion. Journal of Computer-mediated. *Communication, 3*(2), JCMC325.

Knight, V. F., Sartini, E., & Spriggs, A. D. (2015). Evaluating visual activity schedules as evidence-based practice for individuals with autism spectrum disorders. *Journal of Autism and Developmental Disorders, 45*(1), 157–178.

Koirala, A., Yu, Z., Schiltz, H., Van Hecke, A., Armstrong, B., & Zheng, Z. (2021). A preliminary exploration of virtual reality-based visual and touch sensory processing assessment for adolescents with autism spectrum disorder. *IEEE Transactions on Neural Systems and Rehabilitation Engineering, 29*, 619–628.

Krupić, D., Žuro, B., & Corr, P. J. (2021). Anxiety and threat magnification in subjective and physiological responses of fear of heights induced by virtual reality. *Personality and Individual Differences, 169*, 109720.

Kunda, M., & Goel, A. K. (2011). Thinking in pictures as a cognitive account of autism. *Journal of Autism and Developmental Disorders, 41*(9), 1157–1177.

Lemmens, J. S., & von Münchhausen, C. F. (2023). Let the beat flow: How game difficulty in virtual reality affects flow. *Acta Psychologica, 232*, 103812.

Lessiter, J., Freeman, J., Keogh, E., & Davidoff, J. (2001). A cross-media presence questionnaire: The ITC-sense of presence inventory. *Presence: Teleoperators and Virtual Environments, 10*(3), 282–297. https://doi.org/10.1162/105474601300343612

Lobban, F., Taylor, K., Murray, C., & Jones, S. (2012). Bipolar disorder is a two-edged sword: A qualitative study to understand the positive edge. *Journal of Affective Disorders, 141*(2–3), 204–212.

Lockwood, P. L., Apps, M. A. J., Valton, V., Viding, E., & Roiser, J. P. (2015). Neurocomputational mechanisms of prosocial learning and links to empathy. *Journal of Neuroscience, 35*(40), 13720–13727. https://doi.org/10.1523/JNEUROSCI.1703-15.2015

Markey, P. S., Jakesch, M., & Leder, H. (2019). Art looks different–Semantic and syntactic processing of paintings and associated neurophysiological brain responses. *Brain and Cognition, 134*, 58–66.

Maskey, M., Lowry, J., Rodgers, J., McConachie, H., & Parr, J. R. (2014). Reducing specific phobia/fear in young people with autism spectrum disorders through a virtual reality environment intervention. *PLOS ONE, 9*(7), e100374.

Maskey, M., et al. (2019). A randomised controlled feasibility trial of immersive virtual reality treatment for phobias in young people with autism spectrum disorders. *Journal of Autism and Developmental Disorders, 49*(5), 1912–1927.

Mayer, R. E. (2009). *Multimedia Learning* (2nd ed.). Cambridge University Press.

Mazza, M., Pino, M. C., Vagnetti, R., Peretti, S., Valenti, M., Marchetti, A., & Di Dio, C. (2020). Discrepancies between explicit and implicit evaluation of aesthetic perception ability in individuals with autism: A potential way to improve social functioning. *BMC psychology, 8*(1), 74.

McGeachan, C., & Philo, C. (2023). "Hanging around in their brokenness": On mental ill-health geography, asylums and camps, artworks and salvage. *Annals of the American Association of Geographers, 113*(5), 1224–1242.

Miller, S., & Reid, D. (2003). Doing play: Competency, control, and expression. *CyberPsychology & Behavior, 6*(6), 623–632.

Milton, D. (2012). On the ontological status of autism: The 'double empathy problem'. *Disability & Society, 27*(6), 883–887. https://doi.org/10.1080/09687599.2012.710008

Milton, D. E. (2014). Autistic expertise: A critical reflection on the production of knowledge in autism studies. *Autism, 18*(7), 794–802.

Morris, R. G., Rowe, A., Fox, N., Feigenbaum, J. D., Miotto, E. C., & Howlin, P. (1999). Spatial working memory in Asperger's syndrome and in patients with focal frontal and temporal lobe lesions. *Brain and Cognition, 41*(1), 9–26.

Murray, D., Lesser, M., & Lawson, W. (2005). Attention, monotropism and the diagnostic criteria for autism. (White paper / discussion paper). https://monotropism.org/.

Nelson, N., & Wright, S. (Eds.). (1995). *Power and participatory development: Theory and practice* (pp. xi+-225pp).

Nilson, K. M. R. (2025). The case for visual art in overcoming the double empathy problem. https://scholarsarchive.byu.edu/etd/10872/

Nisbett, R. E., & Wilson, T. D. (1977). Telling more than we can know: Verbal reports on mental processes. *Psychological Review, 84*(3), 231–259. https://doi.org/10.1037/0033-295X.84.3.231

Nodine, C. F., Locher, P. J., & Krupinski, E. A. (1993). The role of formal art training on perception and aesthetic judgment of art compositions. *Leonardo, 26*(3), 219–227.

O'Connor, N., & Hermelin, B. (1988). Low intelligence and special abilities. *Journal of Child Psychology and Psychiatry, and Allied Disciplines, 29*(4), 391–396.

Orland-Barak, L., & Maskit, D. (2017). Visuals as 'illustrations' of experience'. In *Methodologies of mediation in professional learning* (pp. 27–36). Springer International Publishing.

Oster, G. D., & Crone, P. G. (2004). *Using drawings in assessment and therapy: A guide for mental health professionals.* Routledge.

Paivio, A. (1991). Dual coding theory: Retrospect and current status. *Canadian Journal of Psychology/Revue canadienne de psychologie, 45*(3), 255.

Pellas, N., Mystakidis, S., & Kazanidis, I. (2021). Immersive virtual reality in K-12 and higher education: A systematic review of the last decade scientific literature. *Virtual Reality, 25*(3), 835–861.

Philo, C., & Andrews, J. (2017). Introduction: Histories of asylums, insanity and psychiatry in Scotland. *History of Psychiatry, 28*(1), 3–14.

Plechatá, A., Morton, T., Perez-Cueto, F. J., & Makransky, G. (2022). A randomized trial testing the effectiveness of virtual reality as a tool for proenvironmental dietary change. *Scientific Reports, 12*(1), 14315.

Pink, S. (2015). Going forward through the world: Thinking theoretically about first person perspective digital ethnography. *Integrative Psychological and Behavioral Science, 49*(2), 239–252.

Premack, D., & Woodruff, G. (1978). Does the chimpanzee have a theory of mind? *Behavioral and Brain Sciences, 1*(4), 515–526. https://doi.org/10.1017/S0140525X00076512

Prosser, J., & Loxley, A. (2008). Introducing visual methods. https://eprints.ncrm.ac.uk/id/eprint/420/1/MethodsReviewPaperNCRM-010.pdf

Pryke-Hobbes, A., Davies, J., Heasman, B., Livesey, A., Walker, A., Pellicano, E., & Remington, A. (2023). The workplace masking experiences of autistic, non-autistic neurodivergent and neurotypical adults in the UK. *Plos One, 18*(9), e0290001.

Qela, B., Damiani, S., De Santis, S., Groppi, F., Pichiecchio, A., Asteggiano, C., et al. (2025). Predictive coding in neuropsychiatric disorders: A systematic transdiagnostic review. *Neuroscience & Biobehavioral Reviews, 169*, 106020.

Quesque, F., & Rossetti, Y. (2020). What do theory-of-mind tasks actually measure? *Current Directions in Psychological Science, 29*(6), 595–602.

Rajagopalan, A., Kumar, S. S., & Mukkadan, J. K. (2017). Effect of vestibular stimulation on auditory and visual reaction time in relation to stress. *Journal of Advanced Pharmaceutical Technology & Research, 8*(1), 34–38.

Rapaport, H., & Sowman, P. F. (2024). Examining predictive coding accounts of typical and autistic neurocognitive development. *Neuroscience & Biobehavioral Reviews, 167*, 105905.

Richard, V., Glăveanu, V., & Aubertin, P. (2023). The embodied journey of an idea: An exploration of movement creativity in circus arts. *The Journal of Creative Behavior, 57*(2), 221–236.

Richardson, J. F. (2022). *Art as a language for autism: Building effective therapeutic relationships with children and adolescents*. Routledge.

Richesin, M. T., Baldwin, D. R., & Wicks, L. A. (2021). Art making and virtual reality: A comparison study of physiological and psychological outcomes. *The Arts in Psychotherapy, 75*, 101823.

Riva, G. (2009). Is presence a technology issue? Some insights from cognitive sciences. *Virtual Reality, 13*(3), 159–169.

Riva, G., & Waterworth, J. A. (2014). Being present in a virtual world. In *The oxford handbook of virtuality* (Vol. 4, pp. 205–221). Oxford University Press.

Riva, G., Waterworth, J. A., & Waterworth, E. L. (2004). The layers of presence: A bio-cultural approach to understanding presence in natural and mediated environments. *CyberPsychology & Behavior, 7*(4), 402–416.

Robertson, A. E. (2012). Sensory experiences of individuals with Autism Spectrum Disorder and autistic traits: A mixed methods approach (Doctoral dissertation, University of Glasgow).

Robertson, A. E., & Simmons, D. R. (2013). The Glasgow sensory questionnaire: A measure of sensory processing in adults. *Journal of Autism and Developmental Disorders, 43*(4), 775–784. https://doi.org/10.1007/s10803-012-1608-

Robertson, C. E., & Baron-Cohen, S. (2017). Sensory perception in autism. *Nature Reviews Neuroscience, 18*(11), 671–684.

Rolin, R. A., Fooken, J., Spering, M., & Pai, D. K. (2018). Perception of looming motion in virtual reality egocentric interception tasks. *IEEE Transactions on Visualization and Computer Graphics, 25*(10), 3042–3048.

Rose, G. (2014). On the relation between 'visual research methods' and contemporary visual culture. *The sociological review, 62*(1), 24–46.

Roth, I. (2020). Autism, creativity and aesthetics. *Qualitative Research in Psychology, 17*(4), 498–508.

Ruzich, E., Allison, C., Smith, P., Watson, P., Auyeung, B., Ring, H., & Baron-Cohen, S. (2015). Measuring autistic traits in the general population: A systematic review of the AQ. *Molecular Autism, 6*, 2. https://doi.org/10.1186/2040-2392-6-2

Rzepka, A. M., Hussey, K. J., Maltz, M. V., Babin, K., Wilcox, L. M., & Culham, J. C. (2023). Familiar size affects perception differently in virtual reality and the real world. *Philosophical Transactions of the Royal Society B: Biological Sciences, 378*(1869).

Sapey-Triomphe, L. A., Moulin, A., Sonié, S., & Schmitz, C. (2018). The Glasgow Sensory Questionnaire: Validation of a French language version and refinement of sensory profiles of people with high autism-spectrum quotient. *Journal of Autism and Developmental Disorders, 48*(5), 1549–1565.

Savickaite, S., Morrison, C., Lux, E., Delafield-Butt, J., & Simmons, D. R. (2022). The use of a tablet-based app for investigating the influence of autistic and ADHD traits on performance in a complex drawing task. *Behavior Research Methods, 54*(5), 2479–2501.

Schopbach, R. R. (1967). Art in psychotherapy. *Henry Ford Hospital Medical Journal, 15*(3), 229–239.

Schubert, T., Friedmann, F., & Regenbrecht, H. (1999). Embodied presence in virtual environments. In *Visual representations and interpretations* (pp. 269–278). Springer London.

Schubert, T. W., Friedmann, F., & Regenbrecht, H. (2001). The experience of presence: Factor analytic insights. *Presence: Teleoperators and Virtual Environments, 10*(3), 266–281. https://doi.org/10.1162/105474601300343603

Shah, A., & Frith, U. (1983). An islet of ability in autistic children: A research note. *Journal of Child Psychology and Psychiatry, 24*(4), 613–620. https://doi.org/10.1111/j.1469-7610.1983.tb00137.x

Shah, A., & Frith, U. (1993). Why do autistic individuals show superior performance on the block design task? *Journal of Child Psychology and Psychiatry, 34*(8), 1351–1364. https://doi.org/10.1111/j.1469-7610.1993.tb02095.x

Shamri Zeevi, L. (2021). Virtual reality–based art therapy for adolescents with social anxiety: A pilot study. *Frontiers in Psychology, 12*, 584943. https://doi.org/10.3389/fpsyg.2021.584943

Silverman, C. (2015). NeuroTribes: The legacy of autism and the future of neurodiversity by Steve Silberman. *Anthropological Quarterly, 88*(4), 1111–1121.

Silvia, P. J. (2012). *Human emotions and aesthetic experience. Aesthetic science: Connecting minds, brain and experience* (pp. 250–275). Oxford University Press.

Sorkin, D. L., & Zwolan, T. A. (2008). Parental perspectives regarding early intervention and its role in cochlear implantation in children. *Otology & Neurotology, 29*(2), 137–141.

Sperber, D., & Wilson, D. (1986). *Relevance: Communication and cognition* (Vol. 142). Harvard University Pres.

Spielberger, C. D., Gorsuch, R. L., & Lushene, R. (1983). *Manual for the State–Trait anxiety inventory.* Consulting Psychologists Press.

Stenberdt, V. A., & Makransky, G. (2023). Mastery experiences in immersive virtual reality promote pro-environmental waste-sorting behavior. *Computers & Education, 198*, 104760.

Tan, C., Makransky, G., & Mayer, R. E. (2022). Immersion and flow in virtual reality learning environments. *Computers & Education, 176*, 104360. https://doi.org/10.1016/j.compedu.2021.104360

Treffert, D. A. (2009). The savant syndrome: An extraordinary condition. *Philosophical Transactions of the Royal Society B: Biological Sciences, 364*(1522), 1351–1357. https://doi.org/10.1098/rstb.2008.0326

Van der Hallen, R., Evers, K., Brewaeys, K., Van den Noortgate, W., & Wagemans, J. (2015). Global processing takes time: A meta-analysis on local–global visual processing in ASD. *Psychological Bulletin, 141*(3), 549–573. https://doi.org/10.1037/bul0000004

Võ, M. L. H., & Wolfe, J. M. (2013). Differential electrophysiological signatures of semantic and syntactic scene processing. *Psychological Science, 24*(9), 1816–1823.

Wagemans, J., Elder, J. H., Kubovy, M., Palmer, S. E., Peterson, M. A., Singh, M., & Von der Heydt, R. (2012). A century of Gestalt psychology in visual perception: I. Perceptual grouping and figure–ground organization. *Psychological Bulletin, 138*(6), 1172.

Wakabayashi, A., Baron-Cohen, S., & Wheelwright, S. (2006). Are autistic traits an independent personality dimension? A study of the Autism-Spectrum Quotient (AQ) and the NEO-PI-R. *Personality and Individual Differences, 41*(5), 873–883.

Wallerstein, N., Duran, B., Oetzel, J. G., & Minkler, M. (2017). On community-based participatory research. *Community-based Participatory Research for health: Advancing Social and Health Equity, 3*, 3–16.

Wang, Y. M., Chiu, W. C., Lin, H. H., Wang, Y. S., Wang, Y. Y., & Chen, I. F. (2024). Determinants of students' adoption of virtual reality-based learning systems: An individual difference perspective. *Innovations in Education and Teaching International, 61*(1), 143–153.

Williams, G. L., Wharton, T., & Jagoe, C. (2021). Mutual (mis) understanding: Reframing autistic pragmatic "impairments" using relevance theory. *Frontiers in Psychology, 12*, 616664.

Williams, J. H., Waiter, G. D., Perra, O., Perrett, D. I., & Whiten, A. (2008). An fMRI study of joint attention experience. *NeuroImage, 39*(1), 115–123. https://doi.org/10.1016/j.neuroimage.2007.08.003

Winkel, M. (2022). Our changing role: Expanding the reach of art therapy. In *Virtual art therapy* (pp. 1–10). Routledge.

Woo, M., Kim, J., Park, J., & Lee, S. (2023). Understanding cybersickness in immersive virtual environments. *Virtual Reality, 27*, 1–15. https://doi.org/10.1007/s10055-022-00667-5

Yeh, S.-C., Li, M.-C., & Chen, S.-Y. (2019). The relationship between flow experience and learning outcomes in virtual environments. *Educational Technology Research and Development, 67*(3), 531–548. https://doi.org/10.1007/s11423-019-09637-5

Zabelina, D. L., & Beeman, M. (2013). Short-term attentional perseveration associated with real-life creative achievement. *Frontiers in Psychology, 4*, 191.

Zeisel, A., Thiel, T., Gaigg, S. B., Roessner, V., & Ring, M. (2023). Validation of the German Glasgow Sensory Questionnaire and replication of sensory processing differences in students with higher and lower Autism-Spectrum Quotient. *BMC Psychiatry, 23*(1), 426.

Zhang, C., Yao, C., Liu, J., Zhou, Z., Zhang, W., Liu, L., … & Wang, G. (2021, May). StoryDrawer: A Co-creative agent supporting children's storytelling through collaborative drawing. In *Extended Abstracts of the 2021 CHI Conference on Human Factors in Computing Systems* (pp. 1–6).

Zhang, M., Ding, H., Naumceska, M., & Zhang, Y. (2022). Virtual reality technology as an educational and intervention tool for children with autism spectrum disorder: Current perspectives and future directions. *Behavioral Sciences, 12*(5), 138.

CHAPTER 5

Beyond Words: Creativity, Communication, and Empowerment in VR

Despite increasing awareness, autism research has traditionally prioritized behavioral symptoms above perceptual experience (Robertson & Baron-Cohen, 2017), frequently overlooking the internal, first-person narratives that are critical to comprehending the condition. This mismatch between the quantifiable and the felt has created a gap between lived experience and empirical study, which participatory, arts-based, and person-centered research is now attempting to close (Happé & Frith, 2020).

As more researchers adopt neurodiversity-affirming paradigms, there is growing interest in techniques that enable autistic people to convey their experiences in non-verbal, creative, and self-directed ways. Drawing, for example, has long been utilized in therapeutic settings to encourage expression and contemplation (Oster & Crone, 2004; Guillemin, 2004), and it represents a promising route for capturing perceptual differences that might otherwise go unnoticed.

In parallel, Virtual reality (VR) is emerging as a strong tool for psychological research, providing immersive, interactive worlds that are less socially demanding and more ecologically valid, particularly for autistic individuals (Maskey et al., 2014; Iachini et al., 2019). VR allows people to express and share aspects of their perspective through embodied movement and creative interaction. When combined with drawing activities and Think Aloud protocols (Eccles & Arsal, 2017), which require participants to recount their ideas while performing a task, VR has the potential to

S. Savickaite, *Exploring Neurodiversity Through Virtual Reality*,
https://doi.org/10.1007/978-3-032-19636-1_5

expose not just what is experienced, but also how it is processed in the present.

Synedelica: Mixed Reality Reimagined (Desnoyers-Stewart et al., 2025) is a great illustration of how virtual reality may be utilized to look at perception differences. Synedelica is different from regular VR or AR apps because it changes how the user sees reality directly, rather than just adding digital items to the real world. The passthrough feature of a Meta Quest headset lets the system change the way things seem in real time, creating changing gradients, contours, and colors that change with sound. This design converts any place, from a quiet street to a festival crowd, into an immersive, synesthetic canvas that combines sounds with visual changes. Participants are not taken to another world; instead, they are encouraged to experience their own surroundings in a new way, enhanced and rearranged by technology (Kasunic et al., 2024).

For neurodivergent individuals, this method is very meaningful. Individuals with autism, ADHD, synaesthesia, or aphantasia often report perceptual experiences that deviate from neurotypical standards, characterized by increased sensitivity to sensory stimuli, cross-modal connections, or the lack of visual images. People typically use a lot of words to explain things, which can make it hard to communicate these private experiences effectively. expression that words alone hand, let users share and externalize their perceptual states directly. This gives people a way to communicate without words that others can immediately experience. This ability to "show" instead of "tell" opens up new methods for empathy and understanding, filling in gaps in expression that words alone cannot always fill (Kasunic et al., 2024).

VR sketching environments further demonstrate the significance of non-verbal expression. People can reproduce perceptual experiences that might not be available to others by using apps that let them doodle in the air or use hybrid 2D/3D techniques. For instance, persons with synesthesia can show the shapes, colors, or textures they see when they hear certain sounds, and people with aphantasia can communicate the lack of mental images by comparing their work to that of others. Drawing in VR is perfectly positioned to portray the volumetric, dynamic characteristics of perception—something flat, 2D drawings often fail to represent. Additionally, these platforms lessen motor strain by using limitations and affordances, making them a more accessible way for persons who have physical or cognitive challenges that make traditional sketching hard to do.

When you put together initiatives like Synedelica and VR-based painting, you can see how immersive technology could help people talk to each other without using spoken or written language. They enable the re-creation of experiences that are not only profoundly personal but also frequently challenging to express in traditional symbolic representations. This makes it possible for neurodivergent communities to express themselves in more interesting ways and to connect with others in novel ways. Rather than making differences seem like things that keep people apart, these technologies show how perceptual variety can be made real, interactive, and even collaborative. They point to VR as an interesting and new way to connect individuals through their own senses.

In the next three case studies I will present three studies we have conducted using VR Arts-based method to explore perceptual differences in autistic individuals, synesthetes, and those with aphantasia. This hopefully serves as a rich illustrative portfolio of how this multimedia and multimethod tools can be adapted to different context.

Autistic Expression in Virtual Reality

The first study I present used quantitative and qualitative methods to investigate how autistic persons experience creativity and perception in virtual reality (VR). The quantitative measures—the Autism Spectrum Quotient (AQ), the Glasgow Sensory Questionnaire (GSQ), and a Technical Proficiency Questionnaire (TPQ)—were used to describe individuals' background characteristics, including sensory sensitivities, autistic symptoms, and familiarity with technology. These data were only used for demographic and contextual analysis. The primary goal of the study was to conduct a qualitative investigation into participants' experiences with VR tools such as theBlu (an underwater simulation) and OpenBrush (a 3D sketching environment), as well as their reflections during and after the sessions. Six participants (4 male, 2 female), aged 19–27 years, took part in the study (all had formal autism diagnosis).

After the drawing task, participants were invited to complete a semi-structured interview based on previous research into autism diagnosis, perceptual experiences, and communication with neurotypical people (Milner et al., 2019; Russell et al., 2019; Thompson-Hodgetts et al., 2020). Interview questions included:

1. What is your diagnosis journey? Could you tell us anything more about it?
2. What could you share about your perceptual world that would help us understand it better?
3. Are you artistic? Does creativity help you express your perceptual experiences?
4. Do your perceptual experiences change? Do you think they differ from those of other autistic individuals?
5. How did you feel during the experiment? Any suggestions for improvement?
6. Do you think VR could help others understand autistic perception?

If participants were uncomfortable answering any questions, they were skipped. In many cases, participants spontaneously addressed these topics during the drawing task and were later asked to elaborate. All drawing sessions were recorded (video and audio), transcribed, and anonymized.

Quantitative Data

Three participants (1, 4, and 6) had overall GSQ scores that showed a low frequency of hyper- and hyposensitivity. These scores were much lower than the UK average of 46, demonstrating the variability of autism. In contrast, Participant 2 had a much higher GSQ score, especially in the visual, tactile, auditory, and olfactory subscales. The literature implies that synesthesia may improve several autistic features (Ward et al., 2017), and in our study, Participant 2, who disclosed a synesthetic experience, scored a GSQ total of 120, which is significantly higher than the population mean. They also scored high on the AQ attention-to-detail subscale, which supports previous findings.

The majority of subjects had higher GSQ hypersensitivity subscale scores compared to their hyposensitivity scores. This conclusion is consistent with prior research that found a positive link between AQ and GSQ scores (Robertson & Simmons, 2013). Participant 5 also scored higher on the GSQ, emphasizing individual differences.

The analysis of subscale scores from both questionnaires revealed more information on individual characteristics. Participant 1 scored low on AQ-Imagination (score = 4), indicating a strong ability to generate ideas, as seen by their self-report of “I have a lot of ideas.” Participant 2 had a high AQ-Imagination score of 10 while reporting limited creative imagination and trouble understanding unfamiliar concepts. Participant 6, who reported being hypersensitive to auditory stimuli, got higher GSQ auditory scores.

Most individuals scored highest on the AQ attention-switching subscale, which measures the difficulty of shifting focus between stimuli (Baron-Cohen, 2001). This is consistent with Reed and McCarthy's (2012) findings that autistic children exhibit difficulties with cross-modal attention switching. Given that VR uses several senses (visual, aural, and tactile), this element should be included in future research designs.

Qualitative Data (Fig. 5.1)

All qualitative data—including think-aloud content during drawing and interview responses—were analyzed using reflexive thematic analysis (Braun & Clarke, 2006). This six-step process involved familiarization,

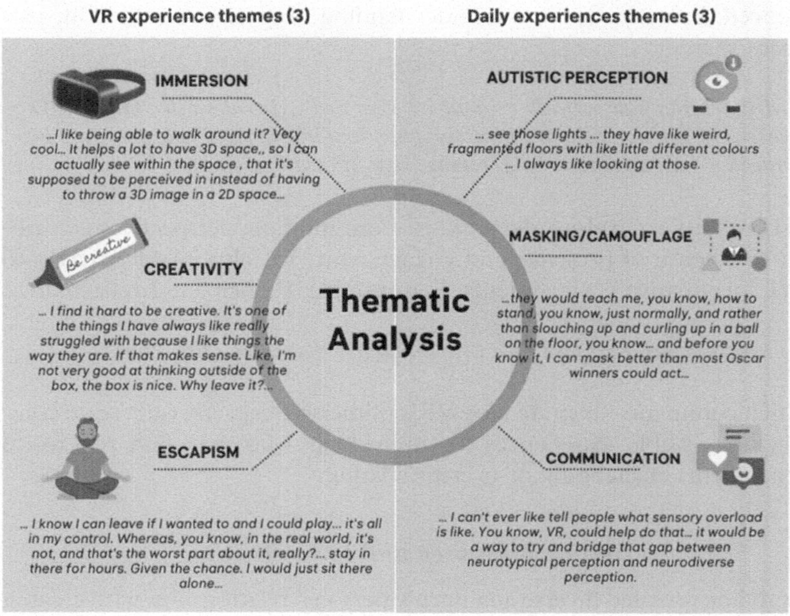

Fig. 5.1 Summary of six themes identified through thematic analysis

initial coding, theme development, theme review, naming and definition, and producing the report. Due to the small sample size, results were presented on a case-by-case basis. Two researchers independently analyzed the data and collaboratively finalized the coding and themes.

Thematic Analysis: Interaction with the Virtual Worlds (Theme 1)

To evaluate the suitability of VR for autistic participants, we examined their experiences during the OpenBrush drawing task and follow-up debrief discussions. Three overarching themes emerged: Immersion, Artistic Expression and Individuality, and Escapism.

Immersion

The immersive nature of the 360-degree VR space was consistently appreciated. Participants described how moving within the environment enhanced their experience and understanding of space and scale. One participant shared:

> *…I like being able to walk around it? Very cool… It helps a lot to have 3D space,, so I can actually see within the space, that it's supposed to be perceived in instead of having to throw a 3D image in a 2D space…*

This ability to explore the artwork from multiple perspectives contributed to a sense of presence and engagement. VR also enabled access to novel, imaginative environments. For example, Participant 2 reflected:

> *…Look, you never get presented with things like that in real life. I love it…*

Such comments illustrate how VR's immersive capacity can create compelling, accessible experiences for individuals who may find real-world environments challenging or overstimulating.

Artistic Expression and Individuality

This theme revealed diverse and deeply personal relationships with creativity. All participants used their drawings to express identity and interests, although in very different ways. While Participant 2 voiced discomfort with open-ended creative tasks:

> *… I find it hard to be creative. It's one of the things I have always like really struggled with because I like things the way they are. If that makes sense. Like, I'm not very good at thinking outside of the box, the box is nice, why leave it?…*

Others found drawing in VR to be a therapeutic and grounding activity. Participant 3 described:

> *…it calms me, I have done it since I was a wee girl…*

In contrast, Participant 5 emphasized the simple enjoyment of art:

> *I don't really like when people say does it express, I don't really understand words like that, I, I just like to do it. There's no such thing as expresses who I am, no, I just like it.*

These reflections highlight that creativity need not be symbolic or deeply conceptual—it may instead serve as a stabilizing and joyful form of self-expression.

Escapism

VR offered a safe space to retreat, experiment, and exert control over one's surroundings—something often difficult in the real world. Participant 3 noted the freedom to undo or reset changes:

> *… like, I didn't like the snow, so I could easily say, no, no, no. Return to the beginning…*

Participant 2 also valued the controlled exposure VR could offer:

> *… So for example, like a bus station, um, it would give me different stimulus. Stimuli, but I know I can leave if I wanted to and I could play it's all in my control. Whereas, you know, in the real world, it's not, and that's the worst part about it, really?…*

They later added:

> *...stay in there for hours. Given the opportunity. I would just sit there alone...*

The VR environment's calming nature resonated widely. Participant 3 described the tranquil effect of the night sky:

> *... I'd just love the stars, go into the night and just look at the stars and relax...*

Similarly, Participant 6 commented on the peace enabled by the reduced auditory input.

Thematic Analysis: Daily Experiences (Theme 2)

To further understand participants' perspectives on autism and perception, we analyzed their responses to the debrief questions. Three themes were identified: Situational Adjustment, Autistic Perceptual Differences, and Sharing the Autistic Perspective through VR.

Masking and Situational Adjustment

Participants had diverse diagnostic journeys, with some noting delays in support. Participant 5, diagnosed at age 10, recalled:

> *... lack of understanding. Lack of caring...*

Participant 3, diagnosed at 18, shared how stigma influenced their choice to keep their diagnosis private:

> *... I 'feel as if I have been judged a lot more cause people see autism as a disability. Like something to be disgraced with... if you don't look as if you have autism then you are treated differently than people that do look like they have autism...*

Several participants described how they learned to mask autistic traits. Participant 2 explained:

> *...they would teach me, you know, how to stand, you know, just normally, and rather than slouching up and curling up in a ball on the floor, you know... and before you know it, I can mask better than most Oscar winners could act...*

Participant 5 highlighted how their home environment supported desensitization to overwhelming stimuli and rapid situational adjustments.

Autistic Sensory Differences Affect Perception

Participants reported highly individualized sensory responses. Participant 2 explained:

> *I could be having sensory overload in the same environment as someone else's perfectly fine, but we could both be autistic.*

Participant 5 noted:

> *it's more like the IKEA lights, when you go to IKEA you see those lights.*

Others struggled to differentiate their experience from others. Participant 3 said:

> *everyone's different*

While Participant 1 reflected:

> *... I've never, I've never had any experience where I thought to myself, I would've, I would've done this differently if I didn't have autism like I couldn't point to a part of my personality and go that's definitely autism...*

These observations reflect the heterogeneity of autistic sensory and perceptual experience.

Sharing the Autistic Perspective Through VR

Participants were largely enthusiastic about the potential of VR to help others better understand autistic perception. Participant 3 suggested family members might benefit from trying it, while Participant 2 expressed:

> *... I can't ever like tell people what sensory overload is like. You know, VR, could help do that... it would be a way to try and bridge that gap between neurotypical perception and neurodiverse perception. But for sure, it's a very good tool...*

However, concerns about overstimulation were raised:

> *... it is actually really quite hard to focus in on those, those particular things that might send you a bit crazy, uh, that would cause sensory overload. But I think given enough time and enough implementation. It would be fantastic...*

Participant 5 questioned the true impact of such tools:

> *... I don't really think you can understand autism to an extent...*

And added:

> *...Do the neurotypicals want to come meet us, or do you want us to jump into your own border... like jump into your world? Cause that's not going to do any good...*

Our findings support several previously published observations, notably those related to environmental regulation. Previous research has found that the capacity to control sensory input helps lessen stress in autistic individuals (Robertson & Simmons, 2015). Our participants also emphasized the necessity of being able to customize their VR environments. This sensation of control may have allowed people to experiment with OpenBrush aspects that they would normally avoid in real life, such as bright colors (as seen with Participant 2).

The visual examination of drawings (Fig. 5.2) revealed the participants' creative preferences and perceptual styles. Many people preferred to use bright, contrasting colors against black backgrounds. Drawing styles varied, reflecting a wide range of cognitive and aesthetic preferences.

Participant 1 made a highly realistic self-portrait with exact colors for skin tone, eyes, and facial hair. Although such precision is frequently associated with a low creative profile in the literature (Scott & Baron-Cohen, 1996), it differed from their AQ-Imagination score. Participants 2 and 6 drew inventive characters with complex features like goggles and shoelaces, demonstrating a detail-oriented cognitive preferences (Darewych et al., 2018).

Fig. 5.2 Series of OpenBrush screenshots capturing drawings created by participants during the VR session

Participants 3, 4, and 5 exhibited a lower interest in painting human figures. This may mirror a larger tendency in autistic expressive art, where non-social subjects are frequently preferred (Darewych et al., 2018). However, this does not necessarily indicate a lack of inventiveness. For example, Participant 5's usage of floral components as eyes in cat drawings demonstrated originality and inventiveness.

The social nature of the stimulus may also influence imaginative responses to drawing activities. Ten Eycke and Müller (2015) discovered that autistic youngsters produced more inventive output when asked to draw a house rather than a person. Thus, future research should carefully examine task framing.

Despite the 3D aspect of VR, the majority of participants struggled with depth perception, drawing predominantly in 2D. This is consistent with findings from art therapy research indicating that depth perception can be difficult for some autistic people (Alter-Muri, 2017; Vaisvaser, 2019). The fondness for familiar drawings may reflect autistic' traits such as stress on consistency. Importantly, this propensity may also be present in neurotypical participants who are using unusual tools such as VR for the first time, and it should be examined further with control groups.

None of the participants felt motion sickness or dizziness (Riva et al., 2021), while several took time to adjust to the lighting in VR, which corresponded to their GSQ-visual ratings. Notably, OpenBrush enabled users to manage their sensory surroundings, a feature previously found as useful to autistic people (MacLennan et al., 2021; Robertson & Simmons, 2015). The ability to remove drawings facilitated creative exploration.

Participant 2 described their virtual reality drawings as a "little palace," emphasizing the tool's sense of ownership and immersion. VR provided a mechanism to detach from real-world stressors, in line with research on escapism and gaming in autistic people (Sundberg, 2018; Engelhardt et al., 2017). Participants regularly lost track of time and were reluctant to leave the virtual reality space. This was not an issue in our environment, however it should be observed in longer use situations. These immersive and expressive properties indicate a high potential for therapeutic uses.

Participants reported a variety of sensory sensitivities. Most experienced hyper-reactivity, although Participant 5, who reported little sensory problems, scored higher on the GSQ for hyposensitivity. Participants also described sensory episodes as physically uncomfortable, which is consistent with earlier research (Robertson & Simmons, 2015; Kirby et al., 2014; Robertson, 2012). Several participants stated that emotional mood, weariness, and uncertainty influenced their sensory processing, which could explain some of the intra-individual heterogeneity observed here. These parameters should be formally assessed in future studies.

Participant 2's comment about fragmented perception in supermarkets recalls descriptions of perceptual fragmentation in autism (Kanner, 1943; Booth & Happé, 2018). Qualitative insights may disclose aspects of perception that questionnaires cannot capture.

Understanding perception in autism necessitates a participant-led approach. This study described an innovative usage of VR, specifically the OpenBrush drawing tool, to investigate autistic individuals' perceptual worlds. Combining visual, aural, and narrative data allowed for a thorough investigation of personal experience. VR was warmly appreciated by all participants, who characterized it as immersive, relaxing, and creatively liberated.

These findings lend weight to the idea that virtual reality can be used for both study and therapy. Future research should build on this foundation by including bigger and more diverse samples, repeated sessions, and neurotypical comparison groups to gain a better understanding of perceptual experiences in autism.

The Case of Synesthesia

In synesthesia, people have sensory or cognitive experiences when they see or hear things that do not seem to be connected (Simner, 2011). For instance, auditory stimuli such as speech or music may evoke sensations of color or taste, or letters may be intrinsically interpreted as colored. The estimated incidence in the general population has ranged from 0.5% (Baron-Cohen et al., 1996) to 4.4% (Simner et al., 2006). Current estimates posit an absence of significant sex bias; earlier beliefs suggested a higher prevalence in women, perhaps because to variations in self-referral (Simner & Carmichael, 2015).

Stimuli that cause synesthetic experiences are called "inducers," and the resulting perceptual or cognitive experiences are called "concurrents" (Grossenbacher & Lovelace, 2001). Inducers and concurrents might exist within the same or distinct modalities (Rothen et al., 2013). It is customary to write synesthetic variants in the inducer–concurrent format, and this report will follow that convention. Certain synesthetes perceive their concurrents as spatially expanded (Simner, 2011); for instance, individuals with grapheme-color synesthesia may visualize the triggered colors as projected onto the text they are reading. These synesthetes are regarded as "projectors." Some individuals possess awareness of their concurrent experiences or visualize them "in the mind's eye," categorizing them as "associators" (Ward & Simner, 2020).

Synesthesia can be developmental, acquired, or provoked. This study will concentrate exclusively on developmental synesthesia, characterized by its onset in early childhood and representing the majority of documented occurrences of synesthesia (Ward & Simner, 2020).

More than 100 different types of synesthesia have been reported so far (Ward & Simner, 2020). Individuals with synesthesia may exhibit many forms of the condition (Ward, 2019). The most prevalent type of synesthesia is colored days, which 64% of people with synesthesia have (Simner et al., 2006). Cognitive components, including graphemes and words, constitute the majority of inducers, comprising 88%, but color is the predominant concomitant, representing 95% of all elicited experiences. This research will concentrate mostly on grapheme-color and auditory-visual synesthesia.

Grapheme-color synesthesia is the most often examined variety, comprising around 45% of synesthetes, or 1.4% of the entire population (Simner et al., 2006). People with grapheme-color synesthesia see letters as having their own colors. Each synesthete will have their own colors, although some graphemes are more likely than others to be a certain hue. For example, A is red and D is brown more often than would be predicted by chance (Rich et al., 2005; Simner et al., 2005).

In auditory-visual synesthesia, the perception of sounds elicits supplementary visual information (Neufeld et al., 2012). The literature predominantly emphasizes additional color sensations; however, any visual attribute, including shape (Chiou et al., 2013), texture, and movement (Moos et al., 2013; Eagleman & Goodale, 2009), may be triggered. Moreover, concurrents can be perceived in three dimensions (Eagleman & Goodale, 2009). The automatic visual content perceived by auditory-visual synesthetes frequently exhibits parallels with the general cross-modal associations observed in the non-synesthetic population regarding sound and vision, such as high-pitched tones being perceived as elevated in spatial position and characterized by smaller, less rounded forms and lighter hues compared to lower-pitched tones (Ward et al., 2006). These cross-modal correspondences are referred to as "synaesthetic congruences" and are believed to facilitate information processing (Spence & Youssef, 2019).

Recreating Synesthetic Experiences

Many studies have portrayed synesthetes' grapheme-color connections using color pickers. Nonetheless, these are predominantly employed as a means of evaluating the authenticity of grapheme-color synesthesia (Rothen et al., 2013), rather than representing the entirety of concurrent phenomenology. Chiou and colleagues elaborated on this by employing GIMP software alongside hand drawings, verbal descriptions, and Adobe Photoshop (1990) to replicate the simultaneous experiences of synesthetes who perceived colored geometric shapes in specific spatial locations in response to auditory stimuli (Chiou et al., 2013). In a related study, a professional animator made animated reconstructions of auditory-visual synesthesia. These were then utilized in performance at the event people who do not have synesthesia prefer them to control animations (Ward et al., 2008).

In a more general sense, a lot of artists have made works based on synesthetic connections. Mikalojus Konstantinas Čiurlionis and Wassily

Kandinsky made Sonata of the Stars (1908) and Fuga (Fugue) (1914), which were both meant to turn music into paintings (Ward et al., 2008). More recently, artists Melissa McCracken and Jack Coulter have become known for their paintings of their auditory-visual synesthesia. McCracken paints oil paintings of popular songs, and Coulter paints a picture of the 2016 Glastonbury Festival after listening to every performance at the event. The artist Carol Steen made the painting "Vision," which shows how she felt during an acupuncture session when she had tactile-visual synesthesia (Steen, 2001). Steen elucidates her motivation for creating "Vision" as a result of her inadequacy in articulating the essence of her experiences through language (Steen, 2001). Billie Eilish, a musician, has more recently used art installations to reproduce her personal synesthetic experiences of the songs on her first album (Billie Eilish Experience, 2019) (see https://web.archive.org/web/20190403020359/billieeilishexperience.com/).

It is evident that synesthetic experiences are more complex than what can be represented solely by color pickers, a notion supported by several research and the endeavors of synesthetic artists. This report seeks to expand upon prior research, specifically the study of Ward et al. (2008), by introducing an exploratory feasibility study that replicates synesthetic connections within a Virtual reality (VR) environment utilizing the art software OpenBrush (2016) 1. Openbrush (2016) lets people paint in a 3D space that feels real, using a variety of brushes that can provide dynamic and textured effects. Compared to animation packages, VR is a more accessible medium because it does not take as much time or talent to make sketches. Moreover, VR is a very authentic and realistic medium with good ecological validity (Savickaite et al., 2021), and its immersive nature enables people beyond the creator to "enter" the 3D environment and engage with it. Consequently, the objective of this research is to present virtual reality as an innovative approach to investigating the phenomenology of synesthesia, with the possibility for dissemination to individuals who do not experience synesthesia.

The sole investigation employing VR technology to replicate synesthesia concentrated exclusively on spatial sequence synesthesia. The authors utilized WorldViz VR software in this study to enable participants to position elements from familiar sequences (e.g., the months of the year) in three-dimensional space, reflecting their experiential perception of these sequences (Eagleman, 2009). This was not immersive, and an avatar stood in for the participants. A recent project developed VR musical representations based on synesthetic associations, although it did not include synesthetes in this process (Weinel, 2021). Recent studies have concentrated on the utilization of VR technology in domains such as art therapy (Hacmun et al., 2018) and visual processing styles for autism and ADHD characteristics (Savickaite et al., 2021).

This study details two interconnected experiments examining the representation of synesthetic sensations through conventional color pickers and immersive virtual reality drawing. The initial experiment, carried out amid COVID-19 constraints, utilized a "VR-by-proxy" design, with the researcher serving as an intermediary. Six synesthetes participated, articulating grapheme–color and auditory–visual correlations through Zoom, whereas fundamental recreations were constructed utilizing Google Slides and HEX color codes. When participants talked about more complicated concurrents, including movement, texture, or three-dimensional shapes, the researcher used OpenBrush to make short movies of these and then asked the participants to rate them. After the epidemic, the second experiment was done. Participants used OpenBrush directly in VR to draw their experiences, and the data was analyzed thematically. This mix of non-VR methods (questionnaires, color pickers, structured interviews) and VR-based art-making gave us an extraordinarily rich multimodal picture of how people with synesthesia feel and talk about it.

Feedback from participants (first experiment) showed both the good and bad sides of "VR-by-proxy" for this purpose. For some, VR representations caught remarkable characteristics of their perceptual worlds: Participant 3, for instance, was surprised by how well OpenBrush matched her synesthesia for birdsong. She said that the "*movement and rough edges are very accurate*" and gave the image a near-perfect fit, even though other details like fading and peripherals were lost. She said that her synesthesia is "*very hard to explain, so there would always be a loss in accuracy when someone else tries to reproduce it.*" This shows both the problem and the potential of VR in trying to recreate experiences that are hard to express. Participant 2, on the other hand, thought that many of the OpenBrush recreations did not catch the subtle, unclear parts of his experiences. However, he did say that some stimuli, including the number 7 and the month of June, were reproduced better. He pointed out that if he could use the VR system himself, it may better recreate the feeling of being "*alone in his head.*" This suggests that using VR equipment directly and actively may be very important for authenticity. Participant 4 was particularly pleased, valuing "*the 3D element and how it was possible to move around and interact within the environment,*" and characterizing certain representations, like glittering speckles for birdsong, as quite akin to his experiences.

The trials demonstrated that traditional tools such as color pickers can accurately depict stable grapheme-color correlations, but they fail to encapsulate the dynamic, volumetric, and textural characteristics of auditory-visual or more intricate forms of synesthesia. In contrast, VR painting let people show movement, depth, and mood on the outside. One participant even said it was "*a good representation of how speech patterns can be*" through forms that change and flow. These results indicate that VR art-making may serve as an effective adjunct to conventional methods, especially for conveying perceptual distinctions that are difficult to articulate (even in "VR-by-proxy" mode). The research shows that VR can create an immersive "middle ground" where people's private sensory worlds can be seen by others. This opens up new possibilities to learn about synesthesia and, more generally, to talk about neurodivergent sensory experiences.

Second Experiment

The second experiment investigated whether immersive, participant-operated virtual reality sketching may capture elements of synesthetic concurrents that static, non-VR technologies fail to detect. Three audiovisual synesthetes entered the lab, put on an HTC Vive Pro, and used OpenBrush to reproduce what they "see" while listening to five everyday sounds: birds singing, cars passing, the phone ringing, rain, and white noise. After each sound, which lasted about 30 seconds and could be played again if necessary, they judged how well their drawing matched their experience on a scale of 0 to 5 and talked about how they did it. Two participants came back about 19 weeks later for a retest. This study builds on a previous mixed-methods experiment in which non-VR measures (screening questionnaire, structured interviews, and HEX color picker matching) were effective for basic, stable grapheme-color pairings but were clearly inadequate for dynamic, volumetric, or textural concurrents.

Most of the participants gave high marks, with mean scores for birdsong, automobiles, and phone ringing clustering around 4–5. Their comments also made it clear what VR provided that pen-and-paper or 2D software did not. "*This is the best I've ever gotten,*" one person said. I never managed to explain my experiences so plainly. "*I want to show it to my family.*" Another person pointed out the change from flat representation to located making: "*There's so much more I can say... because I can use a 3D space instead of trying to draw on paper. So, yes, a huge benefit.*" One person was very clear regarding traditional media: "*Pen and paper are too small and [don't] get the same accurate representation.*"

One of the main benefits was the ability to stage movement and texture, which are important parts of many auditory-visual concurrents. Animated brushes helped get the dynamics right. One participant said that the phone's "*circular motion*" was "*slower in the middle, but on the outside it moves a lot more, almost like a sort of gravitational vacuum.*" When speed gradients or size changes over time were too much for the tools to handle, participants came up with solutions, such as combining expanding and contracting cycles into a single "*mean ring.*" People were saying that textural brushes, notably Smoke and Sparkles, felt real: "*This smoke will really help because a lot of my synaesthesia looks kind of like that,*" and "*Oh my God… this is… the kind of stars in your eyes.*" One participant summed up the tactile realism well when they said, "*I feel like I could just touch them.*" They look extremely real.

Dimensionality and the ability to position forms relative to one's own body were equally significant—capabilities that static 2D media lack. Participants identified concurrents in the periphery ("*I'm just in the corner of my eye*"), articulated experiences of being within or across drawn objects, and indicated alterations in perspective—"*beside… and then… behind it.*" These embodied positions were important for accuracy. For example, a concurrent that sounded like white noise was felt like a blade coming straight at you, but if you looked at it from the side, it would look like "*TV interference.*" The spatial stance is not an annotation to the image; it is part of the perception.

The study focused on visualizations (Figs. 5.3 and 5.4), although the sessions revealed cross-modal spillover and autobiographical memory, enhancing our understanding of lived synesthesia. One person said, "*I feel like I can taste this… little tubs of pears,*" and another said, "*thinking my feet are going to get wet.*" The immersive, creative setting also made linkages to music, crafts, and everyday activities, giving a fuller sense of how concurrents run through everyday life. Interestingly, people really enjoyed it—"*It would never stop like amazing me*"—without losing attention on the work at hand. This suggests that VR painting is both fun and structured enough for research application.

At the same time, the tools had obvious and helpful restrictions. When OpenBrush's animated brushes could not show more complicated kinematics (such objects changing size over time or multi-rate pulsations),

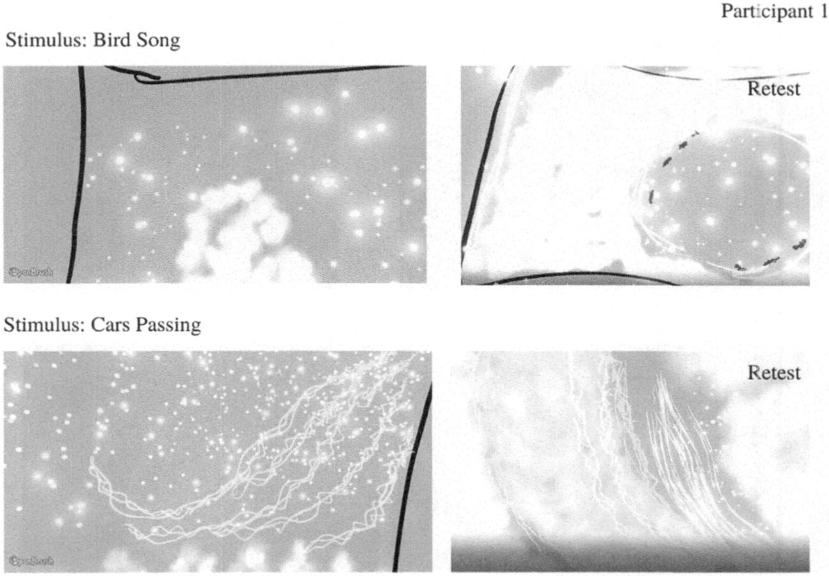

Fig. 5.3 Screenshots of OpenBrush drawings created by Participant 1 during the VR session

when the time it took to learn about brush sets limited exploration, or when the synesthetic intensity for a specific stimulus was low, accuracy went down. Retest drawings, on the other hand, indicated that the overall shape, color range, and "gist" were similar enough to suggest that the tool will be reliable for each person if they had more time to learn how to use it.

The findings suggest that participant-led VR drawing is a semi-structured but flexible method. It is structured enough to allow for ratings, comparisons between stimuli, and systematic analysis of recurring features (such as color, form, motion, texture, and spatial placement), but it is also flexible enough to respect individuality and embodiment. Non-VR experiments are still useful for simple, stable mappings, but immersive sketching is essential when concurrents are dynamic, volumetric, and located in space. In this way, Experiment 2 shows how VR may make private sensory worlds shareable without making them less interesting. This method works well for various types of neurodivergent perception where words and 2D diagrams often fail.

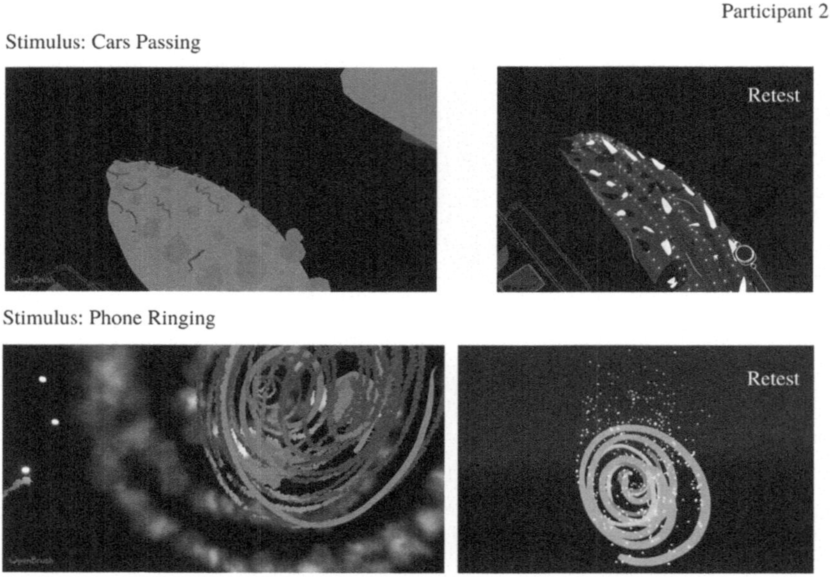

Fig. 5.4 Screenshots of OpenBrush drawings created by Participant 2 during the VR session

This research has detailed two studies examining the application of virtual reality to investigate the phenomenology of grapheme-color (experiment 1 only) and audiovisual synesthesia. Experiment 1 utilized a VR-by-proxy method due to limitations imposed by the COVID-19 epidemic. In Experiment 2, participants utilized the VR equipment independently to generate their own depictions of their synesthesia. Participants in both trials reacted very positively to the VR environment. Some even said that their VR drawings were the best representations of their synesthesia they had ever made.

One evident benefit of utilizing VR to replicate synesthetic associations is that it lets you do sketches in a three-dimensional, immersive world. In both studies, participants indicate the spatial orientation of their contemporaneous experiences in relation to their own bodies. For instance, in Experiment 1, Participant 4 commented on observing the researcher's reproduction of the misty gray mass produced by the sound of rain, suggesting that instead of watching it from afar, we should be positioned extremely close, almost within the mist. In the same way, two views were provided for the speckles that happened in reaction to birdsong: one from a distance and one from closer up. The participant remarked that the far-away version was pretty accurate, but the close-up version was hard to judge because he didn't see it from that close-up perspective. Participant 3 said that the sound of the researcher's voice should fade out into the background instead of staying around a clear edge. In all instances, the significance of placement was articulated by participants solely in meeting 2, however they expressed strong sentiments regarding it. This demonstrates the challenge participants faced in articulating their supplementary perceptual experiences, a result that aligns with prior research (Sollberger, 2013). It also shows how important dimensionality is in synesthetic experiences, which is something that VR can only capture.

Participants in Experiment 2 corroborated these findings, consistently referencing the appropriate spatial positioning of objects in relation to themselves. Participant 1 mostly saw their synesthetic experiences in two dimensions, as they were on a screen or in their peripheral vision. Participants 2 and 3, on the other hand, talked about their experiences in three dimensions. For example, Participant 3 said they were "*beside*," "*behind*," "*inside*," "*standing on*," or "*walking through*" their different synesthetic experiences. These differences may indicate whether the participants were associators or projectors. Investigating the distinctions in how associators and projectors portray their perceptual experiences in a virtual world could be a significant direction for future research.

This image shows how the drawings are oriented in space in reference to the participant. Participant 1 (top) saw things as if they were on a screen and felt limited by their field of vision, which made them hesitant to explore the virtual world's three-dimensional space. Participant 2 (middle) drew things in relation to their body and talked about moving through and standing on things in the three-dimensional space. Participant 3 (bottom) drew things in relation to their body, but usually next to, behind, or in front of them.

Participants instinctively illustrated their experiences in spatial contexts, although typically articulated these descriptions only when solicited by the researcher. It is clear that the synesthetes' concurrent experiences are a crucial part of audiovisual synesthesia, and typical 2D media cannot show this. VR enables this mode of expression and permits non-synesthetes to enter the scene and perceive a more comprehensive, immersive representation of another's synesthesia.

Constraints and Prospective Pathways

OpenBrush (2016) was not able to capture some of the experiences that some participants shared, even though they were promising. Certain forms of motion could not be caught, primarily. Both tests showed this. For instance, in Experiment 1, Participant 3 said that the sound of birdsong made her feel like an orange color was "jiggling" back and forth in the bottom right corner. Then, it jumped across to halfway up the left-hand side and turned into a twisting peach octagon. The first minor "jiggling" motion was well recorded, but no tool could make the object go across the screen, change color and shape, and then twist. The sound of white noise also made Participant 3 feel that they were seeing a white wave, like a heart rate monitor going across the screen and fading away as it did. Once more, no tool could record this movement. Also, the tools were preset, which made some colors less accurate by changing them in small ways. For instance, the brush that was used to make Participant 3's pink cascade turned white at the end of each stroke. Participant 3 said, "the color is not quite right, but the movement is good," which means that this tool could accurately duplicate her dynamic concurrent experience, but the predefined coloring made it less accurate overall. In Experiment 2, certain types of motion were not captured, prompting participants to employ various strategies to suggest motion—such as adding lines to indicate the direction of motion or illustrating the "mean" (Participant 2) size of rings that should be moving and gradually diminishing—rather than accurately representing the motion as they perceived it. These examples show that OpenBrush (2016) is a useful tool for capturing some visual aspects of synesthesia, but it does not This is outside the scope needed to effectively capture other aspects.

But a recent move has made OpenBrush (2016) an open-source platform. This means that Google will no longer update it, but anyone may now access the code and make improvements to it. This is outside the scope of this project, but researchers can change the program to fit their needs in the future. This could fix the problems that were mentioned above. To accurately capture motion, on the other hand, you would need animation programs. Michael Gagne and Jeremy Blake made synesthetic cartoons for the movies Sensology (2010) and Punch-Drunk Love (2002) that showed how sounds and sights might interact together when music played. This was in addition to the work of Ward et al. (2008). One of the best things about OpenBrush (2016) is that it is easy to use, even for people who are not very good with computers or do not have a lot of time. So, by making its code open source, it may be possible to add more complicated movements to future works without having to use more complicated animation tools.

A significant disadvantage in Experiment 1 was that participants did not sketch the contemporaneous stimuli themselves. Experiment 2 fixed this problem. One good thing about Experiment 1 was that the participants gave extensive and detailed accounts of their experiences, as well as precise suggestions for how to make the researcher's OpenBrush (2016) drawings better. The researcher also got unlimited access to the VR system, which helped her understand the features of OpenBrush (2016) better and gave her more time to think about how to effectively show what the participants said. In Experiment 2, on the other hand, participants had less time to get to know OpenBrush (2016) and made comments while they were in the VR environment, but they did so less often. Also, participants had a restricted amount of time to finish their drawings because VR can make people unwell (Chattha et al., 2020). A subsequent experiment may integrate the advantages of both methodologies. One way to do this is to show the participants the walkthrough video of OpenBrush's (2016) features used in Experiment 1 before the VR session. They could also be given early access to the stimuli so they can think about how they might recreate their synaesthetic experiences in VR. After the VR session, a semi-structured interview might be utilized to get clear and thorough feedback on what parts of their synesthesia were successfully represented in VR and what more tools, training, or experience they would need to make their drawings more accurate.

Virtual Reality and Aphantasia

Not only do we live in different places, but we also live in separate parts of ourselves. Perception, memory, cognition, and imagination all build each person's inner environment. These invisible landscapes typically go unnoticed because they are private. But when we take a moment to think about it, we see how varied our mental lives may be and how little we really know about the inner lives of the people around us.

Mental imagery is the ability to construct sensory experiences without any outside input. You might "see" an apple, "hear" a song, or "smell" fresh grass in your mind's eye. These internal simulations are not just nice additions; they are often the basis for remembering, planning, and creativity. A lot of us think in pictures, going over scenarios or reading stories with pictures in our heads (Savickaite et al., 2025).

Aphantasia is the opposite of this: the inability to make mental pictures. For an individual with aphantasia, reading a novel fails to elicit vivid mental imagery, despite a comprehensive understanding of the narrative. Studies employing the binocular rivalry task provide robust evidence: when individuals are instructed to visualize a specific visual pattern prior to viewing two competing pictures in each eye, their imagined pattern subtly influences their perception. However, individuals with aphantasia exhibit no perceptual priming; their previous "imagery" does not affect the initial appearance in the rivalry test, indicating that visual mental imagery is indeed lacking in these individuals (Keogh & Pearson, 2021).

Aphantasia and other invisible distinctions in cognition show us that our internal experiences are not the same for everyone. Some minds are full of bright imagery and worlds that can be seen, felt, and heard, while others are quiet, abstract, or not visual at all. Recognizing this diversity enhances our comprehension of the processes of thinking, imagining, and remembering. Aphantasia is not a flaw; it is a divergence in perceptual and cognitive style, compelling us to reevaluate our beliefs regarding the mind and imagination.

We do not talk about what it is really like to think very often because most of it is buried. But looking into those hidden landscapes—through interviews, behavioral exercises, or immersive technologies like virtual reality—can help us understand not only unusual disorders like aphantasia but also the broad range of how minds differ. The more we expose these concealed realms, the better we can foster empathy, challenge preconceived notions, and reevaluate the true nature of "normal" cognition (Savickaite et al., 2025).

The term neurodiversity originated in the 1990s within autistic online communities to characterize natural human cognitive variance and to contest deficit-oriented interpretations of difference. Neurodiversity emphasizes the absence of a singular "correct" mode of thinking, learning, or behaving, asserting that deviations from prevailing norms should not be inherently pathologized (Baumer & Frueh, 2021; Walker, 2017). Conditions including autism, ADHD, dyslexia, dyscalculia, and dyspraxia are sometimes put together under this umbrella (Clouder et al., 2020), however they are not only characterized by weakness. Research indicates that specific types of neurodivergence can provide advantages, such as autism's correlation with meticulousness, systematization, and prolonged concentration (Wheelwright et al., 2006), or synesthesia's associated with improved memory and creativity (Simner, 2019; Smees et al., 2019).

In this context, aphantasia has lately been examined as a possible manifestation of neurodivergence. Aphantasia is the inability or significant decrease in the ability to create mental images. People with aphantasia can still remember what they see, but they cannot see it in their "mind's eye." Self-report instruments, notably the Vividness of Visual Imagery Questionnaire (VVIQ; Marks, 1973; Marks & Isaac, 1995), consistently detect aphantasia and correspond with behavioral validation studies (Keogh & Pearson, 2018; Pearson et al., 2011; Zeman et al., 2015). Population estimates indicate that approximately 3.9% of individuals are aphantasic (Dance et al., 2025), rendering it uncommon yet noteworthy due to its global prevalence (Simner, 2021).

The primary inquiry is whether aphantasia ought to be regarded as a disorder or a cognitive variation. Recent evidence indicates the latter. Some characterize aphantasia as a pathology or "mental illness" (Yang, 2022), while others depict it as an intriguing and non-pathological variety of human experience (Zeman et al., 2020). There is few empirical evidence supporting pathogenic beginnings, and an increasing corpus of study regards it as a manifestation of neurodivergence aligned with overarching trends of individual cognitive variation (Monzel, Vetterlein et al., 2022).

Consequently, aphantasia exemplifies both the potential and difficulties of implementing neurodiversity frameworks. On the one hand, it emphasizes that cognitive differences might exist without necessarily indicating deficiency. On the other hand, it shows that there are still disagreements on how to classify, understand, and evaluate these kinds of conditions in both scientific and social discussions.

Most studies on aphantasia use quantitative instruments like the VVIQ, memory tasks, and other neuropsychological tests (Keogh et al., 2021a). The essence of aphantasia is inherently subjective, necessitating further exploration of this subjective experience. How do persons with aphantasia feel about their minds? What does it feel like to not be able to picture things? How do humans understand the world without mental images?

Virtual reality (VR) is a potential technique to learn more about how people feel about things. Virtual reality environments are immersive, interactive, and can give you a first-person view. These settings have been linked to vivid images and engagement (Savickaite et al., 2022). People with autism and synesthesia have already used VR drawing to show their sensory experiences in ways other than language. Could the same approach also provide insights into the aphantasic inner world?

In our pilot study, four individuals (ages 21–29; two male and two female) participated in a VR drawing activity with OpenBrush. They were asked to draw pictures based on suggestions like "cube," "tree," and "recent dream," and they were also asked to think about what they had drawn in semi-structured interviews. Participants also filled out the VVIQ, the Autism Spectrum Quotient (AQ), and the Glasgow Sensory Questionnaire (GSQ) to help with interpretation. These offered a more comprehensive cognitive and sensory framework in conjunction with their drawings.

Even though this exploratory study was small, it showed some really interesting patterns in how people with aphantasia think about creativity, memory, and perception when they cannot see images (Figures 5.5, 5.6, 5.7, and 5.8). I will discuss each of the primary themes of our findings using some quotes from the participants.

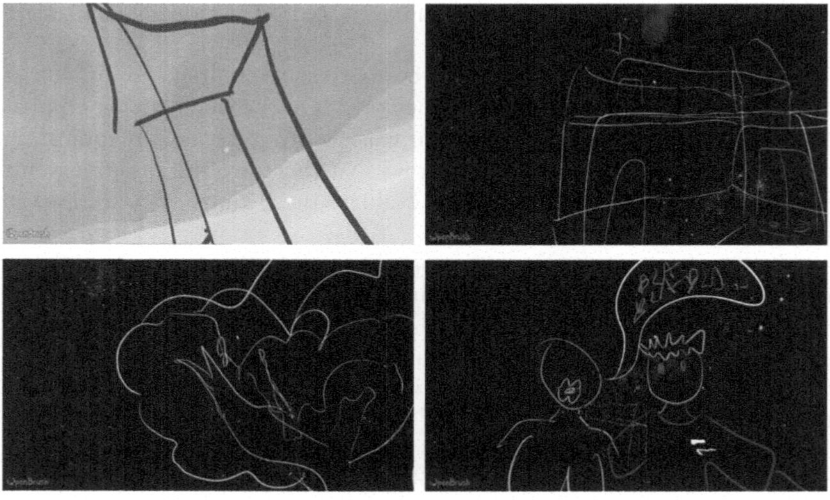

aphantasia 1

Fig. 5.5 Screenshots of OpenBrush drawings created by Participant 1 during the VR session

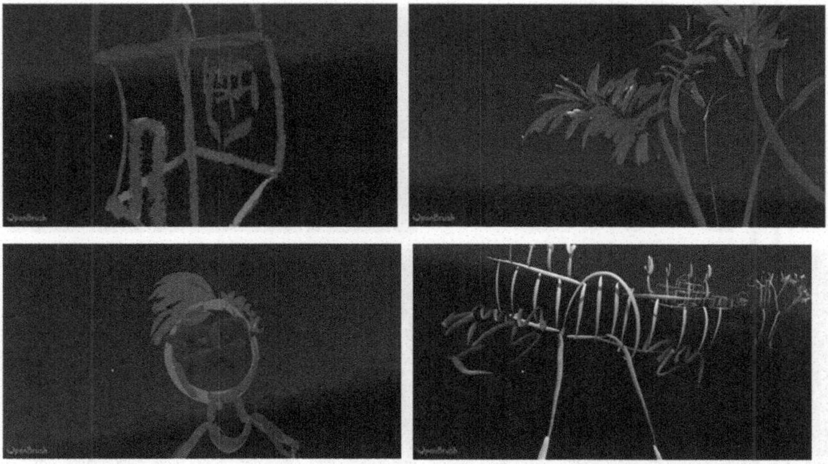

aphantasia 2

Fig. 5.6 Screenshots of OpenBrush drawings created by Participant 2 during the VR session

The "black mind"

The most common subject was the idea of a "*black mind.*" Everyone who took part said that when they closed their eyes, they could only see blackness. They had an idea of what an object should appear like in terms of color, shape, or form, but they didn't actually see it.

One person said, "*I know what the apple looks like, but I don't see it.*" I assumed it was typical. What do you see when you shut your eyes? And for me, nothing.

Another person said that imagination still exists, but in a different way: "*For us, imagination is like a book—words, but not pictures.*"

This differentiation between imagination and imagery corroborates contemporary philosophical discourse (Nanay, 2021; Arcangeli, 2023), which contends that imagination entails far more than mere mental representations.

aphantasia 3

Fig. 5.7 Screenshots of OpenBrush drawings created by Participant 3 during the VR session

Dependence on Citations and External Assistance

A second important theme was the need for references. Participants consistently favored working from external stimuli, colors, or visuals. Even when the duties were open-ended, they still used templates they were used to. One participant said, "*I need a reference… maybe a story.*"

For persons with aphantasia, external stimuli function as extensions of cognition, acting as scaffolds to compensate for the absence of mental images. This is in line with the "*extended mind*" theory (Clark & Chalmers, 1998), which says that things like sketches, models, or stories can become part of our cognitive system. In this way, VR art was not just a way to express yourself, but also a way to help you think.

The Importance of Having Trained Drawing Skills

Three of the four participants had backgrounds in art, which had a big effect on how they did things. They said it was hard to sketch people and that figure drawing needed a lot of practice and reference images. One

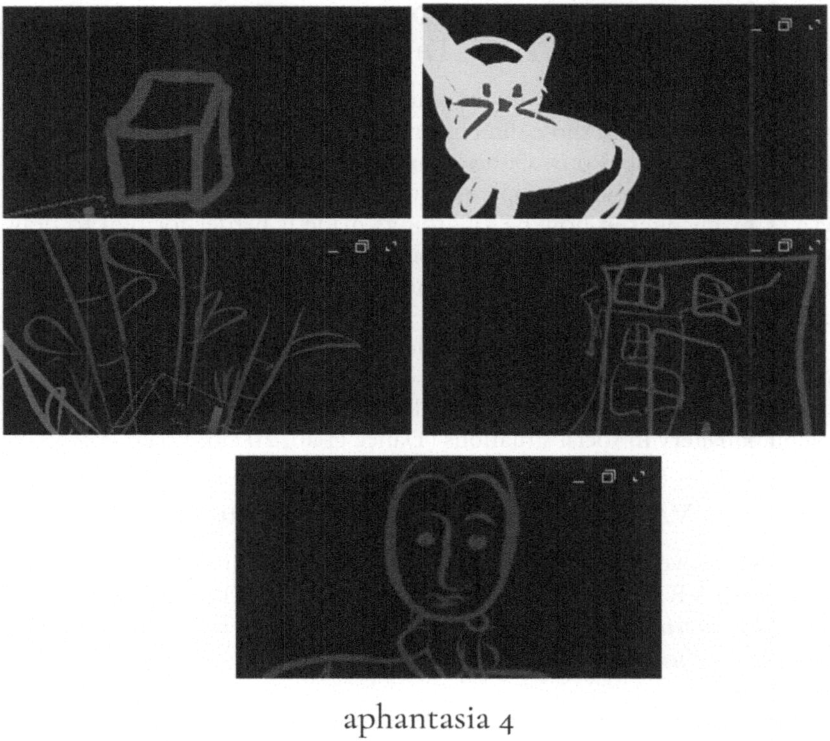

Fig. 5.8 Screenshots of OpenBrush drawings created by Participant 4 during the VR session

participant remembered that painting instruction used images or observation instead of imagining things in their heads: "*As part of life drawing, you have to draw what you can see...*" I guess that taught me to use my eyes instead of my mind.

It's interesting that many of their outputs were abstract or schematic, but drawings were often useful as well, helping with memory or organizing spatial reasoning. One participant said that painting helped him remember times he couldn't otherwise picture.

Drawing in Two Dimensions Against Three Dimensions

Another constant pattern in the data was that when participants drew things, they did so in three dimensions, but when they drew persons, they did it in two dimensions. Cubes, homes, and trees were good for spatial reasoning, but drawing people required work. One participant said that even tiny changes in how he saw things made it harder for him to draw without help from others: "*If I draw an apple a thousand times, I can do that apple.*" However, if I alter the angle or the setting, I need the reference again.

This challenge may indicate the social and perceptual intricacies involved in depicting individuals, resonating with prior research suggesting that aphantasic individuals may depend more on observation than on mental imagery in social situations (Dance et al., 2021).

Variations in Personal VR Experiences

Even while everyone had the "*black mind*" experience, how they interacted with VR was different. One person said that VR drawing was freeing: "*I appreciate VR because I can see what isn't. When I close my eyes, I usually only see black. So I see something that isn't real; it's a different sensation.*"

But another person did not like 3D drawing because it was unpleasant. They preferred modeling software that does not change viewpoint. Some people tried out different brushes and colors. One person used unusual colors (such as white trees and purple skies), while others stuck to more realistic ones.

These changes from case to case remind us that aphantasia is not the same for everyone. Like vivid imagers, people with aphantasia have different ways of making up for the lack of mental pictures.

Beyond Absence: Aphantasia as an Alternative Perceptual Realm

Our examination uncovered multiple prevailing motifs. Together, they show that aphantasia is not just the lack of images, but a different way of seeing things. People with aphantasia generally use language, outside tools, and taught skills to help them remember things, imagine things, and be creative.

This does not limit ingenuity. Many of the people who took part said they were curious and proud to find new ways to do things. Recent studies indicate that aphantasia does not hinder artistic or scientific success (Keogh et al., 2021b). Instead, it modifies how creativity happens by using observation, abstraction, or outside scaffolds instead of mental representations.

This study used VR in a new way. Its immersive settings made it easier for people to talk about experiences they could not put into words. Teleportation, first-person recording, and different brushes were some of the additional features that made it easier to explore the inner world. VR made an important safe and private area for people to express themselves, where they could try things out without the burden of making a finished piece of art.

Looking Ahead

There were clear limits to our investigation. Due to the limited sample size of four individuals, three of whom were artists, the conclusions cannot be generalized. Subsequent study ought to incorporate people from diverse backgrounds, particularly in STEM disciplines, and should also establish a neurotypical comparator group. Larger samples may facilitate the identification of subtypes of aphantasia by examining the correlation between sensory differences, as assessed by instruments such as the GSQ, and specific techniques employed in virtual reality.

There are additional technical paths to follow. More adaptable recording devices would provide the capture of more nuanced in-task commentary, and subsequent research might examine diverse contexts (e.g., light versus dark, realistic versus fanciful) to evaluate their influence on drawing outputs.

Our preliminary study indicates that VR drawing can offer an immersive and expressive means for individuals with aphantasia to externalize their perceptual experiences. The "black mind" is not an empty void; it is richly textured, bolstered by references, molded by training, and articulated through external tools.

We think that VR is a new way to do research and a place for people with aphantasia to learn about, communicate, and think about how they see things in their own way. We can get beyond perceiving aphantasia as just "low imagery vividness" and start to see it as one of many viable ways to experience reality by continuing to investigate these inner realms.

Art, Drawing, and Virtual Reality: Methodological Implications

For arts-based and multimodal research, the review of these studies reinforces the case for treating drawings and VR artifacts as theory-bearing data. Aphantasia uses VR drawing and external media to "offload" imagery, allowing mental scenes to be inspected and co-annotated; hyperphantasia (vivid visual imagery; opposite of aphantasia) uses deliberately sequenced, controllable VR scenarios to channel high-vividness simulation into explicit design choices. This is consistent with our need for protocols that align picture + talk + action traces (e.g., brush choice, stroke timing, viewpoint changes) such that the mechanism (differences in top-down construction) is evident in the record rather than just stated textually.

Synesthesia frequently coexists with vivid imagery (and is more common in hyperphantasic people), but it is a unique neurological type distinguished by automatic, continuous cross-modal concurrents rather than simply "strong images." Treating synesthesia alongside aphantasia/hyperphantasia reveals a neurodivergence spectrum of perceptual construction: imagery precision (low-high) on one axis and cross-modal coupling on another. This framing reinforces our previous stance—overlap without equivalence—and encourages comparative designs that use participant-produced visuals (including VR) as primary data across groups.

The monotropism lens also clarifies synesthete experiences. Synesthesia is a separate neurocognitive variety characterized by automatic, constant cross-modal concurrents; monotropism does not produce synesthesia, nor does synesthesia imply monotropism. Monotropism provides an explanation for why specific synesthetic mappings or synesthesia-related interests may become especially important for a given person (and why interruptions or rapid task shifts can be unpleasant): the attention system prioritizes a small number of highly meaningful attractors. In reality, this complements our arts/VR mission by prompting participant-generated mappings (e.g., color alphabets, music-color spaces), allowing for deep, uninterrupted exploration, and examining the drawings themselves—rather than just the accompanying talk—as theory-bearing data.

Chapter Conclusion

This chapter has shown how VR-based creative practice—especially participant-led drawing in OpenBrush—can operate as a non-verbal, neurodiversity-affirming method for communicating perceptual experience, redistributing epistemic power, and generating new kinds of data about cognition that conventional language-heavy paradigms routinely miss. Across the case studies in autism, synesthesia, and aphantasia, immersive making enabled participants to externalize lived experience through dimensionality, movement, texture, and spatial positioning—features that proved central to "what it feels like" yet are difficult to capture with 2D tools, questionnaires, or interviews alone—while the recorded process (brush choice, stroke timing, viewpoint shifts) created a rich "data trail" for mixed-methods analysis. The findings also clarified that VR is not a universal solution: representational accuracy depends on tool affordances (especially motion), onboarding time, stimulus intensity, and individual comfort with 3D interaction, reinforcing the importance of flexible protocols that align image + talk + action and treat visual artifacts as theory-bearing evidence.

References

Alter-Muri, S. B. (2017). Art education and art therapy strategies for autism spectrum disorder students. *Art Education, 70*(5), 20–25.

Arcangeli, M. (2023). Aphantasia demystified. *Synthese, 201*(2), 31.

Baron-Cohen, S. (2001). Theory of mind in normal development and autism. *Prisme, 34*(1), 74–183.

Baumer, N., & Frueh, J. (2021). What is neurodiversity. *Harvard Health*, 23.

Booth, R., & Happé, F. (2018). Evidence of reduced global processing in autism spectrum disorder. *Journal of Clinical and Experimental Neuropsychology, 40*(3), 365–377. https://doi.org/10.1080/87565641.2017.1374371

Braun, V., & Clarke, V. (2006). Using thematic analysis in psychology. *Qualitative Research in Psychology, 3*(2), 77–101.

Chattha, A., Chen, E. A., & Albaghli, R. (2020). Virtual reality as a tool for social skill intervention in autism spectrum disorder. *Frontiers in Psychology, 11*, 556718. https://doi.org/10.3389/fpsyg.2020.556718

Chiou, R., Stelter, M., & Rich, A. N. (2013). Alternative conceptualizations of synaesthesia. *Cerebral Cortex, 23*(12), 2912–2921. https://doi.org/10.1093/cercor/bhs373

Clark, A., & Chalmers, D. (1998). The extended mind. *Analysis, 58*(1), 7–19.

Clouder, L., Karakus, M., Cinotti, A., Ferreyra, M. V., Fierros, G. A., & Rojo, P. (2020). Neurodiversity in higher education: A narrative synthesis. *Higher Education, 80*(4), 757–778.

Dance, C. J., Meeten, F., & Simner, J. (2025). The role of mental imagery in worry: Insights from aphantasia. *Behaviour Research and Therapy, 193*, 104838.

Dance, C. J., Ward, J., & Simner, J. (2021). What is the link between mental imagery and sensory sensitivity? Insights from aphantasia. *Perception, 50*(9), 757–782.

Darewych, O. H., & Riedel Bowers, N. (2018). Positive arts interventions: Creative clinical tools promoting psychological well-being. *International Journal of Art Therapy, 23*(2), 62–69.

Desnoyers-Stewart, J., Miller, N., & Riecke, B. E. (2025). Synedelica: Mixed Reality Reimagined. *Proceedings of the ACM on Computer Graphics and Interactive Techniques, 8*(3), 1–12.

Eagleman, D. M. (2009). Using time perception to measure fitness for duty. *Military Psychology, 21*(supl), S123–S129.

Eagleman, D. M., & Goodale, M. (2009). Why color synesthesia involves more than color. *Cerebral Cortex, 19*(12), 2896–2905. https://doi.org/10.1093/cercor/bhn175

Eccles, D. W., & Arsal, G. (2017). The think aloud method: What is it and how do I use it? *Qualitative Research in Sport, Exercise and Health, 9*(4), 514–531.

Engelhardt, C. R., et al. (2017). Sensory interests in autism. *Autism, 21*(4), 441–452. https://doi.org/10.1177/1362361317714414

Grossenbacher, P. G., & Lovelace, C. T. (2001). Mechanisms of synesthesia: Cognitive and physiological constraints. *Trends in Cognitive Sciences, 5*(1), 36–41.

Guillemin, M. (2004). Understanding illness: Using drawings as a research method. *Qualitative Health Research, 14*(2), 272–289.

Hacmun, I., Regev, D., & Salomon, R. (2018). The principles of art therapy in virtual reality. *Frontiers in Psychology, 9*, 2082.

Happé, F., & Frith, U. (2020). Annual research review: Looking back to look forward–changes in the concept of autism and implications for future research. *Journal of Child Psychology and Psychiatry, 61*(3), 218–232.

Iachini, T., Maffei, L., Masullo, M., Senese, V. P., Rapuano, M., Pascale, A., et al. (2019). The experience of virtual reality: Are individual differences in mental imagery associated with sense of presence? *Cognitive processing, 20*(3), 291–298.

Kanner, L. (1943). Autistic disturbances of affective contact. *Nervous Child, 2*(3), 217–250.

Kasunic, N., Bracun, S., & Paukovic, M. (2024). Modelling a cybersecurity awareness program at a higher education institution. In *ICERI2024 Proceedings* (pp. 1031–1040). Iated.

Keogh, R., & Pearson, J. (2018). The blind mind: No sensory visual imagery in aphantasia. *eLife, 7*, e33904. https://doi.org/10.7554/eLife.33904

Keogh, R., & Pearson, J. (2021). Aphantasia and visual imagery. *Nature Communications, 12*, 1357. https://doi.org/10.1038/s41467-021-21166-z

Keogh, R., Pearson, J., & Zeman, A. (2021a). Aphantasia: The science of visual imagery extremes. In *Handbook of clinical neurology* (Vol. 178, pp. 277–296). Elsevier.

Keogh, R., Wicken, M., & Pearson, J. (2021b). Visual working memory in aphantasia: Retained accuracy and capacity with a different strategy. *Cortex, 143*, 237–253.

Kirby, A. V., Little, L. M., & Schultz, B. N. (2014). Sensory experiences and ASD. *Neuropsychology, 28*(2), 156–167. https://doi.org/10.1037/neu0000138

MacLennan, K., et al. (2021). Sensory reactivity differences in ASD. *Research in Autism Spectrum Disorders, 83*, 101833. https://doi.org/10.1016/j.rasd.2021.101833

Marks, D. F. (1973). Visual imagery differences and eye movements in the recall of pictures. *Perception & Psychophysics, 14*(3), 407–412.

Marks, D. F., & Isaac, A. R. (1995). Topographical distribution of EEG activity accompanying visual and motor imagery in vivid and non-vivid imagers. *British Journal of Psychology, 86*(2), 271–282.

Maskey, M., Lowry, J., Rodgers, J., McConachie, H., & Parr, J. R. (2014). Reducing specific phobia/fear in young people with autism spectrum disorders (ASDs) through a virtual reality environment intervention. *PloS one, 9*(7), e100374.

Milner, V., McIntosh, H., Colvert, E., & Happé, F. (2019). A qualitative exploration of the female experience of autism spectrum disorder (ASD). *Journal of Autism and Developmental Disorders, 49*(6), 2389–2402.

Monzel, M., Vetterlein, T., et al. (2022). Aphantasia and spatial imagery: OSF preprint. https://doi.org/10.31234/osf.io/r7q3g

Moos, A., Simmons, D., Simner, J., & Smith, R. (2013). Color and texture associations in voice-induced synesthesia. *Frontiers in Psychology, 4*, 568.

Nanay, B. (2021). Unconscious mental imagery. *Philosophical Transactions of the Royal Society B, 376*(1817), 20190689.

Neufeld, J., et al. (2012). Functional correlates of synaesthesia. *Journal of Cognitive Neuroscience, 24*(8), 1730–1740. https://doi.org/10.1162/jocn_a_00267

Oster, G. D., & Crone, P. G. (2004). *Using drawings in assessment and therapy: A guide for mental health professionals*. Routledge.

Pearson, J., Clifford, C. W. G., & Tong, F. (2011). The functional impact of mental imagery on perception. *Current Biology, 21*(4), 304–308. https://doi.org/10.1016/j.cub.2011.05.034

Reed, P., & McCarthy, J. (2012). Cross-modal attention-switching is impaired in autism spectrum disorders. *Journal of Autism and Developmental Disorders, 42*(6), 947–953.

Rich, A. N., Bradshaw, J. L., & Mattingley, J. B. (2005). Are synaesthetic experiences perceptual? *Psychological Science, 16*(9), 661–667. https://doi.org/10.1111/j.1467-9280.2005.01614.x

Riva, G., Malighetti, C., & Serino, S. (2021). Virtual reality in the treatment of eating disorders. *Clinical Psychology & Psychotherapy, 28*(3), 477–488.

Robertson, A. E., & Simmons, D. R. (2013). The relationship between sensory sensitivity and autistic traits in the general population. *Journal of Autism and Developmental Disorders, 43*(4), 775–784.

Robertson, A. E., & Simmons, D. R. (2015). The sensory experiences of adults with autism spectrum disorder: A qualitative analysis. *Journal of Autism and Developmental Disorders, 45*(11), 3473–3483. https://doi.org/10.1007/s10803-015-2540-z

Robertson, C. E. (2012). Sensory processing in autism. *Neuroscience & Biobehavioral Reviews, 36*(1), 271–284. https://doi.org/10.1016/j.neubiorev.2012.07.001

Robertson, C. E., & Baron-Cohen, S. (2017). Sensory perception in autism. *Nature Reviews Neuroscience, 18*(11), 671–684.

Rothen, N., Tsakanikos, E., Meier, B., & Ward, J. (2013). Synaesthesia and cognitive processing. *Cortex, 49*(6), 1740–1751. https://doi.org/10.1016/j.cortex.2012.12.013

Russell, G., Mandy, W., Elliott, D., White, R., Pittwood, T., & Ford, T. (2019). Selection bias on intellectual ability in autism research: A cross-sectional review and meta-analysis. *Molecular Autism, 10*(1), 9.

Savickaite, S., Husselman, T. A., Taylor, R., Millington, E., Hayashibara, E., & Arthur, T. (2022). Applications of virtual reality (VR) in autism research: Current trends and taxonomy of definitions. *Journal of Enabling Technologies, 16*(2), 147–154.

Savickaite, S., Li, H., & Simmons, D. (2025). What can virtual reality reveal about perceptual differences in Aphantasia: A qualitative study. https://doi.org/10.31234/osf.io/7ntpy_v1.

Savickaite, S., McNaughton, K., Gaillard, E., Amaya, I., McDonnell, N., Millington, E., & Simmons, D. (2021). Using HMD Virtual Reality to investigate individual differences in visual processing styles. *PsyArXiv Preprints, 10.*

Scott, F. J., & Baron-Cohen, S. (1996). Imagining real and unreal things: Evidence of a dissociation in autism. *Journal of Cognitive Neuroscience, 8*(4), 371–382.

Simner, J. (2011). Lexical-gustatory synesthesia and food-and diet-related behavior. In *Handbook of Behavior, Food and Nutrition* (pp. 1397–1408). Springer New York.

Simner, J. (2019). *Synaesthesia: A very short introduction* (Vol. 608). Oxford University Press.
Simner, J., & Carmichael, D. A. (2015). Is synaesthesia a dominantly female trait? *Cognitive Neuroscience, 6*(2–3), 68–76.
Simner, J., Mulvenna, C., Sagiv, N., et al. (2006). Synaesthesia: The prevalence and underlying mechanisms. *Nature Neuroscience, 9*(6), 761–762. https://doi.org/10.1038/nn1648
Simner, J., et al. (2005). Synaesthetic colours and graphemes. *Cognition, 95*(2), 1–14. https://doi.org/10.1016/j.cognition.2004.11.005
Smees, R., Hughes, J., Carmichael, D. A., & Simner, J. (2019). Learning in colour: Children with grapheme-colour synaesthesia show cognitive benefits in vocabulary and self-evaluated reading. *Philosophical Transactions of the Royal Society B: Biological Sciences, 374*(1787).
Sollberger, M. (2013). Rethinking synesthesia. *Philosophical Psychology, 26*(2), 171–187.
Spence, C., & Youssef, J. (2019). Synaesthesia: The multisensory dining experience. *International Journal of Gastronomy and Food Science, 18*, 100179.
Steen (2001). Vision. https://www.researchgate.net/publication/249562327_Visions_Shared_A_Firsthand_Look_into_Synesthesia_and_Art
Sundberg, M. (2018). VR & interaction. *IEEE Transactions on Affective Computing, 9*(2), 1–10. https://doi.org/10.1109/TAFFC.2018.2832099
Ten Eycke, K. D., & Müller, U. (2015). Brief report: New evidence for a social-specific imagination deficit in children with autism spectrum disorder. *Journal of Autism and Developmental Disorders, 45*(1), 213–220.
Thompson-Hodgetts, S., Labonte, C., Mazumder, R., & Phelan, S. (2020). Helpful or harmful? A scoping review of perceptions and outcomes of autism diagnostic disclosure to others. *Research in Autism Spectrum Disorders, 77*, 101598.
Vaisvaser, S. (2019). Moving along and beyond the spectrum: Creative group therapy for children with autism. *Frontiers in Psychology, 10*, 417.
Walker, S. (2017). The autism binary: Finding the cause and cure/accepting and helping the affected population-making the case for neurodiversity (Doctoral dissertation, Rutgers University-Camden Graduate School).
Ward, J. (2019). Synaesthesia: A distinct entity that is an emergent feature of adaptive neurocognitive differences. *Philosophical Transactions of the Royal Society B: Biological Sciences, 374*(1787).
Ward, J., Hoadley, C., Hughes, J. E., Smith, P., Allison, C., Baron-Cohen, S., & Simner, J. (2017). Atypical sensory sensitivity as a shared feature between synaesthesia and autism. *Scientific Reports, 7*(1), 41155.
Ward, J., & Simner, J. (2020). Synesthesia: The current state of the field. In *Multisensory perception* (pp. 283–300). Academic Press.

Ward, J., Huckstep, B., & Tsakanikos, E. (2006). Sound–colour synaesthesia. *Journal of Experimental Psychology: Human Perception and Performance, 32*(5), 1197–1207. https://doi.org/10.1037/0096-1523.32.5.1197

Ward, J., Thompson-Lake, D., Ely, R., & Kaminski, F. (2008). Synaesthesia, creativity and art: What is the link? *British Journal of Psychology, 99*(1), 127–141.

Weinel, J. (2021, September). Synaesthetic audio-visual sound toys in virtual reality. In *Proceedings of the 16th International Audio Mostly Conference* (pp. 135–138).

Wheelwright, S., Baron-Cohen, S., Goldenfeld, N., Delaney, J., Fine, D., Smith, R., et al. (2006). Predicting autism spectrum quotient (AQ) from the systemizing quotient-revised (SQ-R) and empathy quotient (EQ). *Brain Research, 1079*(1), 47–56.

Yang, Y. (2022, January). Analysis on Aphantasia's symptom. In *In 2021 International Conference on Social Development and Media Communication (SDMC 2021)* (pp. 1037–1040). Atlantis Press.

Zeman, A., Dewar, M., & Della Sala, S. (2015). Lives without imagery – Congenital aphantasia. *Cortex, 73*, 378–380. https://doi.org/10.1093/cercor/bhu185

Zeman, A., Milton, F., et al. (2020). Aphantasia: The science of visual imagery extremes. *Trends in Cognitive Sciences, 24*(9), 702–712. https://doi.org/10.1016/j.tics.2020.05.009

CHAPTER 6

The Fragile Balance: Ethics, Sensory Design, and Inclusion in VR

One of the key challenges in developing VR-based arts methodologies lies in the difficulty of analyzing participant responses alongside their drawings, as there are currently few established approaches that bring these multimodal data sources together in a coherent way. This issue was a central point of discussion at the QUERY group workshop at the University of Exeter, where we revisited findings from my own work, which is distinctive in its use of VR to explore perceptual differences rather than to serve therapeutic purposes. Our discussions highlighted that this challenge extends beyond VR drawing analysis to the wider use of arts-based methods in psychology, raising questions about how such approaches might connect more productively with ethnographic traditions.

Several potential candidates for an analytic framework were identified, including content analysis, which provides a systematic means of coding both manifest and latent features of material (Krippendorff, 2018), but may struggle with the integration of image and text; the Japanese method of Tōjisha-Kenkyū, which incorporates text and images in parallel (Ayaya & Kitanaka, 2023), though it remains difficult to treat these modes equally in analysis; and possible combinations of Interpretative Phenomenological Analysis (Smith et al., 2009) with ethnographic techniques to account for both lived experience and context. Much of the existing literature on drawing analysis, such as Pridmore and Bendelow's (1995) work with children, tends to treat drawings as prompts to elicit verbal responses or as

S. Savickaite, *Exploring Neurodiversity Through Virtual Reality*,
https://doi.org/10.1007/978-3-032-19636-1_6

illustrative adjuncts to text, but rarely as data with equal analytic weight. In this sense, a substantial amount of meaning is often lost, as the visual dimension is sidelined simply because it does not fit neatly into established protocols such as IPA or thematic analysis.

Related methodological work in video research, for example, where transcripts and video stills are aligned side by side (Heath et al., 2010), demonstrates the possibility of multimodal analysis, but also highlights the time-intensive labor of alignment and the lack of standard frameworks to support it. Further considerations were raised around applying a form of "visual grammar" (Kress & van Leeuwen, 2006), which views images as structured systems of representation with three metafunctions—representational, interactive, and compositional—alongside markers of modality (such as detail, color saturation, or perspective) that shape perceptions of realism. While such frameworks offer valuable conceptual tools, they also risk over-systematizing and quantifying materials that are inherently qualitative, and therefore may not align with the aims of exploring lived, subjective, and perceptual experience. As such, there remains a methodological impasse: a "frozen" status in which existing protocols neither fully accommodate the richness of multimodal data, nor offer sufficient flexibility to capture what might otherwise be missed in VR and arts-based research.

There is a broad toolkit for examining artistic drawing and lived experience that exists largely outside of psychology and is essentially multimodal. Sensory and multimodal ethnography offers a framework for treating images, speech, movement, atmosphere, and material interactions as co-data rather than isolating any one channel (Pink, 2015). Multimodal ethnography goes beyond this by advocating for the systematic integration of different semiotic resources and the publication of hypermedia outputs that maintain image and text side by side, keeping the relationships that produce meaning (Dicks et al., 2006). In practice, qualitative work with hypermedia demonstrates how to link video clips, stills, transcripts, and fieldnotes into navigable "episode cards"—an approach that maps neatly onto immersive sessions or VR drawing walkthroughs where actions, strokes, and reflections unfold simultaneously (Dicks et al., 2005).

Aligning images, actions, and speech analytically is one of the most difficult things to do. It is possible to sync images with gesture, gaze, and talk using multimodal and video-based microanalysis (Heath et al., 2010). Conversation-analytic extensions add more embodied sources to transcription (Mondada, 2018), which lets you record temporal aspects of VR sketching like brush changes, stroke timing, and changes in viewpoint that affect how meaning is made. According to Goodwin's theory of action and embodiment, drawings are active meaning tools that are part of situated interaction (Goodwin, 2000).

A constant challenge—and the central point for this book—is that drawings are too frequently employed as elicitation methods to promote discussion or as visuals to embellish conclusions, while systematic study of the drawings themselves lags behind. Outside of psychology, there are growing models for developing cumulative protocols—visual grounded theory specifies procedures for coding visual segments, memoing with picture snippets, and iterating categories from images instead of forcing images to meet textual codes (Mey & Dietrich, 2017). However, the discipline lacks standardized, clear standards for presenting, annotating, and analyzing drawn data, which is especially important when drawings are the primary or only communicative channel for some neurodivergent participants, or when cross-cultural research requires non-linguistic comparability. Bridging sensory ethnography, arts-based research, multimodal interaction analysis, visual semiotics, and participatory visual methods would enable researchers to specify (a) how drawings are generated and contextualized; (b) how image-talk-action are aligned and displayed; and (c) how visual evidence is coded, warranted, and returned to participants. Without such guidelines, drawings' interpretative effort goes unacknowledged, and a critical route for understanding lived perceptual disparities remains underdeveloped, particularly in neurodivergent populations and immersive, technology-mediated contexts.

Technological Literacy

There is always a link between technology advancement and social and ethical implications (Kenwright, 2018). Because of the growing availability of VR technologies, immersive experiences are moving beyond entertainment and games. While VR has numerous potential benefits, there has been much debate concerning the ethical issues that this new technology brings (Kenwright, 2018). There is currently a scarcity of data on the physiological impacts of VR, both short and long term. Furthermore, nothing is known about who and what types of people utilize virtual reality (age, experience level, and attitudes). Many issues about individual qualities, particularly critical thinking skills, remain unresolved. Any answers to current VR technology difficulties should address VR as a whole, not just individual components (Kenwright, 2018). The connectivity and synergy of various VR system components, which commonly include many senses (audio, touch, visual, and proprioception), affects the overall immersive experience.

The implications of the size, kind, and weight of VR game equipment, such as laptops, huge television displays, tablets, smartphones, and, in particular, HMDs, are of special interest (Wang et al., 2018). Concerns have been raised about the effects of virtual environments on the developing visuomotor system, such as negative effects on accommodation, vergence, and stereoscopic vision, as well as visual-motor coordination (eye-hand coordination), which refers to the matching or mismatching of visual information and hand movements.

Finally, the condition known as cybersickness causes nausea and disorientation when viewing virtual environments on head-mounted displays, large screens, and curved screen systems (Kaimara et al., 2022). When compared to desktop displays and large screens, HMDs cause the most cybersickness (Rebenitsch & Owen, 2016). Since current evidence suggests that cybersickness symptoms persist for some time after leaving the VR without causing long-term or permanent harm (Bruck & Watters, 2009), the greatest concern is the potential impact on the visual system. However, recently graphics update rate, field of view, reduced lag between head tracking and visualization have made VR more accessible for research and education (Zhang et al., 2022). The issues outstanding are related to limited (or nearly non-existent) consensus on the research and education standards for using VR. Complex three-dimensional scenes, avatar use, customization and the level of training required to create comparable good quality content are just some of the issues still needing further investigation. Moreover, there is very limited research on how different senses interact in VR, how basic perceptual and cognitive paradigms translate from the real world, and how comparable experimental paradigms are.

Ethical and Methodological Considerations

The use of virtual reality drawing tools to explore perceptual differences raises important ethical and methodological considerations that sit at the intersection of XR ethics, neurodiversity scholarship, and disability studies. While the present work does not constitute participatory design in a formal sense, it aligns closely with neurodiversity-informed and disability studies approaches by prioritizing individual perspectives and enabling participants to communicate lived perceptual experiences in ways that are not constrained by normative linguistic expectations (Goulet et al., 2025). Art-based and visual methods have long been recognized as particularly valuable for populations whose experiences may be difficult to articulate verbally, and VR drawing extends this affordance by allowing experiences to be externalized spatially and dynamically.

From the perspective of epistemic justice, this approach emphasizes participants as credible experts of their own perceptual worlds, rather than positioning researchers as sole interpreters of experience. Neurodiversity scholarship has repeatedly highlighted how dominant research methods privilege neurotypical modes of communication and sense-making, often leading to the marginalization or distortion of neurodivergent accounts. By allowing participants to express perceptual differences through drawing and embodied interaction, this methodology supports epistemic enablement rather than requiring adaptation to neurotypical norms of verbal reporting. In this sense, the method aligns with disability studies where that accessibility and inclusion emerge not from retrofitting existing tools, but from creating conditions under which diverse ways of knowing can be meaningfully expressed (Dark, 2025; Dwyer, 2022; Grummt, 2024).

Ethically, transparency around data collection is central to the responsible use of XR technologies. As outlined in the broader XR ethics literature (Baeyaert, 2025; Newbutt et al., 2024), immersive systems can collect extensive sensor and behavioral data, including movement trajectories and interaction histories, which may be used to infer identity or internal states if combined with additional data streams. In the present study, OpenBrush, a freely available, open-source VR drawing tool, was deliberately chosen because it does not collect biometric data by default. The data retained consist of three-dimensional drawings and the movement data necessary to preserve those drawings as artifacts. No eye tracking, physiological sensing, or affective inference is collected unless explicitly enabled at the platform level. Participants must therefore be clearly informed about what data are captured, what are not, and under what circumstances additional data collection could occur. Should biometric or behavioral telemetry beyond drawing data be enabled in future adaptations, this would require explicit disclosure and renewed consent, in line with XR privacy and informed consent recommendations.

The use of OpenBrush also demonstrates how ethically sensitive XR research can be conducted without developing bespoke tools that introduce additional risks, costs, or governance complexities. Using an existing, open-source application reduces the likelihood of opaque data practices and avoids the need for custom-built sensing pipelines that might inadvertently increase privacy risks. Moreover, OpenBrush's open-source status creates future opportunities for customization informed by neurodivergent needs, such as adjustable sensory parameters, simplified interfaces, or alternative interaction modes. Such adaptations would align with calls from disability studies and neurodiversity research for greater user agency and configurability, particularly in relation to sensory thresholds and comfort (McGill, 2021; Hadan et al., 2025).

Accessibility and sustainability are further ethical strengths of this methodological setup. OpenBrush is compatible with a wide range of VR headsets, including older and lower-cost devices such as Quest 1 and Quest 2, which are sufficient for the drawing tasks used in this work. This reduces financial barriers and mitigates concerns around technological exclusion that are frequently raised in XR ethics debates. Importantly, it enables practices such as recycling or reusing older headsets that might otherwise be retired as newer equipment is purchased, expanding the reach of XR research and making it more feasible for under-resourced research groups or community-based projects.

Concerns commonly associated with XR use, such as cybersickness, sensory overload, or psychological distress, are also relevant but notably mitigated in this context. XR ethics and mental health literature highlights that immersive realism, prolonged exposure, and complex navigation can exacerbate discomfort or adverse effects, particularly for neurodivergent users with sensory sensitivities. However, the drawing-based tasks employed here involve minimal locomotion, limited visual flow, and a high degree of user control, which substantially reduce the likelihood of cybersickness or sensory overwhelm. This further demonstrates how methodological design choices directly shape ethical risk profiles: the same technology can pose vastly different ethical challenges depending on how it is used (Lukava, 2022; Newbutt & Bradley, 2025).

Chapter Conclusion

This chapter critically examines the ethical and methodological tensions involved in using VR-based drawing to study perceptual differences, arguing that while immersive, arts-based methods offer powerful routes to epistemic justice and inclusion, they also expose gaps in existing analytic frameworks and XR research standards. By situating VR drawing within sensory ethnography, multimodal analysis, and disability-informed ethics, the chapter highlights the need to treat drawings, embodied action, and verbal reflection as co-equal data, rather than subordinating visual expression to text. It demonstrates how careful methodological design, using accessible, open-source tools with minimal data capture and high user control, can mitigate risks such as sensory overload, privacy intrusion, and power imbalance, while enabling neurodivergent participants to communicate lived experience on their own terms.

References

Baeyaert, J. (2025). The philosophy of cognitive diversity: Rethinking ethical AI design through the lens of neurodiversity. Sustainable Futures, 10, 101126.

Bruck, S., & Watters, P. A. (2009). The factor structure of cybersickness. *Displays, 30*(2), 81–88.

Dark, J. (2025). Inclusion by design: A neuro-cognitive trait interaction approach to neurodivergent research. *Methodological Innovations*. Advance online publication. https://doi.org/10.1177/20597991251396144

Dicks, B., Mason, B., Coffey, A., & Atkinson, P. (2005). *Qualitative research and hypermedia: Ethnography for the digital age*. Sage.

Dicks, B., Soyinka, B., & Coffey, A. (2006). Multimodal ethnography. *Qualitative Research, 6*(1), 77–96.

Dwyer, P. (2022). The neurodiversity approach(es): What are they and what do they mean for researchers? *Human Development, 66*(2), 73–92.

Goodwin, C. (2000). Action and embodiment within situated human interaction. *Journal of Pragmatics, 32*(10), 1489–1522.

Goulet, M.-H., Dellazizzo, L., Goyer, S., Dollé, S., Hudon, A., Phraxayavong, K., Désilets, M., & Dumais, A. (2025). What are the ethical issues surrounding extended reality in mental health? A scoping review of the different perspectives. *Behavioral Sciences, 15*(10), 1431.

Grummt, M. (2024). Sociocultural perspectives on neurodiversity—An analysis, interpretation and synthesis of the basic terms, discourses and theoretical positions. *Sociology Compass, 18*(8), e13249.

Hadan, H., Valiquette, M., Nacke, L. E., & Zhang-Kennedy, L. (2025). Immersive invaders: Privacy threats from deceptive design in virtual reality games and applications. *Proceedings of the ACM on Human-Computer Interaction, 9*(7), 1–54.

Heath, C., Hindmarsh, J., & Luff, P. (2010). *Video in qualitative research: Analysing social interaction in everyday life*. Sage.

Kaimara, P., Oikonomou, A., & Deliyannis, I. (2022). Could virtual reality applications pose real risks to children and adolescents? A systematic review of ethical issues and concerns. *Virtual Reality, 26*(2), 697–735.

Kenwright, B. (2018). Virtual reality: Ethical challenges and dangers [opinion]. *IEEE Technology and Society Magazine, 37*(4), 20–25.

Kress, G., & van Leeuwen, T. (2006). *Reading images: The grammar of visual design* (2nd ed.). Routledge.

Krippendorff, K. (2018). *Content analysis: An introduction to its methodology* (4th ed.). Sage.

Ayaya, S. & Katanaka, J. (2023). *Tōjisha-kenkyū*. https://aeon.co/essays/japans-radical-alternative-topsychiatric-diagnosis.

Lukava, T. (2022). Two sides of the same coin: Accessibility practices and neurodivergent users' experience of extended reality (Doctoral dissertation, University College London).

McGill, M. (2021, November). Extended reality (XR) and the erosion of anonymity and privacy (IEEE SA Industry Connections report). IEEE Standards Association.

Mey, G., & Dietrich, M. (2017). From text to image–Shaping a visual grounded theory methodology. *Historical Social Research/Historische Sozialforschung, 42*, 280–300.

Mondada, L. (2018). Multiple temporalities of language and body in interaction: Challenges for transcribing multimodality. *Research on Language and Social Interaction, 51*(1), 85–106.

Newbutt, N., & Bradley, R. (2025). Exploring ethical research issues related to extended reality technologies used with autistic populations. Journal of Responsible Technology, 21, 100102

Newbutt, N., Glaser, N., Sonley Francois, M., Schmidt, M., & Cobb, S. (2024). How are autistic people involved in the design of extended reality technologies? A systematic literature review. *Journal of Autism and Developmental Disorders, 54*(11), 4232–4258. https://doi.org/10.1007/s10803-023-06130-3

Pink, S. (2015). *Doing sensory ethnography* (2nd ed.). Sage.

Pridmore, P., & Bendelow, G. (1995). Images of health: Exploring beliefs of children using the 'draw-and-write' technique. *Health Education Journal, 54*(4), 473–488.

Rebenitsch, L., & Owen, C. (2016). Review on cybersickness in applications and visual displays. *Virtual Reality, 20*(2), 101–125.

Smith, J. A., Flowers, P., & Larkin, M. (2009). *Interpretative phenomenological analysis: Theory, method and research*. Sage.

Wang, P., Wu, P., Wang, J., Chi, H. L., & Wang, X. (2018). A critical review of the use of virtual reality in construction engineering education and training. *International journal of Environmental Research and Public Health, 15*(6), 1204.

Zhang, X., Chen, Y., Hu, L., & Wang, Y. (2022). The metaverse in education: Definition, framework, features, potential applications, challenges, and future research topics. *Frontiers in Psychology, 13*, 1016300.

CHAPTER 7

From Insight to Impact: Shaping the Next Generation of Immersive Neurodiversity Rese arch

Hypothesis-driven research is an essential research paradigm that involves creating and evaluating new ideas and hypotheses to lead future studies (Clark, 1963). This method can be extremely beneficial in the research of complicated and multiple disorders such as neurodiversity, where many elements remain unknown and undiscovered. Aside from hypothesis-generating research, there are several more ways that can help us better understand neurodivergence and related diseases. Mårtensson et al. (2016) suggest that taking a multidisciplinary approach can lead to fresh insights and unique approaches.

Another key aspect to consider how our understanding of neurodiversity might be applied to different situations and contexts. Autism research, for example, could help us comprehend other conditions like ADHD, anxiety disorders, and depression. Similarly, measures created to help autistic persons may be useful in other settings, such as school, healthcare, and the workplace. Giving neurodivergent people a voice and including them in the study process is also essential for producing meaningful insights and establishing relevant and successful therapies (Hart, 2025; Den Houting, 2019). This includes acknowledging the neurodivergent community's diversity of experiences and viewpoints, as well as actively seeking out and respecting the input of those who have lived experience. In this book, I did not actively use Participatory Action Research (PAR) (Kindon et al., 2008), but did emphasize the person-centric approach and

S. Savickaite, *Exploring Neurodiversity Through Virtual Reality*,
https://doi.org/10.1007/978-3-032-19636-1_7

allowed our autistic participants to freely engage with the virtual drawing task. It has also addressed the power imbalance that is frequently reported in empirical investigations (Emerson, 1964), which was an unexpected discovery in our research and should be investigated further.

Furthermore, visual communication is a significant research technique since it may assist express complicated concepts and conclusions in an understandable manner to a non-expert audience (Kenney, 2010). Giving voice to the community is a vital facet of research, especially in subjects like public health and social sciences. Researchers can obtain a deeper understanding of the issue and develop more effective interventions and policies that are responsive to community needs by giving the community a voice and decreasing power imbalances.

Perceptual Style and Neurodivergence

Throughout the empirical chapters, we highlight the necessity of a multidimensional approach to neurodivergence, particularly autism and ADHD. We also show the significance of attention in VR sketching assignments. However, further research is needed to grasp the intricacies of these individual differences, particularly what methods are used and what they imply about perceptual disparities. Unlike the prior studies discussed in Chaps. 1 and 2, none of the groups investigated showed a strong global or local preference. The next question is to conduct direct empirical tests of attentional style on drawing tactics. Another debate is if the relative consistency of drawing technique can be related to masking, which occurs when neurodivergent people acquire the "rules" of how they "should be" drawing early in life. For example, Stephen Wiltshire's savant abilities were discovered early in life, as chronicled by the BBC, and he has been permitted to pursue his unique style of sketching ever since (see Chap. 1). Perhaps we could look into how sketching and other creative activities are taught in schools, and how neurodivergent youngsters may create differently.

Although we did not intend to design a therapeutic tool, but rather to allow neurodivergent individuals to experiment with a new communication tool, we observed that employing arts-based and Think Aloud methods in VR may have therapeutic benefits. Diagnosed and non-diagnosed groups found the simple and controllable atmosphere relaxing, and they frequently communicated their personal experiences and inner thoughts without prompting. This could be attributed to the lower power imbalance between the researcher and the participant in our experimental setup. When participants are in VR, they cannot see the researcher, who only gives general directions and advice verbally. This decreases the "'social' load" of the experiment, as opposed to the traditional circumstance in which volunteers would have to interact with the researcher face-to-face.

Future Research Methods

The neurodiversity movement has improved knowledge, empowerment, and fairness. Further development necessitates a more nuanced paradigm that circumvents two extremes: (i) pathologizing by default and (ii) categorizing every neurodivergence as merely a difference. In light of cognitive continuity, we ought to substitute absolute assertions with context-dependent ones: an identical neurotype may represent a minor variation in certain aspects and contexts, and a deficiency in others, even in the absence of ableism (May, 2025).

Human neurocognitive variety exists within a common psychological framework; disparities frequently pertain to degrees of variation. When neurotypes are treated more as personality qualities, people can keep their identity, community, and accommodations. Diagnostic categories may persist for pragmatic purposes, although they ought not to be reified. A sophisticated understanding of neurodiversity prioritizes respect, inclusivity, and support, while recognizing variety and the validity of varied first-person perspectives on treatment and identity (May, 2025).

From PAR to Co-created XR: Who Decides What the Questions Are and What the Medium Is?

Neurodivergent Participatory Action study (PAR) emphasizes significant, decision-making engagement of neurodivergent individuals throughout the study continuum, encompassing agenda-setting, design, analysis, and dissemination. Millington and colleagues contend that Participatory Action Research (PAR) directly addresses the enduring disjunction between academic and community priorities in autism research, a disparity exacerbated by medical-model frameworks and the "double empathy problem," which refers to the mutual misunderstandings between autistic and non-autistic individuals. They suggest PAR as an ethical perspective and a pragmatic approach for developing VR that accommodates neurodivergent users: co-design identifies sensory stressors to mitigate, interaction affordances that alleviate cognitive load, and the accessibility standards that manufacturers and app developers currently lack. In short, PAR gives a governance structure for who gets to designate which perceptual distinctions matter—and how technology should satisfy them.

When PAR is combined with VR drawing (e.g., OpenBrush/Tilt Brush), users can express perception in a manner that words frequently fail to convey. Research and design reports indicate that VR drawing can facilitate flow, alleviate anxiety, and create therapeutic and art-therapy opportunities for autistic children, while also highlighting deficiencies in existing tools, which were not specifically designed to meet the needs of autistic individuals, necessitating participatory customization (Tan et al., 2025; Andrunyk et al., 2023). Because strokes are volumetric and dynamic, users can "draw" the felt quality of sound, motion, or crowding—as density, vibration, rhythm, or form—co-creating artifacts that researchers and peers can walk about and talk about without having to put them into clinical terms. In practice, PAR promises that participants will not only decide what to study together, but also help create the medium through which they share their experiences.

Intersectionality: Charting Spectra, Not Compartments

Intersectionality tells us that neurodivergence is not just one thing (Fig. 7.1). Developmental stage, co-occurring characteristics (e.g., ADHD alongside autistic features), gender, and culture significantly influence perception and expression. Reviews of visual perception in autism have already revealed heterogeneous profiles influenced by attention and higher-order mechanisms (Chung & Son, 2020). Concurrently, VR-based research programs are employing immersive tasks to investigate individual differences in motion processing and sensory integration among autistic and ADHD traits (Savickaite et al., 2022). PAR-guided VR drawing allows participants to layer different factors. For example, a woman with autism who was diagnosed late and has synesthesia can sculpt how speech "feels" in a busy clinic; an autistic person with ADHD can show how attention "pulls" or "snaps" during a search task; and a teen who does not talk much can mark where a room gets too bright or too loud. Drawings serve

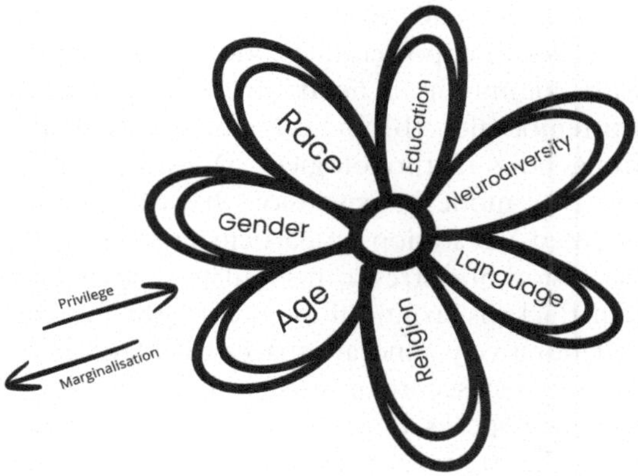

Fig. 7.1 A visual representation of intersecting identity characteristics

as recordings of engagement and avoidance across time, allowing for analysis akin to behavioral traces while retaining their status as expressions owned by individuals.

Considering synesthesia and aphantasia as mere "curiosities" obscures their prevalence and significance in models of perception and images. Recent research employs HMD-VR to simulate synesthetic concurrents, enabling non-synesthetes to experience a semblance of cross-sensory mappings (e.g., tone-to-shape/color, timbre-to-texture) (see previous chapters). This approach explicitly positions VR as a medium for disseminating the phenomenology to others (e.g., clinicians, caregivers, peers). Likewise, qualitative projects are utilizing VR drawing with OpenBrush to investigate how aphantasic participants manage tasks that conventionally rely on visual imagery, rendering the lack of imagery comprehensible through the strategies and 3D artifacts produced (currently ongoing work) (e.g., "What can VR reveal about perceptual differences in aphantasia?"). When viewed through the lens of PAR, these activities stop making rare things seem "strange" and instead show the variety of neurodivergent spectrum.

Culture and Drawing as a Common Language

Cross-cultural studies reveal both universal and systematic cultural variations in the recognition, interpretation, and discourse surrounding autistic symptoms (de Leeuw et al., 2020; Carruthers et al., 2020 (2024)).

Current demands to decolonize autism research emphasize the necessity of reallocating power, methodology, and epistemological practices to align with community-defined objectives and Indigenous or locally situated epistemologies (BPS; Lechene, J., 2024; current viewpoints including Indigenous methodologies). Drawing, akin to music, serves as a nearly universal mode of expression that transcends linguistic barriers. In PAR-oriented VR sessions, a participant from a culture that discourages direct discussion of distress can simulate sensory overwhelm as a darkening field that thickens around fluorescent lights; a recently immigrated family can collaboratively annotate spaces with layered drawings that indicate where routines feel secure or disrupted. These traces do not depend on how well someone speaks English (or any other language), thus they help people from different cultures and languages connect while still keeping the author's identity. They also travel: a clinic in one nation can load and see the same drawing made in another country, which makes it possible to compare sites and cultures in a real time.

A growing body of work shows that participant-led, co-produced research in autism and across neurodivergence is not just ethically preferable—it materially changes *what* gets studied and *how* findings are used. Practice guidelines developed with autistic partners set out concrete standards for power-sharing, accessible consent, fair payment, and role clarity—guardrails that help XR/VR projects avoid tokenism and sustain genuine partnership across the full research arc (Nicolaidis et al., 2019; Gowen, 2019). Empirical case studies echo this: participatory projects repeatedly report shifts in priorities (e.g., from narrow symptom reduction to sensory, mental health, and quality-of-life concerns), richer recruitment of under-heard groups, and outputs that communities actually adopt (Stark et al., 2021; Pellicano & colleagues, 2022). Methodologically, participant-generated media—from sketching to other non-verbal artifacts—capture everyday experiences and values without forcing translation into clinician language, a critical affordance for minimally speaking communicators and for cross-cultural contexts. Beyond autism, participatory translational models now extend to ADHD–autism intersections, positioning neurodivergent youth and adults as co-analysts of data and co-designers of tools—exactly the stance VR drawing benefits from, where people can *author* and *interpret* their perceptual traces (Sonuga-Barke et al., 2024). Recent co-design reports and scoping reviews also stress infrastructure: advisory boards, open practices, and iterative reflection to keep collaborations reciprocal and resilient over time—again, a strong fit for long-horizon XR programs (Le Cunff et al., 2023.). Together, these sources strengthen the claim that participant-led approaches are foundational for VR/drawing work that seeks to represent intersectional neurodivergent experience—spanning speech access, culture and migration, gender, and co-occurring traits—while producing artifacts communities recognize as accurate and useful (Grove et al., 2023).

Decolonizing methodologies in autism research assert that knowledge is produced not solely via written or verbal discourse but also through narrative, imagery, ritual, and many embodied activities. Bruno et al. (2025) contend that the incorporation of Indigenous epistemologies necessitates the acknowledgment of non-verbal and creative expressions as valid evidence, hence redistributing authority from conventional Western research frameworks. This strongly relates to the idea of using drawing in VR as a universal, arts-based language. Similar to pūrākau (Māori storytelling) or Anishinaabe Dream Methodology, which utilize narrative and imagery as legitimate epistemic practices, VR drawing allows autistic individuals—including those who are minimally verbal, from diverse linguistic backgrounds, or navigating multiple cultural identities—to externalize and share their lived experiences without dependence on verbal communication. Situated within participatory action research, this conceptualizes art not merely as an ancillary illustration but as a pivotal communicative instrument for transcending cultural and linguistic barriers, while simultaneously recognizing perceptual variations such as synesthesia or aphantasia as essential components of the neurodivergent spectrum (Bruno et al., 2025; Shawanda & Manitowabi, 2023).

A pertinent example from performance studies is Rai's "Decolonising Attention in and through Live Art," which contends that UK live-art practice is currently redefining the organization of attention by emphasizing embodied, relational, and culturally situated modes of perception as part of a broader decolonizing movement (Rai, 2024). When you read this with neurodivergent PAR and VR drawing in mind, it makes the case stronger that art can be a way to communicate without words. This is because when attention is treated as a shared medium (through gesture, presence, pacing, proximity, and image), participants do not have to rely on text or speech to make knowledge together. In practical terms, VR drawing can be performed as a sort of live art, where players collaboratively construct perceptual realms in real time, encouraging others to join them despite linguistic and cultural disparities. This fits with Rai's decolonizing focus on changing who leads the encounter by changing how they sense it. It also provides a conceptual bridge between arts practice and research that is led by participants and supports neurodiversity.

Urbistondo Cano and Simon (2022) contest the notion of a singular autism spectrum, advocating for Multi-Spectra Living—a perspective that acknowledges individuals as fluid, contextually responsive, and positioned across multiple axes (e.g., agency, sensory load, social roles, cultural rituals) rather than situated on a single linear continuum of "more/less autistic." They demonstrate how diagnostic language can solidify identities and emphasize deficit frameworks, whereas actual lives are influenced by temporal, spatial, interpersonal, and intersecting societal constraints (such as sexism, racism, homophobia, ageism, etc.). A significant caution is their concept of "splintersectionality": quotidian and professional practices that emphasize one characteristic (e.g., "autism") to the detriment of others, thus perpetuating bias and legal shortcomings. In response, they advocate for lenticularity (simultaneously engaging with many perspectives), a decolonial mindset, and epistemic witnessing, ensuring that knowledge about autism is regarded as contextual, relational, and responsible to lived experiences rather than being detached from them (Urbistondo Cano & Simon, 2022).

When you look at it this way, drawing in VR (and other arts-based methodologies) is a good way to do intersectional research since it is both fluid and structured. It is flexible because it lets people talk about changing experiences without having to give a single vocal account. The artifacts are designed so that they leave behind analyzable traces (density, timing, revisitation, layering). This allows for epistemic witnessing that respects authorship while also allowing for systematic comparison across contexts and identities. The multi-spectra perspective validates the inclusion of synesthesia and aphantasia as typical variations within neurodivergence, rather than as uncommon phenomena. Virtual reality drawing can depict cross-modal concurrents or the absence of imagery as first-person spatial forms, positioning these differences in relation to gendered, racialized, and cultural factors rather than in isolation. In practice, lenticular protocols can be included into sessions by rotating perspectives (participant, family, culture-specific facilitators), altering environmental contexts (quiet/home versus public/bright), and iteratively layering drawings to illustrate the dynamic interplay between perception and identity. This puts Multi-Spectra Living into action in a research workflow that is co-authored, culturally aware, and strong in terms of analysis.

Arts-Based Practices and Decolonization

The concept of drawing and other alternative forms of expression as decolonizing techniques is exemplified by Tojisha Kenkyu in Japan. This type of "self-directed research" originated from the Bethel House psychiatric community in Hokkaido, where individuals with mental health and neurodevelopmental conditions commenced documenting their experiences collectively, rather than having them mediated by medical or professional frameworks (Ayaya, 2025). Instead of looking for a cure or a way to diagnose their "problems", participants used different ways of communicating, like diagrams, sketches, personal metaphors, and collaborative storytelling, to map out their symptoms and how they saw them. This movement has been called "radical" since it goes against the authority of psychiatric diagnosis and instead uses lived experience as the main source of proof. Tojisha Kenkyu can be viewed as an integral component of a broader decolonizing movement, aimed at liberating knowledge creation from the hegemony of clinical and predominantly Western psychiatric frameworks, while prioritizing neurodivergent perspectives on their own terms.

In this setting, drawing serves a dual purpose: it functions as both a medium of communication and a means of solidarity. When words do not work, sketches and other shared visual artifacts can help you remember sensory aberrations, interior pictures, or broken perceptual states. The group can then talk about these pictures, come up with new meanings for them, and build on them together. This is similar to how art-based methodologies are being employed more and more in neurodiversity studies to give shape to experiences that are often ignored or pushed aside. For example, Kim (2017) illustrates how lived experience, when artistically externalized, can disrupt the psychiatric gaze and enable neurodivergent persons to regain control over their narratives.

A comparable mindset is evident in research pertaining to cross-cultural and intersectional interpretations of neurodivergence. In a case study on participatory art practices, McGuire (2024) emphasizes that drawing (not in VR) served as a non-verbal medium for autistic individuals to express their inner experiences, especially in situations where spoken language was either unavailable or significantly stigmatized. Through participation workshops, participants were encouraged to depict their sensory environments, feelings, and perceptions through sketching, facilitating a more profound communication not only among autistic peers but also between autistic and neurotypical individuals. The study demonstrated how these images transcended cultural boundaries, rendering them comprehensible to audiences that might typically possess limited or medicalized perceptions of autism. In this context, sketching serves as a decolonizing act: it undermines the authority of clinical categories by providing direct, contextualized narratives of perceptual experience.

Tojisha Kenkyu and participatory drawing techniques combined show how alternate ways of communicating can help people get rid of the stigma of illness and build bridges of understanding between cultures. They also show how neurodivergence is connected to other things: perceptual variations like synesthesia, aphantasia, or autistic sensory profiles are not just exceptional cases, but part of a range of human experiences that can be articulated, understood, and valued in different cultural contexts. These methods use drawing as a universal language, like music, but frequently better at expressing experienced sensory states right away. This opens up avenues for people of all neurotypes, cultures, and beyond the limits of medical or therapeutic discourse to talk to each other.

Drawing and collaborative art have been used as ways for neurodiverse and neurotypical people to communicate with each other in other contexts in East Asia. In Japan, community "participation art" workshops for autistic kids not only helped them express themselves and make friends, but they also had measurable physiological effects that showed they were bonding with others, with autistic kids' salivary oxytocin levels rising more after the activities (Tanaka et al., 2020). A six-week Creative Arts-based Parent Training program in South Korea used drawing to improve communication between parents and children and give adults who care for children a look into how they see the world (Park, 2021; Park, 2022). Kim and Chung (2023) show that tablets and simple creative apps can help teens with intellectual disabilities co-create visual tales in a less-stigmatizing setting, keeping drawing at the center while making it more accessible.

Systematic painting sessions at Beijing's Golden Wings program have long combined expression with public showings. These sessions have helped families and audiences "see" inner sensory logics and reduce stigma through shows (Xu, 2024). In Taiwan, a university enrichment program for young autistic artists showed that drawing could be used for more than just therapy (Kuo et al., 2016), and public exhibitions in Taipei showed children's paintings as part of civic culture, making it normal for different ways of seeing things to be shown in mainstream settings (Taiwan Today, 2014). In West Asia, art has also been used as a way to connect with others.

In Iran, studies of family drawings made by autistic kids and their parents showed everyday differences in how the kids saw things, how space was used, and which symbols they chose. These differences provided non-diagnostic "third objects" for discussion and thought (Saneei & Haghayegh, 2011). In the Levant and Gulf, teachers and services have made drawing a normal part of how they teach and help students. An initiative in Jordan to train teachers has created visual arts programs for autistic students that use side-by-side sketching to help them learn to take turns, make routines, and name their feelings in both school and home settings (Al-Saqer, 2023). Drawing is seen as a low-cost and culturally acceptable way to start a conversation in places where diagnoses perceived negatively.

Drawing is often used as a way for people in the Americas to share their stories and as a museum-level cultural activity. Indigenous-led galleries and workshops in Chiapas, Mexico, work "by–for–with" local families (e.g., Galería MUY). They see drawings and paintings as shared cultural objects and everyday storytelling tools instead of clinical outputs. This is in line with decolonial ideas that people who live it should own their work and knowledge should stay with them (Galería MUY, 2020). Drawing circles and portable image-making are used in psychosocial programs along the US–Mexico corridor so that families can bring visual stories with them to clinics, classrooms, and advocacy meetings (United Nations Children's Fund, 2024). US museums have also changed the way galleries work by turning them into workshops where families work together to make pictures about how they see things and their daily lives. This is done to reduce clinical stigma by showing neurodiverse expression as culture (Dallas Museum of Art, 2017). In the US, American Indian and Alaska Native youth who participate in culturally based art programs say they feel less stressed and have better moods. These programs also offer safe, group ways to talk about sensory and social experiences through drawing and mixed media (Pepic et al., 2022). Community-driven assessments that include art therapy and visual journals reveal priorities that surveys often miss (Basto et al., 2012). There is a lot of writing about Indigenous arts that says traditional visual arts like weaving, beadwork, and symbolic drawing help people feel like they belong and keep their communities together. Pictures are better than questionnaires at getting across language and power barriers, making it easier for people to understand how services work (Kaimal & Arslanbek, 2020).

Supported studio models in Europe and Oceania see drawing as a language that can only be understood in the artist's own words. Inuti's long-running studios in Sweden focus on the sketchbooks, serial drawings, and large-format works of autistic and intellectually disabled artists. Curators learn each artist's visual grammar, and exhibitions and zines let people interact with the work as modern culture (Inuti, 2025; EOA/Outside In, 2019). In Denmark, the GAIA Museum's studio programs show pattern systems, synesthetic mappings, and iterative line-work as modern art, not therapy. For many neurodiverse artists, drawing is their first language (GAIA Museum, 2021). In the same way, the ArtBrut Gallery in Wrocław, Poland, lets guests enter each artist's logic—grids, taxonomies, and schematic maps—through drawing cycles and notebooks, and then continues the conversation through interactive publications (ArtBrut Gallery, 2024–2025). In Australia, Studio A creates professional paths from drawing to murals, illustration, animation, and textiles. Sketches are turned into plans for cross-disciplinary production, which helps neurotypical partners work with neurodiverse perspectives without labeling them (Studio A, 2019–2025). The iNDx exhibitions at Tūhura Otago Museum in Aotearoa New Zealand "show, not tell," with autistic curators in charge of the labels. Susan Te Kahurangi King, who stopped talking as a child, used drawing as a major form of communication for many years, from detailed notebooks to mature abstraction (iNDx, 2023–2025; ICA Miami, 2016; The Guardian (Cocozza), 2017).

Drawing is becoming more and more noticeable as a form of public culture and activism in the Caribbean and Africa as well. Through exhibitions and community partnerships, the mARTism project in Jamaica has made a young autistic artist's drawings more visible. The project uses shared walls and easy-to-find materials to start a talk about autism as a difference rather than a deficit (Jamaica Gleaner, 2020; mARTism, 2023). In Nigeria and Ghana, drawing and comics are used with autistic youth in community arts programs and exhibitions to start policy conversations and turn recurring sensory themes into useful ways to help kids at home and school. More recently, high-profile public art has been used in Nigeria to fight stigma and make autistic artists more visible (Vanguard, 2025; AP News, 2025; Harambee Arts Partners in Ghana, 2024).

Chapter Conclusion

This chapter has argued that the next generation of immersive neurodiversity research must translate insight into impact by shifting both *what* we study and *who* gets to define it. Synthesizing empirical findings with multidimensional theories of perception and attention, it positioned neurodivergence as multi-spectra living—contextual, intersecting, and shaped by culture, gender, development, and co-occurring traits—rather than a single diagnostic axis or deficit narrative. Across autism, ADHD, synesthesia, and aphantasia, VR drawing emerged as a distinctive participatory medium: it allows sensory, emotional, and cognitive experience to be externalized as artifacts that function simultaneously as data, dialogue, and advocacy, while reducing power asymmetries and widening access for those for whom speech is not the primary channel. Framed within PAR and decolonial methodologies, these practices reconfigure immersive technology from a novelty on the hype cycle to an epistemic intervention—one that demands ethical infrastructure, co-governance, and open, adaptable tools—so that immersive research can produce knowledge that communities recognize, can use, and can carry into education, healthcare, policy, and public understanding.

References

Al-Saqer, M. (2023). Supporting children with autism using visual arts. *Jordanian Journal of Arts, 16*(2), 1–14.

Andrunyk, V., Kalka, N., & Shestakevych, T. (2023, June). Virtual reality in art therapy for children with autism. In *MoMLeT+ DS* (pp. 514–525).

AP News. (2025). Nigerian teenager sets world painting record.

ArtBrut Gallery (Wrocław). (2024–2025). artbrut.com.pl.

Ayaya, S. (2025). Tōjisha-Kenkyū on Autism in Japan: Against Epistemic Injustices and Tokenism. *Journal of Social Issues, 81*(4), e70026.

Basto, E., Warson, E., & Barbour, S. (2012). Exploring American Indian adolescents' needs through a communitydriven study. The Arts in Psychotherapy, 39(2), 134–142.

Bruno, G., Lindblom, A., Tupou, J., Kewene, F., Waisman, T. C., & Magiati, I. (2025). Decolonizing autism research: Integrating Indigenous ways of knowing, being, and doing. *Autism, 29*(11), 2637–2643.

Carruthers, S., Pickles, A., Slonims, V., Howlin, P., & Charman, T. (2020). Beyond intervention into daily life: A systematic review of generalisation following social communication interventions for young children with autism. *Autism Research, 13*(4), 506–522.

Chung, S., & Son, J. W. (2020). Visual perception in autism spectrum disorder: A review of neuroimaging studies. *Journal of the Korean Academy of Child and Adolescent Psychiatry, 31*(3), 105.

Clark, A. (1963). Hypothesis and theory in science. *Philosophy of Science, 30*(4), 311–322.
Cocozza, P. (2017, May 31). Silent witness: The outsider art of Susan Te Kahurangi King. *The Guardian*. https://www.theguardian.com/artanddesign/2017/may/31/susan-te-kahurangi-king-silent-outsiderart
Dallas Museum of Art (C3). (2017). Autism programs & studio making. blog.dma.org
de Leeuw, A., Happé, F., & Hoekstra, R. A. (2020). A conceptual framework for understanding the cultural and contextual factors on autism across the globe. *Autism Research, 13*(7), 1029–1050.
Den Houting, J. (2019). Neurodiversity: An insider's perspective. *Autism, 23*(2), 271–273. https://doi.org/10.1177/1362361318820762
Emerson, R. M. (1964). Power-dependence relations: Two experiments. *Sociometry, 27*, 282–298.
European Outsider Art Association / Outside In. (2019). EOA Conference hosted by Inuti, Stockholm.
GAIA Museum Outsider Art (Randers), https://gaiamuseum.dk/english/
Galería MUY (Chiapas). (2020–2025). galeriamuy.org
Gowen, E. (2019). Autistic adults and participatory research. *Autism, 23*(6), 1–4. https://doi.org/10.1177/1362361319847522
Grove, R., Clapham, H., Moodie, T., Gurrin, S., & Hall, G. (2023). 'Living in a world that's not about us': The impact of everyday life on the health and well-being of autistic women and gender diverse people. *Women's Health, 19*. https://doi.org/10.1177/17455057231189542
Harambee Arts partners (Ghana). (2024). Using creative art forms in managing autism in Ghana.
Hart, D. E. (2025). Is "neurodiversity" the proper nomenclature for mental health gradation?. *AJOB Neuroscience, 16*(1), 46–48.
ICA Miami. (2016). Susan Te Kahurangi King.
INDX Shows. (n.d.). iNDx (2023)–(2025). INDX Shows. https://indx-shows.co.uk/
Inuti Foundation (Stockholm) (2025), https://outsiderartassociation.eu/member/b-i/inuti.
Jamaica Gleaner. (2020). Young autistic artist defies odds with mARTism.
Kaimal, G., & Arslanbek, A. (2020). *Indigenous and traditional visual artistic practices*: Implications for art therapy clinical practice and research. Frontiers in psychology, 11, 1320.
Kenney, K. (2010). *Visual communication research designs*. Routledge.
Kim, E. (2017). *Curative violence: Rehabilitating disability, gender, and sexuality in modern Korea*. Duke University Press.

Kim, J., & Chung, Y. J. (2023). A case study of group art therapy using digital media for adolescents with intellectual disabilities. Frontiers in psychiatry, 14, 1172079.

Kindon, S., Pain, R., & Kesby, M. (2008). *Participatory action research approaches and methods: Connecting people, participation and place*. Routledge.

Kuo, C.-C., Kuang, C.-C., & Dai, L.-T. (2016). Learning experiences of young artists with ASD in a University Enrichment Program (Taiwan).

Le Cunff, Y., et al. (2023). Co-design approaches in autism and neurodiversity research. Frontiers. *Education, 8*, 1183456. https://doi.org/10.3389/feduc.2023.1183456

Lechêne, J. (2024, January 2). Decolonising autism. The British Psychological Society. https://www.bps.org.uk/psychologist/decolonising-autism

Mårtensson, J., Eriksson, J., Bodammer, N. C., Lindgren, M., Johansson, M., Nyberg, L., & Lövdén, M. (2016). Growth of language-related brain areas after foreign language learning. *NeuroImage, 133*, 1–10.

mARTism (Jamaica). (2023). Autism Awareness Exhibition.

May, J. (2025). Neurodiversity with nuance. *Neuroethics, 18*(2), 30.

McGuire, K. (2024). Examining the impacts of mindfulness martial arts intervention on neural indices of auditory Selective attention In Youth With ADHD (Doctoral dissertation, Doctoral dissertation, Mount Saint Vincent University)).

Nicolaidis, C., Raymaker, D., Kapp, S. K., Baggs, A., Ashkenazy, E., McDonald, K., Weiner, M., & Zuckerman, K. (2019). Participatory research with autistic communities. *Autism, 23*(4), 1–13. https://doi.org/10.1177/1362361319830523

Park, J. E. (2021). Effectiveness of creative arts-based parent training for parents with children with Autism Spectrum Disorder. The Arts in Psychotherapy, 76, 101837.

Park, J. E. J. (2022). A parent-focused creative approach as a treatment for a high-functioning child with autism spectrum disorder (ASD) in korea: a case study. *International Journal of Environmental Research and Public Health, 19*(13), 7836.

Pellicano, E., et al. (2022). Participatory autism research and community priority setting. *Autism, 26*(2), 1–18. https://doi.org/10.1177/13623613221077921

Pepic, V., Shuler, S., & Secakuku, A. (2022). Evaluating the impact of a culturally sensitive art program on the resilience, perceived stress, and mood of urban American Indian youth. American Indian and Alaska Native Mental Health Research (Online), 29(1), 37–58.

Rai, A. S. (2024). Decolonising attention in and through live art. *Contemporary Theatre Review, 34*(3), 346–362.

Saneei, A., & Haghayegh, S. A. (2011). Family drawings of Iranian children with autism and their family members. The Arts in psychotherapy, 38(5), 333–339.

Savickaite, S., Husselman, T. A., Taylor, R., Millington, E., Hayashibara, E., & Arthur, T. (2022). Applications of virtual reality (VR) in autism research: Current trends and taxonomy of definitions. *Journal of Enabling Technologies, 16*(2), 147–154.

Shawanda, A., & Manitowabi, J. (2023). Anishinaabe dream methodology. *Turtle Island Journal of Indigenous Health, 1*(3) https://doi.org/10.33137/tijih.v1i3.38566

Sonuga-Barke, E. J. S., et al. (2024). Neurodiversity and participatory priorities. *Journal of Child Psychology and Psychiatry*. https://doi.org/10.1111/jcpp.13889

Stark, R., et al. (2021). Co-produced autism research priorities. *Frontiers in Psychology, 12*, 642498. https://doi.org/10.3389/fpsyg.2021.642498

Studio A (Sydney). (2019–2025). studioa.org.au

Taiwan Today. (2014). Autism painting exhibition wraps up in Taipei. taiwantoday.tw

Tanaka, K., et al. (2020). Art-based programs and oxytocin secretion among autistic children. *Frontiers in Psychology, 11*, 598124. https://doi.org/10.3389/fpsyg.2020.598124

Tan, X., Xu, Y., & Rui, G. (2025). Community mobilisation through translation: A sustainable framework for participatory planning. *Urban Planning, 10*, 1–13.

UNICEF. (2020). *MHPSS for Families at the US–Mexico*. Field Guide.

United Nations Children's Fund. (2024, November). In focus: Protecting children affected by migration and forced displacement. https://www.unicef.org/eca/reports/focus-protecting-children-affected-migration-and-forceddisplacement

Urbistondo Cano, F., & Simon, G. (2022). From autism spectrum to multi-spectra living. *Murmurations: Journal of Transformative Systemic Practice, 4*(2), 101–147.

Vanguard (Nigeria). (2025). FG, Lagos celebrate autistic teenager's historic world record in art.

Xu, X. (2024). Exploring the art rehabilitation model for children with ASD—Golden Wings (Beijing).

Concluding Remarks

Toward Authentic, Inclusive, and Experiential Knowledge

This book began, as outlined in the preface, from a personal and academic convergence: an interest in perception, an artistic background, and a growing engagement with neurodiversity and immersive technologies. From the outset, the aim was not simply to *study* neurodivergence, but to rethink how knowledge about perceptual and cognitive difference is produced, whose voices are privileged, and which methods are deemed legitimate. Across the chapters, this work has argued consistently for a shift away from deficit-led, purely verbal, and laboratory-bound approaches, toward person-centered, creative, and immersive methodologies capable of capturing lived experience in richer and more equitable ways.

Three interlinked commitments introduced in the preface run throughout the book:

1. Centering neurodivergent perspectives as epistemically valuable, not merely as objects of explanation.
2. Challenging traditional research hierarchies by using creative, arts-based, and participatory approaches that redistribute power.

S. Savickaite, *Exploring Neurodiversity Through Virtual Reality*,
https://doi.org/10.1007/978-3-032-19636-1

3. Using immersive technologies—particularly VR—not as novelty tools, but as epistemic bridges between internal experience and shared understanding.

Chapter 1 established the conceptual foundations of neurodiversity, neurodivergence, and neurotypes, positioning perceptual and cognitive variation as a fundamental feature of humanity rather than a deviation from a norm. Importantly, this chapter reframed diagnosis as *contextual and pragmatic* rather than definitive, emphasizing lived experience, sensory worlds, and non-verbal expression as legitimate forms of knowledge. This framing set the ethical and epistemological tone for the book: understanding neurodivergence requires methods that can meet people where language alone often fails.

Chapter 2 deepened this argument by examining perceptual differences—particularly in autism—through theories of local–global processing, sensory integration, and autobiographical accounts. By juxtaposing experimental literature with first-person narratives, the chapter demonstrated how conventional methodologies often struggle to access the *felt texture* of perception. This theoretical groundwork directly informed the need for methods capable of externalizing perceptual experience without forcing it into predefined verbal categories.

Chapter 3 introduced virtual reality as precisely such a method. Moving beyond the constraints of the traditional laboratory, VR was framed as a space where experimental control and ecological validity coexist. Crucially, VR was not treated as inherently beneficial; rather, its value lay in its capacity for immersion, interaction, and presence, which—when thoughtfully designed—can reduce social load, increase agency, and allow participants to engage on their own terms. This chapter positioned immersive technology as a methodological *means*, not an end.

Chapter 4 marked a pivotal shift by emphasizing VR drawing as both method and mode of expression. Drawing—particularly in volumetric, immersive space—was shown to function as a bridge between perception, embodiment, and communication. By engaging with aesthetics, empathy, and the double empathy dilemma, this chapter argued that art-based encounters are not merely expressive but relational: they create shared cognitive and affective spaces in which understanding can emerge across neurotypes. Here, creative practice was reframed as a legitimate research instrument rather than an illustrative supplement.

Chapter 5 provided empirical depth through detailed case studies involving autistic individuals, synesthetes, and people with aphantasia. These studies demonstrated how VR-based arts methods allow participants to *show rather than tell* their experiences, revealing perceptual qualities—fragmentation, absence, intensity, rhythm—that resist conventional measurement. Importantly, the findings highlighted variability within neurodivergent groups, reinforcing the argument against monolithic accounts and underscoring the ethical necessity of flexible, participant-led approaches.

Chapter 6 addressed one of the most persistent challenges raised by this work: how to analyze and ethically interpret multimodal data. By critically examining the limitations of existing qualitative frameworks, this chapter made explicit that methodological innovation must extend beyond data collection to analysis and representation. The discussion of multimodal ethnography, visual grounded theory, and sensory methodologies reinforced the central claim that drawings, movements, and immersive actions must be treated as data in their own right—not merely prompts for speech.

Chapter 7 looked forward, situating immersive, creative neurodiversity research within broader debates about participatory action research, intersectionality, and technological maturity. It argued that future work must move toward co-created XR, where neurodivergent individuals help define not only the questions asked, but also the media through which answers are explored. This chapter reinforced the idea that ethical research is inseparable from governance, accessibility, and shared decision-making.

Taken together, the chapters demonstrate that authentic understanding of underrepresented voices requires methodological plurality. Neurodivergent experiences, particularly those involving perception, imagery, and sensory processing, cannot be fully accessed through verbal report alone. Immersive and creative methods do not replace traditional approaches, but they expand the epistemic landscape, making space for forms of knowing that have long been marginalized.

Limitations

Several limitations must be acknowledged. First, many empirical studies presented involve small samples, which is appropriate for exploratory, qualitative, and arts-based research but limits generalizability. Second, the analytical frameworks for multimodal VR data remain underdeveloped; while this book critiques existing approaches and proposes directions, it does not offer a fully standardized solution. Third, access to VR technology, despite increasing availability, still poses practical and socioeconomic barriers, which must be considered when advocating immersive methods as inclusive tools. Finally, although this work emphasizes neurodivergent voices, participatory governance was not implemented to its fullest extent, leaving room for deeper co-production.

Future Directions

Future research should prioritize:

- Co-designed and participatory XR studies, where neurodivergent individuals are involved from agenda-setting through dissemination.
- Development of robust multimodal analytic frameworks that treat visual, embodied, and temporal data as equal to text.
- Longitudinal and cross-cultural studies exploring how neurodivergent perception interacts with gender, culture, education, and technology.
- Exploration of VR drawing and immersive art not only as research tools, but as knowledge-sharing and public engagement platforms.

Ultimately, this book argues that understanding neurodiversity is not solely a scientific challenge, but an ethical one. If psychology is to claim insight into the human mind, it must continue to expand the ways in which people are allowed to *show*, *shape*, and *share* their inner worlds.

Experimental Protocol/Framework

This work expands on Savickaite's (2024) study, Using Virtual Reality to Explore Individual Differences in Perception Due to Neurodiversity, in which I investigated how immersive virtual reality (VR) environments can support creative expression and perceptual-difference research through a person-centered, arts-based, and mixed-methods design. In a similar vein, the current protocol describes how arts-based research, think-aloud methodology, VR as a research platform, participatory (participant-centered) methodologies, and exploratory/hypothesis-generating approaches can be integrated and used to diverse situations. These are some of the main parts to get started before moving on to the STUDIO framework/protocol, which is intended to help scholars understand how the methodologies presented in Savickaite's thesis (2024) might be applied to other contexts. The protocol outlines crucial steps and their justifications, with accompanying questions and checklists to facilitate their completion.

Key Methods to Consider

Arts-based research involves using creative art forms (such as drawing, painting, theater, and digital art) not just for data collecting but also for meaning-making and dissemination (Nathan et al., 2023).

S. Savickaite, *Exploring Neurodiversity Through Virtual Reality*, https://doi.org/10.1007/978-3-032-19636-1

The think-aloud method involves participants verbalizing their cognitive processes while (or immediately after) executing a task, providing insight into cognition, decision-making, and experience (Sergiou et al., 2024).

Virtual reality as a research platform: VR provides immersive and controllable environments for eliciting behavior, perceptual responses, and creative involvement, hence creating new research opportunities (Mills, 2022).

Participatory research/participant-centered research: techniques in which participants (or their communities) act as co-investigators, co-designers, or co-creators of the research process, therefore shifting power and improving relevance (Vaughn, 2020; Cornwall, 1995).

Exploratory and hypothesis-generating work is research that focuses on examining phenomena, producing insights, improving intervention or measurement ideas, and guiding later stages of work rather than testing a specific a priori premise.

References

Cornwall, A. (1995). What is participatory research? *Social Science & Medicine, 41*(12), 1667–1676.

Mills, K. A. (2022). Virtual reality and embodiment in multimodal meaning-making. *Communication Monographs, 89*(2), 177–193.

Nathan, S., … (2023). The use of arts-based methodologies and methods with young people with complex psychosocial needs. *International Journal of Qualitative Methods, 22*, 1–12.

Savickaite, S. (2024). *Using virtual reality to explore individual differences in perception due to neurodiversity* (Unpublished doctoral thesis). University of Glasgow.

Sergiou, C-S., Gerstner, D., Nee, C., Elffers, H. & van Gelder, J.-L. (2024). Virtual reality-based retrospective think aloud (VR-RTA): A novel method for studying decision-making. *Crime Science, 13*(1), 39.

Vaughn, L. M. (2020). Participatory research methods – choice points in the research process. *Journal of Participatory Research Methods, 1*(1), 1–12.

STUDIO Framework

Skills & Readiness (Technical literacy and readiness)
Theoretical Grounding (Background and variables)
Upholding Data Integrity (Data management)
Design Development (Experimental design)
Involvement & Recruitment (Recruitment and logistics)
Oversight & Safety (Health and safety)

The **STUDIO Framework** provides a structured yet flexible approach for implementing arts-based research within virtual reality environments. Building on the methodological foundations outlined in Savickaite (2024), it translates the key theoretical principles of participatory, exploratory, and creative inquiry into a practical, stepwise protocol. The framework's name—STUDIO—symbolizes both the creative and collaborative space in which arts-based VR research takes place and the six core stages guiding its implementation: Skills & Readiness, Theoretical Grounding, Upholding Data Integrity, Design Development, Involvement & Recruitment, and Oversight & Safety. Together, these stages support researchers in moving from conceptualization to ethical and methodological rigor, while maintaining participant-centered, reflective practice. The STUDIO framework thus serves as a bridge between the arts-based and immersive methodologies discussed in Savickaite's work and their application across diverse research contexts, providing a foundation for consistency, transparency, and creativity in experimental design.

STUDIO One: Skills & Readiness

The first stage of the STUDIO framework, Skills & Readiness, addresses the preliminary considerations that underpin the successful implementation of arts-based research using immersive technologies. This stage focuses on technical literacy, accessibility, and researcher preparedness, ensuring that both the research team and participants are equipped to engage meaningfully with virtual reality (VR) or other digital drawing tools. While this framework can be adapted for two-dimensional or traditional arts-based methods, the use of VR introduces unique affordances such as heightened immersion, presence, and a reduction of power imbalances between researcher and participant. These qualities often make VR a preferred medium for participatory and exploratory arts-based research.

When employing VR drawing tools such as OpenBrush, which is freely available and compatible with standalone headsets like the Oculus Quest 2 or 3, it is important to consider both the technical setup and participant experience. These devices allow for live casting, enabling experimenters to monitor participants' creative processes and provide guidance as needed. Other headsets, such as the HTC Vive (tethered or wireless), may also be used; however, tethered setups require additional attention to participant safety to prevent tripping or entanglement. The physical environment should provide sufficient space for movement, allow for safe supervision, and ensure the experimenter has a clear view of participants' actions.

Equally important is the researcher's own technical proficiency—experimenters should be familiar with the OpenBrush palette, able to demonstrate its functions, and confident in instructing participants during onboarding. Preparation at this stage also involves establishing a clear plan for data recording and communication, ensuring participants understand what data will be captured, how it will be managed, and their rights within the process. These elements of readiness form the foundation upon which the rest of the STUDIO framework is built.

- Have I clearly defined why VR (or immersive technology) is being chosen over traditional 2D tools?
- Have I ensured accessibility to the chosen technology for all participants?
- Have I selected an appropriate headset (e.g., Oculus Quest 2/3, HTC Vive) and tested its suitability for the study?
- Is the research space large enough, safe, and arranged for effective participant monitoring?
- Have I familiarized myself with the functions of the drawing software (e.g., OpenBrush)?
- Can I confidently instruct participants on how to use the tools and troubleshoot technical issues?
- Have I planned how data (e.g., video, audio, or movement capture) will be recorded, stored, and communicated to participants?
- Have I prepared onboarding materials or demonstrations to introduce participants to the headset and controllers?
- Have I considered safety measures for both standalone and tethered headset use?
- Have I identified potential accessibility or sensory considerations for neurodivergent participants engaging in immersive environments?

STUDIO Two: Theoretical Grounding

The second stage of the STUDIO framework, Theoretical Grounding, ensures that the research is conceptually coherent, transparent, and aligned with its overarching aims. While this section is typically developed as part of a formal research proposal, incorporating it into the protocol, especially in a condensed, accessible form, ensures that all researchers involved in recruitment, data collection, or participant engagement are familiar with the study's rationale, variables, and methodological choices. This shared understanding is essential for maintaining consistency and accuracy in participant communication and for ensuring that the research process remains theoretically and ethically consistent.

At this stage, researchers should identify the core variables and research questions driving the study. Virtual reality platforms such as OpenBrush inherently generate a large volume of quantitative data (e.g., spatial coordinates, movement trajectories, timestamps), yet not all of it will be relevant to the study aims. Researchers should therefore specify which data streams will be used, how OpenBrush sketches will be exported, and how coordinate or movement data might be extracted for analysis.

In addition, if questionnaires or psychometric instruments are incorporated, whether as part of a mixed-methods or purely quantitative design, these should be clearly listed, along with references and justifications for their inclusion. Researchers should also plan when these instruments will be administered in relation to VR drawing sessions, allowing sufficient rest and acclimatization time to prevent fatigue, disorientation, or cybersickness.

This stage also provides an opportunity to collate all ethical documentation, including consent forms, debrief sheets, and risk assessments, into a cohesive section of the protocol. Whether these forms are digital or paper-based, integrating them here supports replication, knowledge sharing, and transparency. In doing so, Theoretical Grounding ensures that the study is not only methodologically robust but also communicable and reproducible within and beyond the research team.

- Have I clearly defined the research aims, hypotheses, or exploratory questions driving the study?
- Have I identified which data types from VR (e.g., spatial coordinates, timestamps, sketches) are relevant to the research questions?

- Do I know how to export OpenBrush files and extract coordinate or spatial data if required?
- Have I listed and justified all questionnaires or psychometric tools to be used?
- Are there clear references for each questionnaire and rationale for their inclusion?
- Have I determined when questionnaires will be administered relative to VR sessions to minimize fatigue or cybersickness?
- Have I included ethical documentation (consent, debrief, risk assessment) within the protocol?
- Are all team members aware of the theoretical background and ready to respond to participant enquiries accurately?
- Is this section clear and detailed enough for replication or for sharing with other researchers in the lab or externally?

STUDIO Three: Ensuring Data Integrity

The third step of the STUDIO framework is dedicated to Upholding Data Integrity, which ensures that all data generated throughout the study is gathered, saved, and maintained in compliance with institutional standards, ethical approval, and the project's data management plan. While many procedures will be established at the proposal or governance stages (e.g., GDPR compliance, consent handling, safe storage, anonymization), VR-based arts research adds new levels of technical and procedural considerations. VR art-making studies, like those with OpenBrush, provide a variety of data sources, including audio, video, and drawing files. Each demands a unique method to ensure high-quality capture and secure management.

For audio recordings, the preferred way is to attach a clip-on microphone on the participant, particularly in larger experimental spaces. Stationary microphones placed throughout the room frequently provide irregular or poor-quality recordings when people move, turn away, or speak from varied distances. Wearable microphones reduce unpredictability and contribute to clear spoken data, especially in think-aloud or retrospective verbal activities.

For video capture, casting the participant's first-person view (e.g., from a Quest headset) to a PC and recording using normal screen-capture software (e.g., Windows screen recorder) is usually adequate. These recordings allow experimenters to monitor activity, guide participants as needed, and enable future analysis. Files normally export automatically to a predefined directory and should be renamed and saved securely in accordance with your project's conventions.

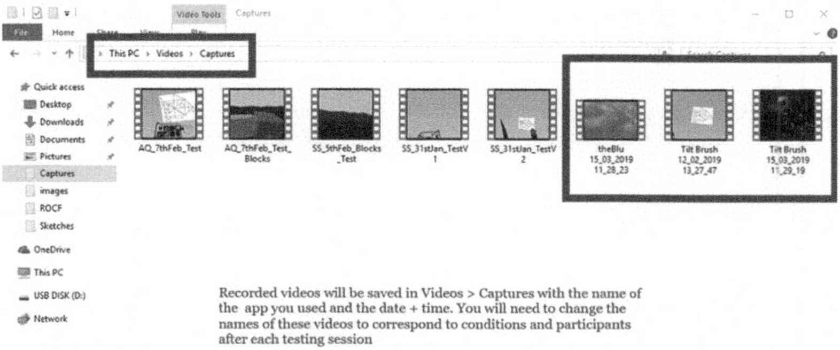

To capture the OpenBrush sketches, participants must save them within the virtual environment. This can be accomplished by leading them through the saving process, or the researcher can re-enter VR after the participant's session to ensure the sketches are properly saved. Saving sketches generates a variety of file formats, including a data file that stores the 3D coordinates of each drawn stroke. These files allow for time-based or spatial analysis of drawing behavior, resulting in a rich dataset. Saved sketches can later be reopened in OpenBrush to recreate viewing conditions or reconstruct temporal drawing sequences, so facilitating mixed-methods or participatory research.

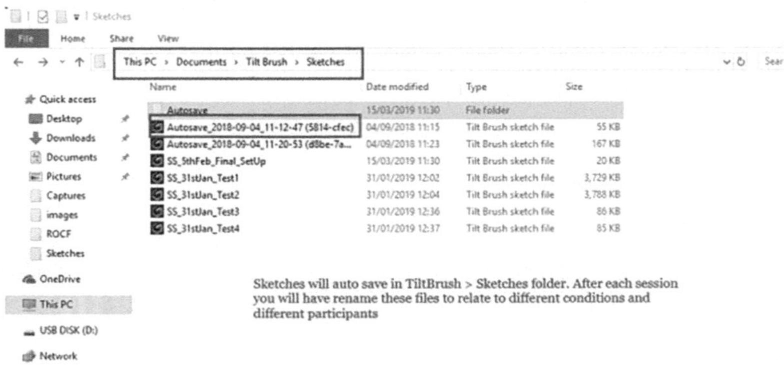

These methods ensure that data, whether qualitative, visual, geographical, or temporal, is preserved, useable, and well documented.

- Does the protocol comply with institutional ethics, GDPR, and the approved data management plan?
- Are consent, pseudonymization, and secure storage processes clear and documented?
- Have I decided which data formats (audio, video, saved sketches, coordinates) are required for my research questions?
- Is a reliable method in place for clear audio capture (e.g., clip-on microphone)?
- If using room microphones, have I assessed whether sound quality will be sufficient?
- Is a consistent video capture method in place (e.g., PC screen recording of headset display)?
- Have I tested the video capture workflow (start/stop, folder destination, file naming)?
- Is there a defined procedure to ensure OpenBrush sketches are saved correctly?
- Do researchers know how to export or extract coordinate-level data from saved sketches?
- Is there a clear convention for file naming and metadata?
- Are data backups planned and consistent with ethics approvals?
- Have team members been trained to follow the same data collection and storage procedures?

STUDIO Four: Design Development

The fourth step of the STUDIO framework, Design Development, is concerned with defining the experimental structure and identifying how the various methodological components—VR immersion, drawing activities, think-aloud procedures, questionnaires, and interviews—interrelate. Although many aspects of research design are discussed elsewhere in this procedure, Stage Four combines these ideas into a cohesive participant pathway. Importantly, the STUDIO stages are not strictly linear; design features may be developed or improved prior to, during, or following other stages.

Design planning begins by determining what participants need to know before coming at the research site. Pre-arrival communications help participants prepare psychologically and practically, lowering uncertainty and facilitating a smoother onboarding experience. Once on site, participants should be led through a well-structured onboarding procedure that the researchers must have practiced prior. The onboarding procedure introduces participants to the VR environment, tools, and researcher support structure, as well as demonstrating how to halt and quit at any time.

VR involvement should be limited to 20–30 minutes every session, therefore the experimental flow must be staged. After the first onboarding and controller familiarization, participants should take a short rest. This break can serve a variety of objectives, including rest, questionnaire completion, or a brief semi-structured talk (e.g., about lived experience or diagnostic journey if studying neurodivergence).

The free-drawing challenge is central to many virtual reality arts studies. A prompt is frequently helpful for participants to get started. This technique, based on art therapy approaches, supports the use of organized prompts as a communication tool rather than as material for direct artwork examination (full list of recommended prompts is available at the end of this document). Drawing, in this approach, serves as a medium for reflecting on perception, lived experience, or other issues. Participants are encouraged to explore, create, and speak out using the drawing as an anchor. During piloting, researchers should try out many prompts to see which ones are the most interesting, eventually settling on a core set (e.g., four to five) to ensure consistency.

The degree of direction provided throughout the drawing will vary depending on the study issue. Some research may recommend minimal intervention, while others may necessitate more systematic inquiry. A key skill for the researcher is learning to follow up meaningfully, relying on art-therapeutic dialogue methods: rather than analyzing the drawing, the researcher uses it as a mediating object to assist the participant in accessing and expressing experiences relevant to the study.

Flexibility is essential. Some participants will only need one or two prompts, while others may need many more. Similarly, some people may speak easily, while others will require more support. Building confidence in conducting these talks is best accomplished by rehearsal—observing experienced researchers, practicing with colleagues, and fine-tuning one's technique before testing with participants.

Design Development determines the study's structure, pacing, and interaction flow, ensuring that VR and arts-based methodologies work together to generate relevant, participant-centered data.

- Is the overall participant pathway clearly structured from arrival to debrief?
- Have pre-arrival expectations been shared with participants?
- Has the onboarding process been tested by the researcher in advance?
- Is the total VR time per participant capped at ~20–30 minutes?
- Is the session broken into manageable segments (onboarding → break → drawing → discussion → break → etc.)?
- Are pre-VR, mid-VR, and post-VR components well defined?
- Have free-drawing prompts been developed, piloted, and refined?
- Is it clear how many prompts participants are likely to receive?
- Is it clear how different prompts support the research question(s)?
- Will the drawing be used as a communication tool rather than for formal artwork interpretation?
- Are procedures in place to support think-aloud or reflective interviewing during or after drawing?
- Have follow-up questioning strategies been developed?
- Has the researcher practiced delivering prompts and guiding conversations confidently?
- Does the design allow flexibility for participant differences in pacing, communication, and comfort level?
- Are breaks embedded to support comfort, prevent cybersickness, and allow for questionnaires/interviews?

STUDIO Five: Involvement and Recruitment

The fifth step of the STUDIO structure, Involvement & Recruitment, is concerned with identifying, recruiting, preparing, and supporting participants, as well as arranging research logistics. While this methodology was originally designed to investigate neurodivergent populations, it is easily adaptable to different groups or research questions. Recruitment can be approached in two stages: first targeting trait-based variability, then recruiting formally diagnosed groups. Many studies have shown that people with high levels of specific neurodivergent traits (e.g., autistic features) can exhibit perception and performance patterns identical to those with formal diagnoses. Thus, piloting work with trait-based samples might be a useful and responsible initial step before moving on to clinical groups.

When working with diagnosed or otherwise specified groups, it is best to recruit through established communities, organizations, or networks. Researchers should be conscious of contextual considerations and accommodations. For example, when working with autistic people, our team noticed that intolerance of ambiguity and anxiety in unfamiliar surroundings can limit engagement. To address this, we developed detailed written instructions (including maps, directions, and schedules), emailed materials ahead of time, and created a brief walk-through video (e.g., using Canva) to demonstrate how to get to the building, what the laboratory looks like, and where researchers would meet. These scaffolds lessen anxiety and ensure that participants understand what to expect, which is an often-overlooked aspect of psychological research in general.

Downloadable link to video template available here.

Clear communication prior to participation should include opportunity to ask questions, thorough explanations of the VR task, and the applicable ethical documents. Participants in VR experiments should receive photos of the VR controllers ahead of time. Controllers are often strange to first-time VR users, particularly those who do not play video games, thus regular visual exposure (by email, video, or onboarding) is beneficial.

Upon arrival, participants should go through an organized onboarding process. Onboarding techniques in VR research vary, but often include orienting participants to the room, reviewing headset handling, clarifying the researcher's role, and establishing expectations for verbal and physical support. Participants must be informed that the researcher may need to touch their hands, shoulders, or adjust the headset to ensure safe and correct controller functioning. They should also be informed that they can remove the headset or discontinue involvement at any time without explanation, which is crucial for autonomy and psychological safety.

During VR tasks, experimenters track activity using casting (e.g., Meta Quest) or platforms like SteamVR (HTC Vive). Video and/or audio recordings may be initiated at this point, depending on the amount of data required. Experimenters should practice giving vocal directions to participants who are unable to see them and be comfortable describing the virtual environment and OpenBrush interface.

Onboarding usually starts in a non-interactive or low-interaction VR environment (e.g., underwater scenes, natural surroundings, Google Earth) to assist users with immersion and locomotion. Because some individuals (e.g., those with hydrophobia) may find underwater situations disturbing, it is best to present several options. After acclimatizing, participants are introduced to OpenBrush. They learn fundamental interactions like teleportation, environment selection, brush selection, scaling, erasing, and deleting. They are then invited to investigate tools, experiment with different brush kinds, and roam around the space to better comprehend boundaries. This exploration phase is critical for reducing fear, boosting confidence, and ensuring that later, more organized drawing activities reflect participants' creative abilities rather than their unfamiliarity with the software.

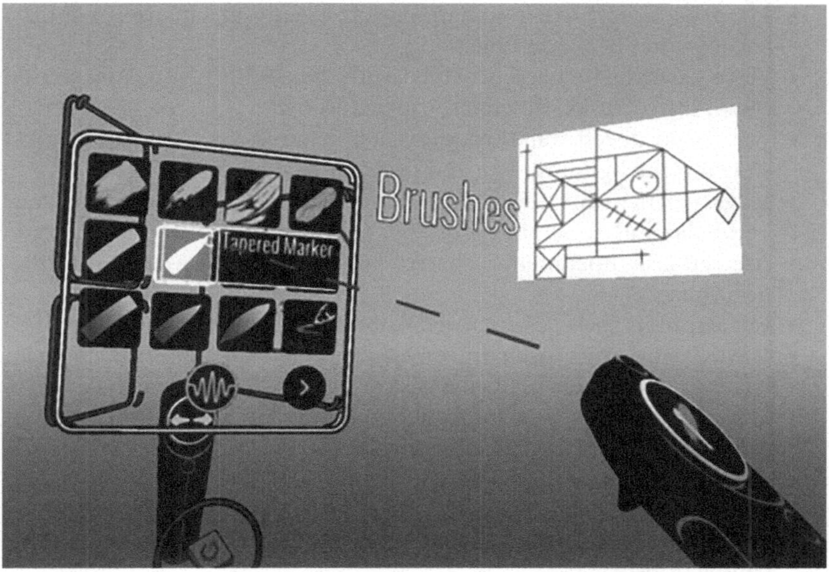

The duration of play-based onboarding varies depending on the participant; researchers should assess when a person is ready to begin formal work. Regardless of the study design, immersion time should be kept to about 20–30 min per session to avoid tiredness, confusion, and cybersickness. Breaks (typically followed by questionnaire completion) are beneficial for preserving comfort and facilitating mixed-methods data collecting.

This stage focusses on relational care, accessibility, safety, and participant autonomy, acknowledging that participation in VR-based arts research is not simply technical, but also experiential, emotional, and embodied.

- Have I clarified whether recruitment will be trait-based, diagnosis-based, or both?
- Is there justification for the chosen population (traits vs. formal diagnosis)?
- Have I established recruitment routes via trusted networks, organizations, or communities?

- Have necessary accommodations for specific groups (e.g., autistic participants) been identified?
- Have participants been provided with detailed pre-visit information (map, instructions, timelines, expectations)?
- Have I produced walkthrough visual materials (e.g., video; photos) showing the building, lab, and process?
- Have participants been sent controller images and guidance before arrival?
- Are ethical documents shared in advance (consent, information sheets)?
- On arrival, is there a structured onboarding process?
- Have participants been informed that physical adjustments (e.g., headset, hand placement) may occur?
- Have participants been informed they can stop at any point without justification?
- Am I prepared to guide VR actions verbally when participants cannot see me?
- Is casting/monitoring available for remote viewing of participant actions?
- Have I rehearsed VR instructions and controller use with colleagues before testing participants?
- Are multiple calm onboarding environments available to suit participant preference?
- Are participants supported to explore brushes, movement, and space prior to task onset?
- Is brush/environment scope restricted appropriately for the study design?
- Are delete/erase functions explained and practiced?
- Are appropriate breaks planned between VR sessions?
- Is VR time limited (20–30 min per session) to avoid fatigue/cybersickness?

STUDIO Six: Oversight and Safety

The sixth and final stage of the STUDIO structure, Oversight & Safety, ensures that researchers prioritize participant well-being throughout the VR study. Because VR immerses people in visually rich worlds that can temporarily impair bodily awareness, experimenters must take proactive measures to prevent physical, sensory, and medical dangers. This level focusses on safe equipment use, pre-screening considerations, symptom monitoring, emergency procedures, hygiene standards, and device maintenance.

Prior to data collection, researchers must be familiar with the VR headset's official setup and operating instructions, as well as the hardware/software requirements. Only authorized hardware and software should be used; unapproved peripherals may result in harm, data loss, or device malfunction. Visual comfort should be assessed for each participant using individual focus adjustment.

Participants should avoid using VR if they are excessively exhausted, ill, stressed, or otherwise physiologically challenged. Pregnant women, the elderly, and people with binocular vision impairments or serious medical issues should speak with a doctor before participating.

VR exposure can cause photosensitive seizures, which are infrequent (about 1 in every 4000 persons). Individuals who have a history of seizures or blackouts should seek medical advice before participation. If a subject has a seizure while testing, they should be placed in the recovery position and seek assistance from a professional first-aider or senior staff member.

Because VR can impair balance and spatial awareness, the research area must be free of obstructions, particularly furniture, wires, stairways, fans, and sharp items. Participants should remain seated unless the study requires standing; standing tasks should be actively monitored. Before using a headset, experimenters should make sure it is properly fastened and displays a single clear image. If headphones are used, keep the level low enough to retain ambient awareness.

Participants should progressively adjust to VR use, taking 10–15 min breaks every ~30 min. They must be told to stop immediately if they feel pain, dizziness, nausea, vision distortion, perspiration, or exhaustion. Post-use symptoms (e.g., drowsiness, decreased multitasking ability) may develop hours later; participants should avoid driving, using machinery, or engaging in physically demanding tasks until symptoms have subsided completely. If content causes unpleasant reactions, users should stop immediately and relax until the symptoms subside. A healthcare professional should evaluate persistent or severe symptoms.

Headsets that are damaged must not be utilized; any flaws must be reported to the primary investigator. To prevent the transmission of contagious illnesses (such as conjunctivitis), the headset should not be shared with symptomatic users. Proper sanitization is required: non-alcohol antibacterial wipes for facial interfaces and microfiber towels for lenses are advised. Skin irritation should be monitored; if irritation occurs, participants should discontinue use and seek medical attention if symptoms worsen.

Adapted from https://www.classvr.com/health-and-safety

- Has the research team reviewed all official headset setup and operating instructions?
- Is authorized hardware/software being used exclusively?
- Has each participant's headset focus been individually adjusted?
- Has the participant been screened for fatigue, illness, stress, or medical contraindications?
- Have participants with relevant medical histories (e.g., seizures) been advised to consult a clinician?
- Is the lab prepared to respond to a seizure (recovery position; first-aider available)?
- Is the VR area cleared of tripping hazards, furniture, sharp objects, cables, and obstructions?
- Are participants advised to remain seated unless otherwise required?
- Is the headset securely fitted and presenting a clear image before use?
- Are headphone volumes kept at safe levels?
- Are session lengths limited to 20–30 min with breaks every 30 min?
- Are participants informed they may stop at any time?
- Are participants instructed not to drive or operate machinery after VR if symptomatic?
- Is the headset inspected for damage before use, and damage reported promptly?
- Is equipment sanitized between participants using non-alcohol wipes and microfiber cloths?
- Is there a procedure for responding to skin irritation or allergic reactions?

Drawing Prompts

Below are series of prompts that can be used for free drawing tasks. They have been adapted from art therapy, however, are not intended to be used for therapeutic purposes in this context (unless the researchers are trained to do so). Provided prompts are based on the following papers:

Buck, J. N. (1948). The H-T-P technique: A qualitative and quantitative scoring manual. *Journal of Clinical Psychology Monograph Supplement, 5*, 37–74.

Ter Laak, J., de Goede, M., Aleva, A., & van Rijswijk, P. (2005). The Draw-A-Person Test: An indicator of children's cognitive and socio-emotional adaptation? *The Journal of Genetic Psychology, 166*(1), 77–93.

Draw how you feel right now.
Draw your heart.
Use colors and shapes to show your mood.
Draw a safe place.
If your feelings were weather, what would they look like?
Draw a self-portrait—as you feel inside, not how you look.
Draw yourself as an animal.
Draw your family doing something.
Draw your home as a place of emotion.
Draw your family as a tree (family tree metaphor).
Draw a bridge—where you are now and where you want to go.
Draw your future self.
Draw the event as symbols or shapes.
Draw patterns that repeat—lines, circles, spirals.
Draw a tree, a house, and a person (HTP test style).
Draw an island—what's on it?
Draw a journey—where are you, where are you headed?

Index

S. Savickaite, *Exploring Neurodiversity Through Virtual Reality*,
https://doi.org/10.1007/978-3-032-19636-1

The manufacturer's authorised representative in the EU is Springer Nature Customer Service Centre GmbH, Europaplatz 3, 69115 Heidelberg, Germany. If you have any concerns regarding our products, please contact ProductSafety@springernature.com

Printed and bound by CPI Group (UK) Ltd, Croydon, CR0 4YY

17/09/2026

02218454-0004